Meeting Goals

Protocols for Leading *Effective, Purpose-Driven* Discussions in Schools

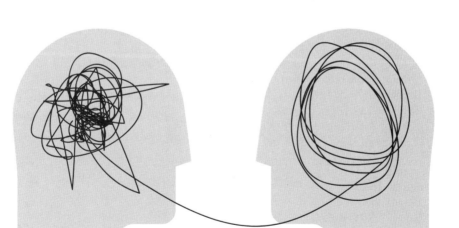

Solution Tree | Press

a division of
Solution Tree

Thomas M. Van Soelen

Copyright © 2021 by Solution Tree Press

Materials appearing here are copyrighted. With one exception, all rights are reserved. Readers may reproduce only those pages marked "Reproducible." Otherwise, no part of this book may be reproduced or transmitted in any form or by any means (electronic, photocopying, recording, or otherwise) without prior written permission of the publisher.

555 North Morton Street
Bloomington, IN 47404
800.733.6786 (toll free) / 812.336.7700
FAX: 812.336.7790

email: info@SolutionTree.com
SolutionTree.com
Visit **go.SolutionTree.com/leadership** to download the free reproducibles in this book.

Printed in the United States of America

Library of Congress Cataloging-in-Publication Data

Names: Van Soelen, Thomas M., author.
Title: Meeting goals : protocols for leading effective, purpose-driven
   discussions in schools / Thomas M. Van Soelen.
Description: Bloomington, IN : Solution Tree Press, 2021. | Includes
   bibliographical references and index.
Identifiers: LCCN 2020047462 (print) | LCCN 2020047463 (ebook) | ISBN
   9781951075736 (paperback) | ISBN 9781951075743 (ebook)
Subjects: LCSH: Meetings--Planning. | Teachers--Professional relationships.
   | School management and organization.
Classification: LCC LB1751 .V36 2021 (print) | LCC LB1751 (ebook) | DDC
   371.2--dc23
LC record available at https://lccn.loc.gov/2020047462
LC ebook record available at https://lccn.loc.gov/2020047463

Solution Tree
Jeffrey C. Jones, CEO
Edmund M. Ackerman, President

Solution Tree Press
President and Publisher: Douglas M. Rife
Associate Publisher: Sarah Payne-Mills
Art Director: Rian Anderson
Managing Production Editor: Kendra Slayton
Copy Chief: Jessi Finn
Production Editor: Miranda Addonizio
Content Development Specialist: Amy Rubenstein
Copy Editor: Kate St. Ives
Proofreader: Elisabeth Abrams
Text and Cover Designer: Kelsey Hergül
Editorial Assistants: Sarah Ludwig and Elijah Oates

Acknowledgments

This book has been years in the making—I just didn't know it at the time. My colleagues Kerise Ridinger and Shawna Miller kept telling me there was a book among the slew of Google documents I provided participants during professional development. They were right. Kerise always made time to discuss content, in particular, the changes Amy Rubenstein and Miranda Addonizio from Solution Tree were asking me to make! Thanks to Amy and Miranda for ensuring a clear message in a *reasonable* number of pages.

I am so thankful for observing and learning from fantastic facilitators: my initial trainers Frances Hensley and Betty Bisplinghoff, as well as others who facilitated with me in various professional development institutes: Jana Claxton, Connie Zimmerman Parrish, James Cowper, Jean-Jacques Credi, Ileana Liberatore, June Long, Nancy Marsh, and Christine Knox. My interactions with these fine folks helped me find and develop words, phrases, explanations, and metaphors that are present in the Language You Can Borrow sections.

As I continue to uncover and understand the privileges of being white, male, and inordinately tall (6'6"!), co-facilitating with Tyese Scott is a gift. She prompts me to think, and most importantly, articulate my thinking, even at times when I might not want to. Particular thanks I also render to Nelson Orta, who latched onto infinitive-agenda setting and kept asking me questions that clarified my thinking.

None of these materials would be available to educators around the world without the authors of many protocols, some of which include David Allen, Gene Thompson-Grove, Nancy Mohr, Daniel Baron, Marylyn Wentworth, Frances Hensley, and Debbie Bambino. The work of the School Reform Initiative (www.schoolreforminitiative.org) is critical to the artful use of discussion protocols and their impact on adult learning and development, resulting in increased achievement for each student. All of the author royalties for this book go directly to the School Reform Initiative. Many thanks to the former executive director, Deirdre Williams, for continuing the fierce fight for educational equity.

Shannon Kersey, principal of Alpharetta High School in Georgia, is an incredible colleague and strategic leader. Proof of our decade of collaboration is present throughout this book. Leading her staff to collaborate across departments using these protocols prompted me to examine all of my facilitation notes, creating more accessible documents to her staff.

I am in debt to Beth Brockman: when I sent my first email about starting a leadership consulting and professional development company, she replied in all caps: "CALL ME." We keep calling each other, and I am appreciative we can learn together.

Julie, my wife, deserves many awards for enduring time spent with me. She has watched me spin out of control numerous times after misplacing my own protocol resource book. After a celebratory hooray, she would then gently remind me to tape together the tattered pages because she knows I may not recover if I lost my notes. Julie, as a small token of my love, I vow to keep the markers in my car trunk in containers that will not constantly roll around while driving or spill out onto the driveway. You did marry a professional developer, but I can practice my own mantra of continuous improvement!

Solution Tree Press would like to thank the following reviewers:

Mark Benson
Principal
Harriet G. Eddy Middle School
Elk Grove, California

Johanna Josaphat
Social Studies Teacher
The Urban Assembly Unison School
Brooklyn, New York

Stevi Quate
Independent Consultant
Public Education and Business Coalition
Denver, Colorado

Anastacia Galloway Reed
Professional Development
Eagle Rock School
Estes Park, Colorado

Rebecca Savage
ELA Coordinator
Lee County Schools
Fort Myers, Florida

Larry Zuares
Instructional Coach
Pemberton Township Schools
Pemberton, New Jersey

Visit **go.SolutionTree.com/leadership** to download the free reproducibles in this book.

Table of Contents

Reproducible pages are in italics.

Chapter 2: Protocols to Build Shared Understanding   35

Chapter 3: Protocols to Refine Products   87

Chapter 4: Protocols to Seek Perspective   111

Chapter 5: Protocols to Explore and Manage Dilemmas   147

Chapter 6: Protocols to Generate Ideas   177

Afterword: Debriefing   203

Appendix A: Consistent Approaches to Common Steps in Protocols   215

About the Author

Thomas M. Van Soelen, PhD, has focused on developing adults for over a decade. His work in the areas of instructional strategies, learning communities, critical friendship, leadership development, and teacher evaluation is known in several states and countries. His collaborative practices, quick wit, and deep experience make for an engaging and meaningful learning experience. Prior to his full-time work as a professional developer and leadership coach (www.vansoelenassociates.com), Thomas worked in multiple states and in public and private schools, teaching every grade level, preK through grade 12, at some point in his career. In addition, he prepared undergraduates at the University of Georgia and conducts both face-to-face and online courses at the graduate level for three institutions. He also held the school district leadership position of associate superintendent in the City Schools of Decatur, Georgia, a post he held for eight years.

Thomas is a member of national organizations (the American Association of School Administrators, American Association of School Personnel Administrators, Learning Forward, and the Association for Supervision and Curriculum Development) and was elected to serve on the national board of the School Reform Initiative. Several journals, periodicals, and organizations have published his writing: *Journal of Staff Development, Principal Leadership, Education Week, School Administrator, National Association of Elementary School Principals, American School Board Journal,* and *Phi Delta Kappan.* His book, *Crafting the Feedback Teachers Need and Deserve: A Guide for Leaders,* is the chronicle of a five-year teacher quality initiative he led in his last district.

Thomas holds bachelor's degrees in elementary education, music education, and vocal performance from Dordt University (Iowa), a master's degree in elementary education and an educational specialist degree in educational leadership from Florida Atlantic University, and a doctoral degree in elementary education from the University of Georgia.

To learn more about Thomas's work, visit www.vansoelen associates.com and follow @tvansoelen on Twitter.

To book Thomas Van Soelen for professional development, contact pd@SolutionTree.com.

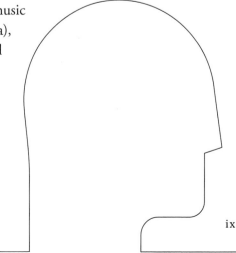

Grounding

As Claire settles in at the monthly principals' meeting, she takes a casual glance at the agenda. There's something new as the last agenda item this month: Consultancies With Principals Only—sounds interesting. After all the repeated monthly topics, focused on operational issues, some time with just principals might be valuable.

As she expected, many agenda items drag on, and as the operational district leaders eventually exit, there are less than fifteen minutes left before the scheduled end of the meeting.

Janise, the assistant superintendent, seems nonplussed as she steps forward and says, "Principals, this is just perfect timing. As I've told some of you, I was recently on an accreditation visit in a neighboring district, and I heard them talk about using discussion protocols with each other. Essentially, they are really fast ways to get things done—sounds good, right? Today, we are going to try one called Consultancy. Some of you will talk in a small group about something that isn't going great at your school, and the other members of the group get to offer some advice. You have been asking for more time in these meetings to just meet with each other, so I thought this would be perfect."

Principals split into triads, and since Claire's birthday is closest to today's date, she draws the short straw: being the presenter and talking about a problematic situation on her campus. Feeling on the spot, Claire doesn't have time to carefully weigh her options and decides to discuss a particularly tricky problem with a staff member.

Janise lays out the protocol structure by saying, "So, here's how this works: first, the presenter will talk for two minutes about the situation. I will let you know when that time is up. The second step is when the other two group members ask a few clarifying questions, and the presenter answers briefly. You'll have one minute for that. Finally, in the last step, the presenter will listen in—no talking now!—as the other two principals give some ideas. I'm positive this will be rewarding for everyone!"

Claire's situation has many layers, and after two minutes, she feels she has only touched the surface, but the group needs to move on. The clarifying questions that follow, such as Have you tried calling HR?, feel more like suggestions. Claire is honest each time a colleague asks a question, usually answering with, "Yes, I've tried that." When it is time for her principal colleagues to give her suggestions, she knows she isn't supposed to talk, but they are looking right at her! Claire nods a lot, writes down what they say, and breathes a sigh of relief when it is over.

"So," Janise begins, "we have just a few minutes to talk about that protocol. Who found that helpful?"

In the preceding scenario, Claire was *protocoled* at the monthly meeting. This happens when a discussion protocol is thrust upon a group of participants. The protocol is done *to* them instead of *with* them. In these situations, the purpose of using a particular protocol is often unclear or unknown, sometimes even to the person who convened the meeting. For protocols that require facilitation, effectiveness depends on the depth of understanding the facilitator has about the specific discussion protocol as well as the features of what makes protocols really work.

If you are new to discussion protocols, or have limited experience with them, I believe this book has the potential to change the collaborative culture of your school in an enormously positive way. It's common to dread or feel ambivalent about meetings—but what if meetings were a way to really get work done? What if your meetings exemplified what meetings are capable of while meeting your goals at the same time? What if your meetings actually created a culture where meetings really mattered? The title of this book was conceived with that double meaning in mind. The preparation and the goal setting of each individual meeting topic are critical—as only then can you have clear meeting goals. At the same time, effectively using discussion protocols creates a culture of effectiveness and efficiency so the goals can be met with excellence while practicing equity. In this introduction, I discuss the features and history of discussion protocols, describe what this book offers to discussion protocol users of all experience levels, and highlight some common misunderstandings.

Features of Discussion Protocols

Many discussion protocols have a deceptive simplicity that often lulls educators (Allen & Blythe, 2004). They enjoy the productivity as well as the collaborative discipline these protocols seem to engender. Before the educators know it, they are hooked, and it isn't just facilitation skills they lack—it's a common definition of a discussion protocol. Here's my operational definition: *a discussion protocol is a structured conversation.* As people talk and listen (*conversation*), they apply certain parameters or constraints (*structures*; McDonald, Mohr, Dichter, & McDonald, 2013).

The preceding scenario involving Claire is an example of something that really happened to one of my colleagues in a meeting that was not well-grounded by the facilitator. *Grounding* is a facilitator's critical first step when sharing an agenda. This move is meant to "shepherd people into the work of the day" (Murphy, 2016). Just as effective facilitators create explicit purpose in agendas (see chapter 1, page 21), they also sequence the agenda carefully and artfully so participants can be intellectually and socially ready for whatever the agenda requires. As Murphy (2016) says, "Bring people into space with care and purpose and you'll likely get the best of their thinking."

Grounding is more than an icebreaker, which is often purely social and disconnected from the actual agenda outcomes. Instead, a grounding experience is intentional and advances the agenda it precedes. Consider a few examples of activities that may ground an agenda.

- **Sentence stems:** Everyone starts with this sentence stem without any dialogue: "I believe the purpose of homework to be . . ." when beginning a meeting on creating a new homework policy.

- **Connections:** This is a chance for groups to make connections with others' experiences without commenting. Instead, individuals who choose to speak simply say what they want to say; everyone else just listens.

- **Cookies:** Use actual fortune cookies or virtual cookies from www .fortunecookiemessage.com to ask each participant to read a fortune and make a connection to the content of the day's agenda.

While the preceding activities, among others, may ground an agenda, this opening text serves to ground *you* in the underlying assumptions and research around using discussion protocols. Chapter 1 focuses on the agenda within which a protocol might be used. Then chapters 2–6 discuss various protocols, including several examples to help you envision similar situations in your work context.

When these constraints, or structures, work well for a group, a set of conditions exists. You can remember these conditions with four words that all start with the letter *E*—discussion protocols are designed to be *e*ffective and *e*fficient, characterized by *e*quity and *e*xcellence. Collectively, these ideal conditions might be referred to as E^4.

Effective

Discussion protocols help educators add meaningful constraints to conversations to create more effective collaborative spaces. Adult learning and development are achievable through the purposeful use of protocols. Although the two sound similar, learning and development are different, and these differences are important. "Adult learning is necessary when educators implement the district's new math program or literacy initiative" (Fahey, Breidenstein, Ippolito, & Hensley, 2019, p. 19) while adult development involves the "entire school community developing new capacities for seeing and understanding complex dilemmas, staying in difficult conversations, and reframing current assumptions" (Fahey et al., 2019, p. 33). Education professor Jacy Ippolito offers definitions of these two notions using some of his own thoughts as well as those of psychologist Robert Kegan (1998), the developer of the constructive developmental theory:

> Personally, I see "adult learning" as the kinds of learning that adults do to inform and expand their knowledge base . . . but this kind of "adult learning" doesn't change the *way* we think about the world, or the ways in which we learn or act in the world. Whereas "adult development" changes the very ways in which we see/think about the world. Bob Kegan used to talk in his classes about the adult brain as a container. Adult learning "fills" the container. Adult development changes the very nature of the container! (J. Ippolito, personal communication, January 3, 2021)

Depending on the context and the purpose, the same protocol could be useful for adult learning or adult development. An effective facilitator uses deep knowledge about each step in the protocol and about potential pitfalls to focus on adult learning or adult development. Adult learning in schools is necessary, but it is not enough. Stories and tangible examples can help leaders become "chief adult developers" (Fahey et al., 2019, p. 36).

Later in this introduction, I offer categories for helping agenda designers choose a protocol that matches the purpose of the meeting. However, I have not designed this book to offer a recipe for facilitators—creating a false belief that there is one right path in facilitating a protocol. A simple download of a discussion protocol does not create the conditions necessary for a group to reach the ideal potential of many discussion protocols, adult development. Instead, this text seeks to empower two groups of educators to improve their preparation and implementation of collaboration: (1) those who have the power to form agendas and facilitate meetings, and (2) those who have influence to improve the process of said meetings.

Protocols support the understanding of school culture while promoting adult development. The shared language that discussion protocols build creates a holding environment (Heifetz, Grashow, & Linsky, 2009) where individuals and groups can reflect. In the holding environment, individuals have the opportunity to reconsider their positions and assumptions while groups can consider their development. Groups are like biological organisms—any organism that ceases to develop will die. Protocols intentionally include a debriefing step (also the name of the afterword of this book, page 203) where groups can explicitly discuss their development (or lack thereof).

These holding environments are places where "heat" can be regulated (Fahey et al., 2019). A leader may turn up the heat in a group by presenting quantitative data that illuminate a gap. Conversely, identifying consensus rather than agreement as a goal for a particular agenda item can reduce the heat.

Although we often see heat regulation as a job for leaders, the discussion protocols themselves are effective heat mitigators. The creators of these protocols designed sequences that strategically and methodically create conversations wherein educators can take risks. Specifically, protocols ask participants to slow down and use only one cognitive structure at a time. Readers who have been part of a discussion protocol before may recall a colleague who jumped a few steps ahead. Perhaps facilitators reminded him or her about the step the group was trying to implement, which may have caused frustration. "Why can't we just talk?" this colleague may have said. At this point, the facilitator may not have had a better rationale than the following: "The protocol says we can't do that kind of thinking yet." This book offers a deeper background in each step of foundational protocols so facilitators can use them to more effectively manage the eventual out-of-sequence moments. For instance, knowledge about heat mitigation in discussion protocols can help a facilitator more effectively explain why fidelity to the protocol sequence is helpful.

Through the effective regulation of heat in these holding environments, facilitators engender trust. I cringe when I see anything about trust on a set of group norms (for example, "We will trust each other."). I think trust is an *outcome*, not a *behavior*. The immediate goal is *not* for group members to trust one another; it is rather for each person to trust in a well-designed agenda and well-aligned discussion protocol (McDonald et al., 2013).

Protocols have proven effective in school improvement and restructuring efforts. They help meet goals—getting work done. They also use predictable structures to create environments of risk taking, resulting in a higher level of trust.

Efficient

I often have a list of errands for Saturday mornings. If I leave the house and come back twenty minutes later, having only successfully completed one errand, I would certainly not call that an efficient trip despite the short time I was away. Time is not the only indicator for efficiency. Purpose is an inextricable factor in that determination. The purpose of my errands is to complete them. If the time was quick, but the purpose was not fulfilled, I certainly do not feel fulfilled. If I spent more time but finished my entire list, I would feel fulfilled.

The same holds for discussion protocols. Educators will feel they have spent their time effectively and efficiently only if they understand why they are using a particular discussion protocol at a particular time. Successful implementation of protocols demonstrates a tight alignment between protocol uses and purposes. Unfortunately, this often doesn't happen. In the scenario at the beginning of this introduction, Janise misinterpreted efficiency to mean quick and nothing more, so she didn't articulate to the participants why she had chosen to use that particular protocol. In fact, she may not have been clear on which protocol to use for her intended purpose. Therefore, even though the experience didn't take a great deal of time, the learning wasn't efficient. The result was Claire feeling like she was protocoled—she didn't leave the gathering having acquired any worthwhile learning.

Equity

Writers like Paul Gorski (2017; Gorski & Pothini, 2018) and Ijeoma Oluo (2019, 2020) offer their thinking about educational equity and how education plays a part in a much larger inequitable environment where many students and families are marginalized. The use of the word equity in E⁴ is narrower—focusing on how we can create more equitable experiences for *educators* when they meet in collaboration. By intentionally improving the quality of our collaboration (meeting together), marginalized students will benefit, thus reducing the gap in their experience and performance.

Educational institutions, and those who make decisions for them, do not naturally design equitable spaces for collaboration. Hierarchies abound, both explicitly on organizational charts and implicitly in relationships. There is not a genuine discussion protocol called The Loudest Voice Wins, but every April Fool's Day, a copy of this fictitious protocol circulates among many experienced facilitators of protocols, causing a good chuckle but reminding us of the importance of having grounding principles that make discussion protocols opportunities to create more equitable spaces for educators.

Educators do not always love protocols. They can be "unwarranted interference in ordinary business" (McDonald et al., 2013, p. 3). Although the reasons for participant resistance in discussion protocols are varied, one dastardly cause can be that some educators simply *want* the environments to stay inequitable. As long as they, or colleagues they deem worthy, are the loudest voices, their agenda rules the day.

That said, the majority of times when I experience groups having trouble using discussion protocols, the trouble stems not from malicious intentions but rather from a lack of collaborative discipline. Effective facilitators help build the habits participants don't yet have, and discussion protocols are the most apt tools these facilitators can use to create the conditions for change. It is not uncommon for someone to remark after a discussion protocol, "You had such great insights!" referencing someone in the group who often remains quiet when spaces aren't carved out for him or her to speak.

A second way to bring equity into adult collaboration is by supporting preferences for how to learn. As I help designers of adult learning think about their agendas, I suggest they consider the ratio of *tight* and *loose* discussion protocols. Tighter-feeling protocols may have more turn taking in predictable patterns, numerous steps with short time frames, sentence stems, or naming of speakers (for example, A, B, C). More loose-feeling protocols could include physical movement, options for discussion prompts, or group compositions that change during the protocol.

Similarly, in using discussion protocols, agenda designers can strike a balance of inductive experiences with discussion protocols (jump in and try it, then read the steps) and deductive experiences (offer the protocol sequence first for participants to silently read, then proceed). It is impossible to take a middle ground in this case: that would be called *indeductive*—which my word processor spell check does not like!

As inherently selfish human beings, we tend to develop agendas with our own preferences in mind. If you are designing a conference for teachers and you love keynote speeches that move you emotionally, your first order of business is to book a keynoter. If you find high value in networking with other educators at breaks, you might schedule multiple breaks or a longer break with specific encouragement to connect with others, instead of checking email. Discussion protocols do not automatically handle this lack of equity in learning preferences, but they can offer an effective check and balance for personal preferences.

Finally, equity in language use is an important feature discussion protocols can bring to collaborative teams. For instance, discussion protocols push on binaries. Ask teachers about observational feedback they received, and they might indicate it was *positive* or *negative*. Or they might say it was *productive* or *unproductive*. Working skillfully with well-chosen discussion protocols allows educators to look beyond binaries. Robert Kegan and Lisa Laskow Lahey (2002) suggest a third alternative to the posed binary of constructive and destructive language: this is *deconstructive* language. Deconstructive language proposes these notions:

- There may be more than one legitimate interpretation.

- All of us have something to learn from the conversation.

- Our conflict may be the result of the separate commitments each of us holds, including commitments we are not always aware we hold. (Kegan & Lahey, 2002, p. 141)

When discussion protocols reflect these tenets and supportive language (for example, sentence stems, facilitation prompts, and explanations), the group builds on these beliefs.

Possibly most important, the language of group members can start to transform. A teacher who used to talk in very definite ways, saying things such as, "The students just don't know . . ." now may involuntarily (at least, initially) use more conditional language such as, "The students might not know . . ." Changes in language can start to show corresponding changes in thinking. This language also affects facilitators. Instead of facilitator-centric language like, "I am going to stop this step and move on," a shift to "It sounds like it might be time to move on," creates a more open approach to the experience.

These manifestations of equity—voice, learning preferences, and language use—can each become residue as the collaboratively undisciplined start to shift in their interactions, often when they are using a discussion protocol and perhaps even when they are not.

Excellence

During the COVID-19 pandemic of 2020, teachers eloquently (and often humorously) shared their frustrations of suddenly becoming distance-learning teachers. Besides feeling isolated and having their routines shaken up, many lost their feelings of excellence. They found coping strategies to help them manage days when they felt like they didn't know how to teach anymore. Educators, by the very profession they chose, desire excellence in others and in themselves. The word *excellence* has a Latin derivative and means *beyond the lofty*. I have been privy to many discussion protocols where members demonstrate genuine shock at the group's ability to be excellent together. We often accept subpar group experiences; as one high school teacher said to me on day one of a professional development training, "It's a meeting; by definition, it's useless."

Excellence is different than what the first E represents: effective. Effectiveness represents goal completion; it doesn't necessarily represent the quality of how that goal was met. The artful use of discussion protocols can raise the expectation level of educators from *useless* to *effective* all the way to *excellent*.

Discussion protocols have the potential to create E^4 gatherings of adults, where the meeting is effective and efficient, where care is taken toward equity of group members, and where those educators leave the meeting feeling like they did an excellent job together.

History of Discussion Protocols

The idea and use of discussion protocols emerged from organizational theory in the 1980s. Concurrently, Sharon Kruse, Karen Seashore Louis, and Anthony S. Bryk (1994) were some of the first researchers to examine the link between effective collaboration and improving both teacher practice and student learning. A seminal document about school restructuring, *Successful School Restructuring* by Fred M. Newmann and Gary G. Wehlage (1995), finds that authentic pedagogy and student performance both correlate to a sense of schoolwide professional community. Every professional contact within the school forms and impacts professional community, from how they talk to each other to when those conversations happen and what they have the autonomy to decide. A six-year longitudinal study in the large system of Chicago Public Schools continues this line of inquiry, finding that professional community and teachers' capacity for professional learning are highly associated with improvements in classroom instruction and student learning (Bryk, Sebring, Allensworth, Luppescu, & Easton, 2010).

With professional learning clearly a marker of effective school improvement, educators and researchers alike wished to replicate the *how* of school improvement efforts in tangible, practical ways. Researchers out of the Annenberg Institute for School Reform at Brown University authored many original discussion protocols in the mid-1990s. Much of that work (and over a hundred more discussion protocols) is now housed via the School Reform Initiative (SRI; www.schoolreforminitiative.org). Many discussion protocols adapted in this book were originally authored by other outstanding educators who also affiliate with SRI. I have cited SRI and other sources as necessary for each protocol that I discuss in this book. For some protocols that SRI has compiled on its website, it is unclear which educators participated in development. SRI acknowledges this fact by listing "developed in the field by educators" on those respective protocols.

About This Book

Because there are so many kinds of discussion protocols available, some writers and organizations have used various grouping strategies to cluster protocols, making it easier for meeting leaders and agenda creators to choose the one that best aligns with their goal. Sometimes protocols are organized around the audience: protocols for school leaders, protocols for collaborative team leaders, protocols for students, and so on. Sometimes protocols are organized around the type of artifacts being examined: protocols to examine student work, protocols to examine assessments, protocols to analyze data, and so on. I find the most powerful and useful way to organize protocols is around purpose. Toward that end, I have structured this book around *protocol families*, adapting a notion first developed by Gene Thompson-Grove, one of the pioneers of using discussion protocols in schools (Thompson-Grove, Hensley, & Van Soelen, n.d.). In the following sections, I provide an overview of chapters and the protocol families they discuss, some information on using protocols, some specifics on how to use this book, and a powerful example of protocols in action from my own experience.

Understanding Protocol Families

Consider a family reunion where you drew the short straw: you're in charge. As you muck through all the logistics of the campground, communicate with your cousin's daughter's friend's husband (the T-shirt designer), and replay in your mind why you missed the birthday party where they assigned you this task, you are also considering the diversity of your family tree. Yes, everyone is technically family, but there are certain eccentricities.

- If the northern Florida relatives come, we need to make sure and . . .
- If the beach folks from near Miami decide to show, we absolutely have to . . .

Using the family reunion metaphor, I've organized the discussion protocols in this book into different protocol families. As discussion protocols become more and more ubiquitous in educator circles, it is essential that educators advocate for purpose first—group members must know why a protocol is going to be *used*, as opposed to the opposite wherein they are *doing* a protocol, so by definition, it then must be worthwhile. All discussion protocols are structured conversations (having parameters and constraints as well as times for people to communicate), but they do not all sound or feel the same. The reasons to use one protocol or another vary.

After introducing this concept, an educator in Dallas, Texas, aptly describes a connection to her own extended family. This is my recollection of what she said:

> I have family all over Texas. When it is just the metro [Dallas] folks getting together, it's one thing. But when everybody comes—whoa! The tribe who lives down by San Antonio prefers to talk in Spanish. We do a lot more code switching with them. The East Texas group has a whole different vernacular—with them, I feel like I am translating for my kids! And then there's the few from Amarillo in the Panhandle. Yep—it's just interesting. (J. Thompson, personal communication, October 15, 2017)

No offense intended to any Texans (particularly those in Amarillo), but her words make the point that family members may be related by blood, by experience, or by something else, but it doesn't mean they communicate in the same way with the same intent.

Chapter 1 discusses purpose-driven agendas. As discussion protocols become increasingly common in schools, a familiar technology-focused expression now has a protocol iteration. "There's an app for that!" is now "There's a protocol for that!" The goal for using protocol families is for agenda creators to consider the purpose of the discussion protocol they are considering. This pause in planning can ensure tight alignment between purpose and action—a critically important feature of meetings in which educators feel like their time is valued. Only then can protocols feel like they are *used* instead of *done*.

Chapter 2 explores the first protocol family—protocols to build shared understanding. Because this protocol family is very large, this is a much longer chapter compared to the others. There will always be parts of the learning trajectory where team members of all kinds need to build shared understanding. If a team of central office leaders spends 100 percent of its time together looking at and analyzing data, the members are too myopic in their focus. If a teacher team spends 100 percent of its time building common assessments, the members may not be acknowledging their lack of shared understanding about a particular standard which is hindering their efforts. If a group of principals spends 100 percent of its collaborative time discussing dilemmas of practice, the principals may be secretly avoiding bringing up areas where we as leaders need to grow our collective understanding. The protocols in chapter 2 provide processes to capture multiple viewpoints held by members of the group and then, through guided discussion, arrive at some degree of shared understanding of the issues, challenges, agreements, and opportunities facing the group. This chapter provides the most diversity, and the most options, in protocol selection in the book, and even more are available at **go.SolutionTree.com/leadership** to view. Due to the sheer quantity of protocols to consider, a matrix in appendix D (page 243) is available to help match a protocol to the challenge you might be facing and tell you where to find it. Effective leaders of adults in schools consistently work toward the goal of chapter 2: building shared understanding, thus, they need these tools frequently.

In the refining protocols found in chapter 3, presenters seek to refine or improve a student work sample, document, or a project so it is more closely aligned with goals or purposes.

Participants receive parameters to consider in planning their feedback, focused on bridging the current work gap and the original goal or purpose.

Chapter 4 delves into the next family of protocols—protocols to seek perspective. Educators' work is certainly difficult, which became especially evident to the world during the COVID-19 pandemic. As educators create materials and feel personally invested in their students' results, they need discussion protocols to help build space to think. This family of protocols creates the conditions for participants to hear different viewpoints, to see a new angle on something they thought they knew so well.

Chapter 5 looks at protocols to explore and manage dilemmas. A dilemma is a puzzle, an issue that raises questions about some aspect of a relationship, process, or product you just can't figure out. Protocols for dilemmas prompt the presenter to think more deeply or expansively about the situation, not to necessarily find *the* or *an* answer. Many dilemma-based protocols help educators realize sometimes the best advice is no advice at all.

Finally, chapter 6 includes protocols to generate ideas. Protocols in this family often address situations in which participants say they are feeling stuck. In these protocols, participants temporarily take on an issue and generate ideas and possibilities for consideration. Presenters stay silent during the process, removing themselves from the pressure to immediately respond to each idea. Protocols in this family differ from unstructured brainstorming. The constraints they offer artfully and skillfully harness group members' creativity and ingenuity while still creating effective and efficient spaces.

At the very end is an afterword that shares a name with the final, essential step of discussion protocols: Debriefing. Like a debriefing during a discussion protocol, it is an important part of processing and understanding what has just taken place.

Table I.1, co-created by Kerise Ridinger in Lewisville, Texas, and myself, can help agenda designers determine which protocol family may be aligned to a particular purpose on their agenda.

Table I.1: Key Words for Protocol Families

Protocol Family	Key Words and Phrases	Artifact Needed?
Protocols to Build Shared Understanding	• We don't all understand . . . • They don't agree about . . . • We need to learn about . . . • Building community is a goal. • We have a text to read.	Perhaps
Protocols to Refine Products	• I have a goal. • There might be a gap. • It is not quite there. • Some of it is good.	Yes

Protocols to Seek Perspective	• What do others see? • I don't know where to go with it. • I need another perspective. • I need new eyes.	Yes
Protocols to Explore and Manage Dilemmas	• I am stuck or I've tried X, Y, and even Z. • I keep thinking about it. • I cannot figure it out.	Perhaps
Protocols to Generate Ideas	• I'm stuck (maybe). • I don't know where to start. • I might know it if I hear it. • I'm willing to start over or blow it up.	Perhaps

Source: © 2018 Kerise Ridinger & Thomas M. Van Soelen. Used with permission.

Often a facilitator will use this tool in a preconference—a conversation between a facilitator and a presenter to accomplish two goals: (1) determine a purpose and (2) choose an appropriate protocol. A more expansive tool for preconferencing is the "Preconference Key Words and Actions" (appendix B, page 237).

Using Protocols

Even if you are precise about how you align your purpose with a protocol, it's important to remember that protocols are not magic. They are not fairy dust sprinkled on recalcitrant, stubborn, or chronically crabby colleagues, miraculously making them more pleasant to be around. They do, however, create conditions where group members can collectively be better than they are as individuals (Donohoo, 2017). Using discussion protocols effectively not only increases effectiveness in the *content* participants discuss but also the very *processes* they use. This phenomenon increases the probability of having clear meeting goals and actually meeting those goals.

Developing expertise is analogous to becoming excellent. Both breed feelings of accomplishment and productivity, especially when responsibilities are clear. Education researchers David Allen and Tina Blythe (2004) specify this as the "roles different people in the group will play" (p. 9). I choose to use the word *jobs* instead of *roles* because I see jobs as temporary and roles as (generally) more permanent. The role of a mother or a sister is usually a long-term moniker, while a job can be seasonal or could change at someone's whim. Thus, if I am asked (and well prepared) to facilitate at a meeting, I take my job seriously, knowing what it entails. When others take on that job, I can empathize with their responsibilities, engaging in more flexible thinking that can move groups forward more quickly and effectively.

In a discussion protocol, there are usually three jobs: (1) presenter, (2) facilitator, and (3) participants. When a protocol requires a *presenter*, the educator is bringing a product or a situation that needs feedback from others. The protocol *facilitator* helps the presenter decide on a process (a protocol) to use so the feedback is aligned to what the presenter really wants. Finally, *participants* are the colleagues who will offer some heavy lifting for the presenter. Chapters 2–6, which detail each protocol family, will specify which jobs are at play within that family and how the expectations of those jobs may differ. Using the word *job* also connotes *work*; it is not enough to simply show up. With the temporal nature of the word *job*, educators can exhibit excellence—be *beyond lofty*—for as long as the job requires (usually sixty minutes or less!), which seems manageable.

For protocols where a person has the job of presenter, a misconception is that this person is in the hot seat. I contend the seat should be a bit like the porridge Goldilocks liked—not too hot and not too cold. Neither extreme yields benefits for the presenter (for a visual presentation of how this is so, see the Zones of Comfort, Risk, and Danger protocol in chapter 2, page 81).

If presenters share their work with a group, the penultimate step in a protocol is called presenter reflection. The discussion protocols in this book advocate a physical move to help the seat have the heat just right or the right amount of *squirm* (Van Soelen, 2019b). The participants can borrow the work as if it is their own for portions of the protocol to help presenters conceptually step away from their work—to look at it more objectively.

A metaphor I use to bring presenters back into the group after they have listened to feedback calls to mind ducks and the idiomatic expression *like water off a duck's back*. Perhaps the presenter heard a piece of feedback, wrote it down, even considered it briefly, and then knew it wouldn't work—the feedback slides out of mind just like water off a duck's back, while other ideas are intriguing, memorable, or even obvious. These pieces of feedback stick, like water catching in the tail feathers of a duck. In the Language You Can Borrow sections throughout this book you'll see examples of how to introduce this metaphor: "*Think of yourself like a duck: some of the feedback rolled right off your back, and some of it may have gotten stuck in your tail feathers.*"

The scaffolds in this book, such as the duck metaphor, are designed for facilitators to experience more moments of excellence in groups, starting with a purpose-driven agenda. As humans, we learn through patterning, and repeated exposures start to build routines in our language and actions. Just like routines in K–12 learning spaces build consistency and create a foundation for effective learning, the same is true for educator teams. Using consistent language in facilitating and participating in discussion protocols can transform teams (Kersey, 2014). Perhaps the learning in these pages will spur some readers to inquire further into the art of facilitation. Other texts can help that effort, particularly focusing on the skills required to effectively lead discussion protocols (Allen & Blythe, 2004, 2015; McDonald et al., 2013).

Chapters 2–6 each begin with two situations in which educators would benefit from using the family of protocols in that chapter. Those chapters also include application examples after the protocol descriptions. The situations and application examples are all actual examples, though the characters in them are addressed with pseudonyms, and they provide implementation support for you to understand and use the many protocols in the book. Misconceptions or common roadblocks form an important basis of each protocol discussion, and these discussions offer novice facilitators important perspectives.

Some of the first discussion protocols used in schools appeared in the early 1990s. Thus, the truism holds up: there is nothing new under the sun. Some of the protocols in this book contain steps that may be exactly the same (between one protocol and another)—clarifying questions are an example of this repetition. Repeated text also appears with several foundational protocols for the particular step containing this text. Some protocols contain steps that are similar to others—usually with important changes that bring forth different outcomes. Since the goal of this book is to help facilitators grow confident in their artful and skillful use of protocols, it seemed logical to include common discussion and common language in one common place. Chapters 4–6 all reference appendices that facilitators can use to deeply understand the protocols in each of the families.

The phrase from the previous section, "There's a protocol for that!" has an unfortunate consequence—teams might never develop proficiency at any one process or discussion protocol. They (or the person who designed the learning for them) may believe they need a few more protocols in their toolbelt. I believe the toolbelt metaphor is wearing thin for teachers. Teachers don't always need a new strategy in their toolbelt—instead, that toolbelt could be weighing them down, and it might make more sense to put time and effort into a *few* powerful strategies and use them broadly and effectively.

It is important for readers to understand the goal is *not* to learn a new protocol a month, a few new protocols each year, and so on. In fact, I wear it as a badge of honor that I do not set New Year's resolutions to learn new protocols. Instead, I view it this way: I will become dangerously good at a few protocols within each of the protocol families. Then, if I encounter a situation where one of those won't work, I search for something new. At that point, since I have spent the requisite amount of time with the foundational discussion protocols, my facilitation skills are strong enough to apply that learning to a process that is new to me.

Notice that language, "process that is new to me." I strongly believe a genuinely new discussion protocol is a rare bird indeed. Instead, most discussion protocols contain portions that are derivations of another protocol.

Even though some helpful texts exist, like *The Power of Protocols* (McDonald et al., 2013), uneven facilitation occurs in schools. This isn't terribly surprising, considering the current wide availability and easy access of discussion protocols. If only downloading also produced facilitator competency! The ripple effect is even more troublesome. A well-intentioned educator downloads a copy of a discussion protocol, *does* it at a meeting, and now the people at that gathering use that experience as their mental model of how protocols work.

When the Annenberg Institute for School Reform developed many discussion protocols in the mid-1990s, schools opted into the training and committed to significant amounts of time, energy, and implementation measures. The discussion protocols themselves were in hard copy (print) format, and online ones were behind password protection—the password only provided to participants once they successfully completed the five- to six-day professional development. The discussion protocols were presented with live support from a trained facilitator—probably a facilitator who either was an author of one or more of the protocols or who had been one of the very first few educators ever trained. Reliability was high. I don't believe the creators and authors of these protocols could have ever imagined the broad, but in many cases, shallow, use of discussion protocols in today's schools.

Using This Book

This book serves to close a gap. Imagine you had been present for one of these original training sessions in the mid-1990s. You would have received handouts (no Google Drive, no bit.ly link, no QR code), and I suspect you would have written all over the handouts as you learned *what wasn't on the page*. There is much to be learned in the white spaces between text.

The introduction and chapter 1 organize the important concepts you would be learning in those professional development sessions. The remaining chapters give granular details about specific discussion protocols and facilitation guidance. You might only use chapters 2–6 when you are getting ready to consider a discussion protocol for an agenda or when you have the job of facilitating a protocol in one of those chapters.

The protocols presented in chapter 2 represent a broad array of how to build shared understanding in a group. Several options are available, with additional examples and facilitation tips included at **go.SolutionTree.com/leadership** in digital form. The purposes of using the discussion protocols offered in chapters 3–6 are different and require more explanation. I call these foundational protocols, meaning they find frequent use within that family. Knowing them is a boon to any educator who wants to use discussion protocols effectively for collaboration. Because these are so critically important, I provide expanded supports for them.

The first expanded support is an anchor chart that lists the purpose of the protocol, the sequence of steps involved, the time allotments for each step and, when applicable, any recommended sentence stems for participants to use during the process. Posting anchor charts in the room supports all three jobs (presenter, facilitator, and participants). Sample anchor charts for various protocols are available at **go.SolutionTree.com/leadership** so you can see what they look like.

The next expanded support details what facilitators would want to know about why this step exists and what it might take in your job as a facilitator to do that step. I think of these supports as *white space learning*. They are the kinds of quips and notes you would take in the margin if you were in a professional development session. Other texts and authors have provided valuable insight into some of these protocols as well (Allen & Blythe, 2004; Fahey et al., 2019; McDonald et al., 2013; Venables, 2011).

Many educators have been to professional development sessions, felt confident when they left, and then experienced an implementation time lag. By the time they were ready to use what they learned, they may have retained the important concepts and outcomes but lost a sense of how to make them come to fruition; or, an educator may receive a discussion protocol without any requisite professional development about the process. Although I contend the best way to learn how a process works is to experience it facilitated well, a close second-place experience is to at least hear some of the words that help participants transition from step to step. The third expanded support in this book is called Language You Can Borrow. Written in first person, these sections of the book are designed for facilitators to take with them into a meeting, and if they desire, to borrow from to aid in facilitation. Please be clear, well-designed and facilitated professional development is still the best place to learn the power of discussion protocols.

Seeing the Protocols in Action

In some ways, I resisted writing this book. Working with Alpharetta High School in metro Atlanta, Georgia, for over eight years changed my mind. Principal Shannon Kersey believes in transformative experiences. She allocates resources so any staff member at her 2,400-student high school can finish a five-day professional development about effective facilitation of discussion protocols. In 2019, 67 percent of her certified staff had done so—what a significant commitment!

During the 2017–2018 school year, Alpharetta High School began Growth Groups, a program still in operation four years later. These groups, founded on the idea of a growth mindset (Dweck, 2016), posed that growth mindset is not just for students but also for adults. These twenty cross-disciplinary teams of seven to ten teachers, leaders, and paraprofessionals met eight times during the year, with a deceivingly simple agenda: sharing something from their daily work on which they were stuck and using a protocol to get some feedback from colleagues they tend to not frequently see.

The returns on this investment have been extraordinary. Teachers found the interdisciplinary group composition to be effective (5.24 mean on a 1–6 Likert scale). They reported usefulness in the feedback (4.36 mean ranging from *1: couldn't implement any ideas* to *6: immediately implemented*). Table I.2 offers a peek into a typical Growth Group date and the scope of work present across the building.

Table I.2: Number of Growth Group Protocols Used

Protocols to Refine Products	11
Protocols to Seek Perspective	3
Protocols to Explore and Manage Dilemmas	15
Protocols to Generate Ideas	11

In creating the Growth Groups, the school used multiple criteria to create broadly diverse sets of educators. The criteria considered: gender, race, department, job responsibilities, and length of time at the school. One important feature was to make sure each group had multiple educators who had successfully completed the summer facilitation professional development. Prior to each Growth Group gathering, I spent time at Alpharetta High School and briefly (less than fifteen minutes) met with each presenter and facilitator to make sure of two things: (1) the work on which the presenter desired feedback was matched well to the chosen protocol, and (2) the facilitator and presenter were ready for their jobs.

A set of detailed facilitation notes went to both the presenter and facilitator. Teachers have greatly appreciated these facilitation notes, as, even though they experienced the professional development in which they practiced presenting, facilitating, and participating, they do not facilitate often enough to grow expertise. Those various facilitation notes have served as the nucleus for this book.

This seems analogous to how Lucy Calkins and her colleagues at Teachers College have developed reading and writing curricula. For years, Calkins seemed to resist a more structured approach (some might say, a scripted approach) to her materials, but after repeated requests and after observing significant gaps between the intent and desired outcome, she relented, creating more specific and explicit materials.

Learning how to facilitate artfully and skillfully takes immense work and dedication. Protocols can be deceptively simple, and "protocols are designed to help configure—not script—an experience" (Allen & Blythe, 2004, p. 10). However, just like a teacher uses a detailed lesson plan to guide learning, the same could be true about this book. Teachers don't need to scaffold themselves from their plan—they can use it in the lesson! In the Uncommon Schools network, teacher teams collaboratively create reteaching scripts and use them to ensure students receive the very best their teachers can offer (Bambrick-Santoyo, 2019). Similarly, facilitators will prepare for a discussion protocol, remembering they can take their scaffolds with them.

Those who argue a script is too prescriptive for facilitating may argue that, just as in teaching, a facilitator needs to be free to react in the moment to what others are saying and what they are leaving unsaid in the group. I agree, and I have argued that learning to facilitate well is a worthy goal. However, what is left in the meanwhile are lackluster or possibly destructive collaborative experiences. Many teachers have previous teaching experience to call on when they make decisions formatively in the moment. Facilitators in schools often do not have a deep well of facilitation experiences from which to draw. Additionally, teachers have had feedback on their teaching and consciously or unconsciously use those inputs in deciding what to do next. Most facilitators have not received helpful feedback on their facilitation. Finally, many teachers have seen high-quality teaching in practice and use those exemplar experiences. In schools, many facilitators of discussion protocols have never seen a discussion protocol facilitated *really well*.

Promote Clarity

As protocols are used in many schools, they are also misused in many places, usually from a lack of understanding—not malintent. When users are clear on the purpose of each step, they are much more likely to have a positive experience. In order to ensure clarity, I discuss many of these misunderstandings in the context of specific protocols and families throughout the book. However, it is worthwhile to address two areas here in which misunderstandings often happen: (1) group norms and (2) debriefing, which occurs at the end of each protocol in chapters 2–6.

Group Norms

Just using a protocol doesn't a productive experience make; it is a similar case with group norms. Simply having a set of norms, often on a wall poster, doesn't equate to positive impact. As you will note in this section, a lack of shared understanding about what norms even are is a critical gap to fill. Read on to examine the alignment between your current understanding about norms and mine. In fact, having a set of norms that are meaningless to the group probably does more harm than good. I identify three misconceptions many educators seem to have about norms: (1) they are rules, (2) they should be made right away, and (3) they are about logistics.

Norms Are Rules

Norms are designed to be contractual in nature—agreements between or among two or more parties. It is true a contract can be broken, but usually, we think about parties not living up to their responsibilities in the contract. This difference is important because group members would think less about *breaking* norms and instead just not *embodying* them enough. I find group roles such as norm checker (or a particularly unfortunate title, *norm police*) encourage the wrong notion.

The television show *Cheers* sheds helpful light here. One of the most memorable characters, Norm (played by George Wendt), was inspired by a real person who frequented a particular bar in Boston (Kerr, 1983). This particular man was so genuine, so salt of the earth, so *norm*al—hence what an appropriate name: Norm. One could surmise that the show's writers wanted to evoke a simple baseline for the viewers of what's normal among the bar's patrons. That's what norms are: the written explanation of what will be normal in a group. If a group isn't exemplifying those agreements, then they are being abnormal.

Norms Should Be Made Right Away

I find groups often create norms too soon in a group's development. Their product becomes shortsighted and more about individual desires for behaviors than the desires and needs of the group. Four hours of group time seems to be the tipping point beyond which group members may create meaningful and realistic norms. Sometimes the process takes even longer and may require a few in-service days, or it might take a few weeks. After a group has spent that much time together, its members have most likely seen authentic behaviors from one another—which means delaying the creation of the group norms (even for just four hours of group work) often results in a more genuine product. Putting a chevron around a set of norms and then laminating them does not make them effective.

Norms Are About Logistics

Groups certainly need procedural agreements about how they operate. A teacher team needs to decide when it will meet (for example, immediately when the bell rings or give five minutes first to use the restroom?), where it will keep common resources (for example, Google Drive? Microsoft OneNote?), and the like. Unfortunately, procedural content, which is often binary in nature, dominates the norms of most groups. For instance, either someone comes to the group on time or not. Teachers update their data sheets before the Thursday noon deadline—or don't. There isn't a middle ground.

Behavioral norms are more dynamic in nature, as they align more to the notion of living up to contractual obligations. A group may sometimes identify multiple perspectives and viewpoints but do so inconsistently. An educator may enjoy giving feedback but has trouble with the receiving part.

Both types—behavioral norms and procedural agreements—are necessary. Dividing them in a T-chart can be a remarkable strategy for groups to see their tendencies and also ensure they have carefully thought about their needs for both categories. Figure I.1 shows an example from a middle school leadership team.

We do our best leading and thinking when we . . .

Behavioral Norms	Procedural Agreements
Invite multiple perspectives, identifying when the perspective is not our own.	Keep meeting notes in OneNote. Grade-level teams should add these notes to their agenda each month.
Stay engaged in the conversation.	Use technology as the agenda's content requires.
Pay attention to who is participating.	Start and end on time: the first Wednesday of each month, 3:30–4:30 p.m.
Go to the source, or let it go.	Use agendas with clear infinitives about purpose.
Come with a willingness to be influenced.	

Figure I.1: Middle school leadership team norms.

Highly effective teams have dynamic norms—these kinds of norms contain the flexibility to change (DuFour, DuFour, Eaker, Many, & Mattos, 2016) as one or more of three things change: (1) the members, (2) the work or content, and (3) the context. COVID-19 is a memorable example of circumstances requiring flexibility in norms, and Alpharetta High School in Alpharetta, Georgia, met this need for flexibility when it added this norm to its leadership team during the spring 2020 months of emergency teaching: "Hold each other accountable to not slip into traditional thinking about school and our roles as leaders and teachers."

No matter what group norms you may have in place, the introduction of discussion protocols may cause them to change. The powerful practices in this book build skills in educators that become normal—which is exactly what group norms attempt to document.

Debriefing

The final step of the protocol process is called debriefing, and it is prone to facilitator misunderstanding. A facilitator may inadvertently re-open a topic by engaging in a misstep during this important processing time. Highly functional groups do not stop at the initial and obvious layer—they persist past talking about learning to development. Instead of repeating the following sections with each protocol in this book, I discuss this area of misunderstanding here, offer facilitation support, and describe how debriefing could center around the protocol itself or the facilitation, as well as focus on the individual or the group.

The Protocol Itself

As groups use protocols, it is valuable to bring to the surface how a particular step felt tricky, helpful, or just plain hard. This happens every time the group uses a process, whether or not the group has experience with it or not. One of the beautiful elements of discussion protocols is they are designed to be recursive. A group could use a particular protocol multiple times during the year, and it may not ever feel redundant because the content may change, the participants within the protocol may have grown and changed since the last time they used the protocol, and the facilitator may be different as well. A common way I might start a debrief is by asking, "So, how did that go?"

Facilitation

A well-facilitated protocol means educators walk away talking about the content, not the facilitation. The facilitative moves described in this book are not designed to center the *facilitator* nor the *presenter*, rather they should center *the work*. During the debriefing, it may be helpful to articulate certain parts of the facilitation that helped (made facile) or hindered the group's work. A facilitator may wish to raise this query, saying it in such a way to not prioritize the work of the facilitator but instead focus on the work of the larger group. Asking a question like, "What parts of the facilitation made it easier for people to do their jobs today?" could spark this debrief focus.

The Group

Whether or not a group uses a particular protocol ever again in its lifetime, the experience will still yield learning about how the group functions. Perhaps the group had trouble following the constraints. Perhaps participants needed some coaxing to be more honest in their talking. If the group has norms, this could be a time to hearken back to them. Debriefing is a time to make that *process* learning just as valuable as the *content* learning. *Content learning* addresses the *what*, while *process learning* makes explicit *how* the group functions. A third-grade team might discuss computation interventions (*what*), and it would also debrief the protocol it used to raise those ideas (*process*). A potential prompt might be the following questions: What specifically in our norms or agreements did we live well today? What behaviors were missing in our interactions today that we had agreed on?

The Individual

Discussion protocols are not designed to be events in the lifespan of a group; instead, they are designed to be the lifeblood of a group—this is how we operate; it's not how we live! Over those shared and layered experiences, adults can both learn and develop (Fahey et al., 2019). A debrief could certainly offer space for individuals to share what they have learned, but highly functional teams talk during a debrief about how they as individuals are starting to develop—how they are looking at the world differently, starting to see inequities in their daily practices, and finding the courage to practice care-filled radical candor with their colleagues. Groups who leverage discussion protocols toward these ends include members who are truly transformed (Kersey, 2014). If this might be the focus in a debrief, possible questions to ask might include the following: "So, what changes might you specifically make in your own practice based on today's learning? Why did it matter that we met today—for you?" After these questions, as a facilitator, you might also say, "Let's go around the circle, asking each person to finish this prompt, 'As a result of today, I commit . . . .'"

It may be tempting to layer a debrief and force all four of these learning layers (the protocol itself, facilitation, group, and individual) by having individual prompts for each one. That is certainly possible. Another approach would be a more organic one—include each of these as a potential back-pocket move if the group needs a change of direction.

And Now, a Look Ahead

Here is where the danger lies. Remember, discussion protocols are not magical—a bit of fairy dust from the facilitator does not suddenly transform a group or its members. Look at your current calendar and count the meetings in the past two weeks in which you wanted to raise your hand and ask, "Why are we talking about this?" However, you enjoy getting a paycheck, so you probably kept your hand down—at least until the parking lot, where suddenly your courage emerged. That meeting where you were lacking purpose may have even *had a protocol included*—and that didn't make it better. In fact, the misuse of a protocol without clear purpose probably made it worse.

This book is written for anyone who wants to believe meetings *can* matter. These pages are helpful for those who chose to be in leadership positions and also for the accidental grade-level leader or department chair. In particular, if you have been protocoled or you think you may be protocoling your colleagues with no modeling or professional development about how to facilitate some discussion protocols well, this book may be for you.

Just like collaborative teams thrive within a larger environment of professional community (Kruse, Louis, & Bryk, 1994), discussion protocols work best when agendas are designed carefully and with clear purpose. Keep reading—creating such purpose-driven agendas is the focus of the first chapter.

1

Ensuring Purpose Before Protocols

Well-intentioned leaders do not intend to lead meaningless meetings. Their circumstances cause them to prioritize other work—often the urgent, sometimes the important, and occasionally, items that are both urgent and important.

Regardless of the reasons why meetings occur without proper planning, agendas without purpose abound in schools and central offices, damaging an often-tenuous culture. Gaps already exist when hierarchies are present in a room, such as certified and classified, principals and teachers, principal supervisors and principals, and superintendent and cabinet. Adding in a required and poorly designed meeting is a recipe for a dish no one wants to eat.

Instead, as educators, we each yearn to be part of gatherings where we actually *want to be*. Imagine putting a meeting on your calendar because you want to, not because you have to. To review, there are four characteristics of those sorts of gatherings (the E⁴), as I discussed in the introduction: you feel (1) effective and (2) efficient, and the meeting is characterized by (3) equity in voice and (4) excellence.

E^4 is not designed to be alliterative just for the sake of wordplay. During a summer multiday professional development about how discussion protocols can be effective tools in creating a positive and inclusive school culture, these words kept popping up. We decided to write them down and coined the term *E⁴*.

As the introduction explains, purpose is a prerequisite for discussion protocols to thrive. As an associate superintendent in Georgia for almost a decade, I had been using discussion protocols whenever possible, but there was something missing. It felt like we were *doing* them and not really *using* them. My team and I set a goal to try and create more meaning out of required meetings, but we needed to tread carefully. In trying to practice more purpose-first leadership, I needed to work within my area of influence.

The superintendent held monthly leadership team meetings, requiring all building principals and central office cabinet members to attend. The agendas were typical in nature to most agendas in schools and school districts, that is, numbered, topical, and unprioritized. Here's an example of six items on one such agenda.

1. New human resources system for applications
2. School Thanksgiving meal schedule
3. Construction update
4. International Baccalaureate implementation
5. Technology inventory
6. Most recent standardized test scores

And the list went on.

As step one in working within influence, I lobbied to create more categories in the agenda, particularly using the natural division between instructional and operational items. The superintendent wished to be present for operational items, so those occurred first. Once those items were completed, operational central office staff were dismissed (after a mandatory lunch, of course). With this new space and freedom, we decided to innovate with purpose in mind. The year 2009 marked the beginning of our plan to create an environment where our discussion protocols could truly make an impact. I'll start by discussing the method we devised to create purpose-driven agendas, move on to putting this method into practice, and finally offer some advice on facilitating a meeting that flows well.

The Method

Facilitative leaders create collaborative experiences where participants learn with and from each other (Garmston & von Frank, 2012). "These 'meetings that matter' do not simply happen—they are crafted with care" (Van Soelen, 2013, p. 24).

We knew we needed a pathway to accomplish our goals, so we got to work. The method we developed almost began out of desperation. As the curriculum directors and I were looking at topics, someone asked, "*Why* are we talking about _____?" Several minutes of discussion ensued, and at the end of our debate, we still didn't have an answer until we stumbled on the real learning with the breakthrough question, Then, *why* is it on the agenda? The answer then was so simple—take it off the agenda.

We discovered the first benefit of a purpose-driven agenda—clarity in what needs to be on the agenda and what does not. As we celebrated our small win, we were annotating our own copy of the agenda with purposeful words and phrases, like *decide* and *ask for feedback*. Right before we were going to declare the agenda final, one of us called out a working assumption, "If our goal is to make more purpose for the principals, why are we the only ones who get to know that purpose?"

Our methodology was born. As curriculum-focused educators, we used a piece of the student curriculum for English language arts (ELA) and identified our written notes as infinitives ("to _____" statements with a verb as the second word, whose function is to indicate the purpose of an action). Interestingly enough, three years later, we discovered Robert J. Garmston had a similar idea of using infinitives publicly with groups (Garmston & von Frank, 2012). We knew we were on the right track!

We still built agendas in drafts with topics as placeholders, similar to how a school leader may keep a Google Doc, a OneNote page, or the comment box in an Outlook event as the dumping ground for current thinking. The next step is where the real thinking took place.

Each item required us to generate an infinitive, which, as mentioned, is a verb form that begins with *to*, such as *to see*. Some infinitives in meetings were standard and repetitive, others were unique to a situation and content. Early on, we realized we were getting caught in a trap, one that author and educator Parker J. Palmer (2009) calls the *tragic gap*. We were claiming more engagement in these meetings but then using infinitives such as *to announce* or *to tell*. We weren't living what we knew was right and true. The curriculum directors would debrief meetings, and they often noted that the most problematic moments occurred during those segments of the agenda.

Another innovation was born: using the infinitive *to inform*. The actual words were not magical—it was the process we used with all topics with that infinitive that is important. Each principal received a paper copy of (or could access online) each relevant item with that particular infinitive. These items should not generate extensive conversation or questions—agenda creators must write enough to provide clear direction (for example, due dates or actions). *To inform* items were defined as one-way communication. Generally, we spent six to ten minutes in each meeting to read the *to inform* segment of the agenda, followed by three to five minutes of clarifying questions, defined as the *who, what, when,* or *where* questions—definitely not the *why*—that should already be apparent in the written communication which we had just read. *Why* questions were unnecessary as we had already decided on *to inform* items, often by others who were not in the room. Spending time discussing (that is, complaining) about a particular decision is unproductive. The *to inform* section was a radical departure from previous practices where already-communicated items were reviewed.

We saw palpable changes that included participants reading information, opening emails to communicate with relevant parties at the school, scheduling events, and adding items to other school-based agendas—in essence, they were using the *to inform* information to *act*.

NOTES

- Having *to inform* items as electronic and all in one place provides a single storehouse of information that is easily searchable.

continued →

- In an effort to save time, some may wish to post the *to inform* items ahead of the meeting for participants to peruse. However, consider the assumption that adults will, when given the opportunity, read the document before the meeting. In one group where I organized the agenda, two of the twelve members insisted on seeing it ahead of time, so we sent it to both of them. They were also the same two members who wanted paper copies of everything at the meeting, rather than URLs. So, we differentiated and made two paper copies of everything.

To inform needed to be monitored. The question, May I make an announcement? wasn't permitted at the meeting if the announcement should have been included in the *to inform* document. Additionally, principals held district office leaders to their commitment about using *to inform*—if emails were going out that didn't require immediate action, that meant district personnel were not maximizing the power of the *to inform* concept. Principals experienced a drop in the quantity of emails as a result of this structure. An amazing feat, no doubt!

This is a monumental difference from the practice of sending information items electronically, virtually removing them fully from an agenda. Principal Shannon Kersey in Alpharetta, Georgia, heard her teachers cry out for more time, so she removed most faculty meetings for a school year. Administrators replaced the face-to-face time with screencast videos of vital information when needed. Unfortunately, this method of meeting teachers' needs had two deleterious effects.

1. Many staff members were not watching the videos, and of those who did, some did not act on the information to align their practices to expectations. One of the videos detailed the teacher requirements to ensure the Curriculum Night experience for parents included the same three components in every class period. The video was launched, but the expectations did not consistently occur.

2. The school's culture took a hit. Privatism started to emerge, even though the school had taken specific steps in previous years to shrink the school so the 130 certified staff members would more frequently interact together.

The next year, Kersey started innovating the calendar to create time blocks where teachers could collaborate and work but kept the necessary staff meetings. Staff members have a choice: they can come after school on a particular day or come before school the next day. The information in either case is the same, and it allows high school teachers to balance the many time commitments they make (for example, clubs, coaching, or tutoring).

Using *to inform* gave a protected time and place for school leaders to actually read the information that otherwise could have been an email they might not have read. Not only did this practice help the participants act, it also provided a guarantee to the originator of the information—an assurance that each person in the room read the material, as opposed to the assumption we might have that is well-communicated with the words, "You're a professional; read your email." I challenge anyone to find an organization with 100 percent compliance to that!

Nothing gets on an agenda without purpose. No infinitive means no reason to include. These agendas are characterized by fewer, more thoughtful items, all of which require participant interaction.

Infinitives will likely change from meeting to meeting. They are designed to be unique to the purposes of the group as well as the content and outcomes for the meeting. Here are some examples of infinitive statements some groups have used.

- To learn about content-area literacy practices
- To create action plans informed by data
- To build consensus
- To give feedback
- To meet compliance for state assessment proctoring
- To draft
- To refine a document
- To articulate expectations
- To generate potential options
- To vision our future using one-to-one devices
- To explore and manage a dilemma
- To look for gaps
- To articulate a response to the community

These are powerful infinitives that can help teams realize their purpose. Not all infinitives are created equal, however, and just having a good infinitive isn't enough without some attention to the agenda's sequence and chosen process or protocol. But when the agenda designer considers all these details, the results are very positive. We'll discuss these considerations in more detail in the following sections.

Two Infinitives to Avoid

Almost anything could be a potential infinitive. We were only limited by our discussions about why something was on the agenda in the first place.

However, we learned over time that two particular infinitives were less productive for the group: (1) *to discuss* and (2) *to decide*. As we reflected on meetings, we realized those infinitives caused the most ineffectiveness for the group. I discuss why in the following sections.

To Discuss

Discussion is a *process*, not an outcome or purpose. Thus, *to discuss* isn't an infinitive in this context. I have coached many leaders where the discussion goes like this:

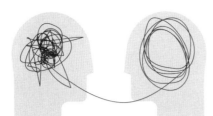

Thomas:	So, we are building an agenda for the next leadership team meeting. I see you have an RTI [response to intervention] process here. What is the goal of that item?
Leader:	It's not going well. We really need to talk about it.
Thomas:	So, what is the intention for having that discussion?
Leader:	The implementation is uneven across the building. We really need to discuss it.
Thomas:	So, what do you hope to accomplish in that particular meeting?
Leader: *(a bit frustrated with me)*	To really dig into it together.
Thomas:	I think we may be having a cyclical conversation. Let's try this another way . . .

The next time you are thinking about writing *to discuss* or *to talk about* as an infinitive, ask yourself, "*Why* are we discussing _____?" Imagine if the previous conversation with the leader was more productive, and one of these was the response.

- "To surface our assumptions about RTI"
- "To assess how well we are doing with RTI"
- "To build consensus on the tight and loose of our RTI process"

With this clear declaration of a purpose or goal, the facilitator can artfully choose a process (perhaps, a discussion protocol).

In a graduate class, I teach about collaborative teams; one assignment asks learners to redesign an agenda for a meeting they attended using infinitives. These teacher leaders often experience quite a bit of cognitive dissonance as they struggle with finding purpose for several items on their chosen agenda. One graduate student took a whole faculty meeting and moved seven of the eight items to a *to inform* section, and took the last item off completely, writing:

> I really struggled with finding purpose to the last item. I honestly think we aren't ready to talk with the whole faculty about it. It makes more sense to put this on a leadership team agenda until they can articulate the infinitive. (T. Vogel, personal communication, April 18, 2018)

What an amended agenda!

To Decide

To decide is the other infinitive *non grata* on an agenda. Instead, consider using *to agree* or *to build consensus*. *To agree* connotes a great deal of power attributed to each individual person. Each person has the power to thwart the decision for all. *To build consensus* (*I can live with it* was this group's working definition) provides more flexibility in moving past the decision to action. This group found *to agree* was rare on its agendas and *to build consensus* more frequent. When they used *to decide*, group members often lacked a shared understanding about what that really means.

Groups often work too long and too hard to reach agreement. This truism occurs in all sorts of gatherings, including in leadership teams, in grade-level teams, within departments, and in schoolwide or districtwide professional learning communities (PLCs). Agreement is a higher bar for a group to reach. When I talk to educators about this notion, they vigorously nod in agreement, and then ask the obvious next question: "Is there a protocol that could help us build consensus?" In this case, the group needs to build shared understanding, so reading about The Fist to Five strategy (page 247) would be a great next step.

Artful Sequencing Using Infinitives

When using this agenda-building process, adults receive opportunities to work within one cognitive function for a longer period of time. Sometimes the agenda designer pays very little attention to sequencing agenda items. There are four basic methods I see educators use when they put their agendas in order.

1. **Running file or calendar entry:** These automatically sequence each time something comes to mind (honestly never coming back to it to put in a meaningful order).

2. **Morse code or alternate items due to length:** The agenda designer starts with an item that will potentially take a while, then puts in a short item, then repeats: long, short, and so on.

3. **Morse code or alternate items due to assumed difficulty of the item:** The agenda designer alternates harder with easier or softer topics.

4. **Morse code or alternate items due to expected emotion:** The agenda designer alternates hot topics (tough to talk about it) with cold (not fraught with emotion).

My colleagues and I knew sequencing items was critical to a meeting's success. We were already implicitly doing this in the *to inform* section by putting informational items together—now the rest of the agenda aligned to the strategy.

We made a discovery that was a game-changer. The preceding methods are less effective than actually thinking about the cognitive function required by the participants for each item. Grouping similar infinitives together prevented constant transitions of expectation. For example, when all the *to-give-feedback* items were clustered together, participants could focus on expected behaviors and not have to return to them during a meeting. Imagine the opposite in this agenda.

1. **To give feedback:** Professional learning days for next school year
2. **To build consensus:** Recertification procedures
3. **To give feedback to the District Diversity Team:** Equity framework
4. **To agree:** Date of summer instructional retreat

Participants would need to constantly change their approach to each agenda item, and frankly, some wouldn't be able to do it very well. For instance, on item 3, the group may start aggressively advocating for changes on the equity framework—wanting a decision today, forgetting their job today is to give feedback to another team.

Results

With this newly found belief system, we experienced the following immediate benefits.

- **Engagement had an important uptick:** Participants were participating! By sorting and sifting content as the agenda was being built, the actual agenda became an artifact of our intent. Educators in the meeting knew the agenda was intentionally designed from the very first minute, which prevented wasting time and energy.

- **Better decisions were made, with collective responsibility:** As authors plead for educators to practice self-care (Boogren, 2018), these agendas aligned toward a similar purpose. Educators only have a finite amount of energy, and misplacing focus happens all too frequently. The new agendas prioritized our thinking, saving our very best for making decisions that impact students and teachers.

- **Relationships improved:** Since the work of school improvement is designed to be a partnership between the district office and schools, the afternoon agendas were critical—some might argue, our most important monthly work. I believe central office personnel could buy shirts embroidered with *They* or *Them*. It is easy to complain about decisions or products developed by unnamed individuals. Over time, the pronoun *we* became far more evident in our school and central office interactions.

Purposeful Agenda Building in Practice

Hickory Hills Elementary School in Marietta, Georgia, brought this chapter's agenda-setting structure to scale. Combined with a knowledge and use of structured conversations (protocols) and promulgated by SRI (www.schoolreforminitiative.org/protocols), the school experienced the nearly impossible. After starting the structure with the leadership team, its members asked if they could use the structure with their own collaborative teams. Each group that meets predictably (for example, grade-level teams, leadership teams, administration teams, intervention teams, and school-governance teams) has adopted this framework and joyfully reports more engagement and high efficiency.

However, Principal Kristen Beaudin needed to address the staff members' many questions about this process, as it was a drastic change from their previously open meeting structure.

In response to their need for clarity, Principal Beaudin collected questions and I answered them all. Figure 1.1 represents the FAQ document I created.

Frequently Asked Questions About Infinitive Agenda Setting

Could one infinitive lead to another?

Absolutely! One meeting might ask a group *to provide feedback* to the administrative team. The administrative team then works and creates options for the grade level to consider. The next meeting might be *to build consensus* as the preferred option for the grade level.

Do participants have input on the agenda?

This format for framing agendas could have a collaborative agenda construction or not.

Is there time for communication, or is it simply directive?

The agenda is designed to provide exactly what the group needs. The infinitive *to inform* may feel more directive because it offers informational items as one-way communication.

What if there is something of urgency that must be informed but it wasn't sent through email?

Then the item would be placed on the *to inform* document wherever it is (for example, Google Docs or OneNote). Email is used less frequently with this process.

How was time managed? How did the group members move on?

Similar to other meetings, time frames are assigned to specific items. When the time frames do not work out, facilitators can explicitly share options for how to move forward.

How are infinitives determined, with a preselected list or as needed?

As needed. Some infinitives may repeat across meetings.

What happens if the time frame does not provide enough time for clarifying questions during the to inform item?

If the group consistently has this issue, then the people who write the *to inform* items know they need to provide more detail in future submissions.

Does to inform mean brand-new items educators have not heard about yet?

Not necessarily. Some items may simply be a reminder of past conversations; others may be new information that is simple to comprehend and probably does not need discussion. These items already have been decided, often by others in leadership, either at the school or district level.

Figure 1.1: Hickory Hills Elementary School FAQs.

Rebecca Williams, principal of Webb Bridge Middle School in Alpharetta, Georgia, discovered she needed to build more autonomy in assistant principals as well as teacher leaders. A culture of micromanagement existed (whether actual or perceived), and in her words, "I spent most of my first year helping others realize *they* can make the decisions they are asking me" (R. Williams, personal communication, January 27, 2020). Explicitly coaching others has certainly helped, but agenda building using infinitives has also been a key structure in the development of agendas where educators are purposefully meeting.

Williams learned about the method in her years at Webb Bridge's matriculating high school, Alpharetta High School. The culture there had grown to rely on purposeful meetings under the leadership of Principal Shannon Kersey, so Williams changed the organization and planning for end-of-year leadership retreats.

As is typical for many organizations, a call went out for agenda items. However, this time, Williams and I changed the Google form. Here were the directions:

> Please decide what topics you believe need to be part of the end-of-year retreat. For each item, please first list the topic and then the outcome. You might use an infinitive like *to clarify* or *to revise*. *To discuss* is not an outcome—that is a process. So really think about *why* you wish to discuss a certain topic.

This form wasn't the game-changer, just like a process, tool, or discussion protocol isn't magical. Instead, a thoughtful agenda with carefully aligned protocols offers the potential for people to change their own behaviors. Williams needed to follow up with several submissions to truly understand the goal or outcome. Then she and I carefully chose discussion protocols to match the outcomes. That is what the rest of this book does. It builds a tighter match between purpose (infinitive) and process (discussion protocol), and it offers scaffolds for facilitators to use as they improve. Then facilitators can reach their goal of E[4] meetings, those that are effective and efficient, characterized by equity in voice and excellence.

Kerri-Ann Williams, first-year principal of Ocee Elementary School in Johns Creek, Georgia, started using infinitives in 2020 to guide her leadership retreat. To her surprise, it became a habit and now pervades all meetings where she gets to design an agenda. She commented, "I find I am using more protocols now, too. It isn't intentional to use protocols—I guess it's because I am just more focused on purpose" (K. Williams, personal communication, December 2, 2019).

Marcus Miller, professional learning coordinator, and his central office team at the Plano Independent School District in Texas, have been using infinitives in their own internal planning since 2019. Once they made their practice public, it became so popular, they were asked to teach the agenda-constructing technique to principals and multiple departments. "The infinitive agenda has become such a cornerstone for our culture that it is the very first thing we create when we plan for professional learning," mentions Miller (M. Miller, personal communication, December 3, 2019).

I Have the Infinitive—Now What?

Leading with the purpose in designing gatherings for educators is an excellent start. It could provide a significant step in building trust between members and the agenda designer. However, a strong purpose (infinitive) combined with slipshod facilitation is still problematic. A planning template like the one shown in figure 1.2 can provide a link between clear purpose and a carefully chosen discussion protocol.

Why	When	What or How	What Happened?

Figure 1.2: Planning template.

Visit go.SolutionTree.com/leadership for a free reproducible version of this figure.

This template strikes a balance between careful planning and excessive detail. I liken the journey of using a planning frame to finding the *just right* lesson-planning template. Standardizing a personal process for all is often deflating for educators and may produce less-than-desirable products. The same would hold true for this planning frame as you design experiences. It is more important for you to have *a frame* to use as opposed to using *this one*.

The following agenda excerpt in figure 1.3 (page 32) is from a technology leadership team meeting in a large urban district. It references two discussion protocols, Chalk Talk and Compass Points, both of which I discuss further in chapter 2 (page 35). The team includes fifteen members, including four from the central office and eleven who are school based. There are multiple layers of leadership and authority. Part of this face-to-face meeting needed to focus on how this group was being neither efficient nor effective.

I use the term *connective tissue* in this agenda. Connective tissue is a generalized anatomical word referring to the parts of the body which connect, support, or bind things together. Connective tissue can be found in many body parts, for example, tendons, ligaments, and cartilage. Kerise Ridinger, coordinator for professional learning in Lewisville Independent School District, and I use the term *connective tissue* to ensure a logical and meaningful flow in agendas. She and I have both been participants in professional learning experiences where a set of activities is *done* in a sequence but participants are left unclear about why *that* process at *that* time. As Kerise and I co-design agendas, we sometimes cannot write effective connective tissue. In those moments, we realize it would be more effective to modify the agenda sequence.

Why	When	What or How	What Happened?
To surface our gaps	9:15 a.m.	Chalk Talk: two prompts—(1) What are the current barriers in our way of being productive together? and (2) What might be at the heart of those barriers?	*Amazing! Members took risks to honestly assess the current state. Led beautifully into the next phase of the meeting. Documented with a picture and going to strategically address more of the gaps in subsequent meetings.*
To build group vocabulary	9:45 a.m.	*Connective tissue: We have started to honestly identify the gaps in our shared work, and now it's time to productively start to shrink them. One important dimension of working together is realizing our own personal preferences as well as the group habits. We will start that learning using this process . . .* Compass Points	*Started about 10 a.m.* *Surprisingly, group members saw a balance among participants standing in the four corners at one point during the Compass Points protocol, but started to understand how they are personally different when this group comes together.*
To draft	10:40 a.m.	*Connective tissue: As the Chalk Talk indicated, there is general confusion about who makes what decision when. This next process is complicated but so is your work! Pushing you through the minutia of this next experience will result in better clarity for everyone.* Decision-making continuum: 1. Generate the junctures on the continuum (for example, executive committee decides together; executive director decides by himself, executive director decides by asking others). 2. Generate the specific items. 3. In pairs, do the sorting. 4. Build consensus in ever-increasingly large groups (for example, pairs join other pairs). Will be important to heterogeneously group so multiple levels of the organization are present in the triads or quads. Ask them what groups would make the most sense.	*Grouping worked out really great—everyone was easily able to see the importance of heterogeneity. The task was not complete when lunch came, but members were happily working and decided to eat and continue to work!*

Figure 1.3: Agenda excerpt.

Figure 1.3 lists some discussion protocols, or structured conversations, in the What or How column. However, these protocols do not exist for their own sake. For instance, Compass Points was not *done* for the group so they could then *do* Compass Points back at their school sites. Chalk Talk was not *modeled* for them simply for the sake of application. Instead, the discussion protocols were necessary for the group's learning, and if any members end up lifting the experience to use with another group at another time, that is an exciting development.

As mentioned in the book's introduction (page 1), being protocoled involves not seeing or hearing a relevant purpose for using a discussion protocol. This chapter provides guidance on how to use infinitives in agenda construction to ensure explicit purpose. Once the purposes are clear, a facilitator can choose a discussion protocol to help the group reach that outcome.

Chapter 2 begins a five-chapter sequence that discusses each of the five protocol families previewed in the introduction. I've written these five chapters so facilitators can both study specific discussion protocols prior to facilitation and refer to pages during the actual facilitation itself. Chapter 2 focuses on protocols to build shared understanding.

2

Protocols to Build Shared Understanding

This chapter represents the largest family of protocols in this book. The following protocols are designed to assist educators in finding common ground, common definitions, or common inquiries. Peggy Schooling, Michael Toth, and Robert J. Marzano (2013) call a common language critical while Anthony S. Bryk (2010) and Michael Fullan and Joanne Quinn (2016) describe the need for it as a lack of coherence. Coherence in learning standards, instructional expectations, and leadership monitoring positively impacts student learning.

The discussion protocols in this chapter are useful in a host of different settings, from those where teachers have worked together for years to those where groups might come together one time for just one specific reason or task. In both situations, E^4 characteristics, effective and efficient, characterized by equity and excellence, are desirable. The discussion protocols in this chapter often require *shared* risk, in that it is infrequent that the group is examining only one person's product or issue. This family of protocols usually considers topics or texts equally relevant and important to everyone in the group.

In the following two situations, the educators considering a discussion protocol are seeking group learning. They both would benefit from one of the discussion protocols explained in this chapter.

SITUATION A

Laura is an instructional coach focused on mathematics. As she works with the fifth-grade team, she believes the members of the team all have very different understandings about what a particular standard means in practice. The team participates in divide-and-conquer planning, and there is disagreement on the team between the two educators who wrote the plans for this week. Rather than spend the collaborative planning time revising the plans, Laura believes this plan would be more empowering for the two teachers who plan mathematics instruction.

Laura has been hoping the team would start using various resources in their planning (many of which she has provided to the team already), so she goes to websites with unpacked standards from Virginia and California. Laura's state doesn't provide unpacked standards for teacher access. Searching out just this particular learning standard, Laura creates a document with less than four pages for the team to read during the planning time. She needs some sort of discussion protocol to help them really study the standards and the related texts.

SITUATION B

The beginning of the year always seems to require such balance. Rodney, an assistant principal, feels like they never get it quite right. If he and his principal plan many whole-faculty experiences, complaints emerge about group and individual time. If they offer fewer, the staff feel disjointed and fractured into teams, which are also important and need adequate group time.

Rodney also is not a fan of useless games. Someone may get hurt if he needs to fill out *one more* matrix where he collects initials of colleagues who have been on a cruise to Jamaica, are the youngest child in their family, and are allergic to something. What his staff members really need is a whole-staff experience where they can laugh together, mix among the various teams, and learn something about themselves, which will help their teacher teams this year. He needs more than an icebreaker.

The family of discussion protocols in this chapter differs from others in that they do not focus on only one person's work or dilemma. *Thus, these protocols often do not feature a presenter.* Or said differently, *everyone is a presenter* in these experiences. Laura isn't examining content standards for her personal benefit—it is for each member of her team. Rodney wants to create a group experience so that all staff members feel value for the time they spend together at the beginning of a school year. Hearing the multiple points of view or ideas around a common question, experience, or other prompts, such as texts, is a first step toward building shared understanding.

Due to the quantity of protocols in this chapter, they are divided into the following categories: text-based protocols, reflection protocols, equity and diversity protocols, and community-building protocols. The categories are not mutually exclusive; some protocols may fit into more than one. Common across all categories is the purpose of building shared understanding among members of a group. Each discussion protocol begins with a short description, followed by group size and protocol sequence. Most of the protocols end with a set of notes and application examples. The application examples are all based on experiences of real educators that occurred when educators chose a specific protocol to match their purpose. For protocols with complex facilitation, the notes are integrated into the sequence itself.

I'll include a quick reminder about debriefing. Debriefing means discussing the process of learning for individuals and groups, not reopening content that was just discussed. See the introduction (page 1) for more detail as well as for possible questions to use to frame a debrief.

Text-Based Protocols

All educators read texts. Discussion protocols can help groups more effectively discuss the texts they read in community with others. Several are listed in this section, with other protocol options available at **go.SolutionTree.com/leadership** in digital form.

Coffee Talk

Frances Hensley initially developed the Coffee Talk protocol, then it was published with refinements by Susan Taylor and Connie Zimmerman Parrish (Hensley, Taylor, & Parrish, n.d.), and then I further adapted it. Coffee Talk is conceptually similar to the sketch popularized by comedian and actor Mike Myers (1991–1994) on the television show *Saturday Night Live*, "Coffee Talk with Linda Richman." The character's famous line, "Talk amongst yourselves," offers insight into the loose nature of this text-based discussion protocol. Originally designed for text specifically about education equity and social justice, a variety of texts works well. An effective text set has multiple text types, including articles, book excerpts, poetry, videos, audio clips, blog posts, academic writing, and practitioner-friendly writing.

Purpose

Participants aim to enlarge their thinking as they read, write, and talk about a text set.

Group Size

Usually the larger, the better. It would be difficult to use Coffee Talk with a group of fewer than eight people.

Pre-Protocol Preparation

Coffee Talk requires a facilitator to design a text set. After choosing a variety of texts that intersect around a theme or idea, make copies or another path for participants to access the texts.

Sequence

1. Give brief introductions of each text (for example, type and origin of text, possibly facts about specific authors). (Less than five minutes)

2. Offer participants time to read whatever they wish in the text set. The goal is *not* to read the entire text set, rather, the goal is to spend time engaged in professional reading. (Twenty-five to forty minutes)

3. Gather participants together, asking them to write about what they just read. Post the following prompts as optional fodder for their writing. (Seven to ten minutes, prompts not required)

   a. What was comforting or comfortable?

   b. What did you find challenging or confusing?

   c. What are you wondering about? What questions do you now have?

   d. What do you most want to remember?

4. Participants leave their seats with readings and reflections in hand, finding two to three others. They do not need to gather with others who read the same texts they did; rather, the theme of the text set brings everyone together. Therefore, their grouping can be anyone in the room, not to be limited by the text titles. (Five to seven minutes)

5. Ask participants to change *something*: change groups, change topics, change speakers, or change texts, then continue for another round. (Five to seven minutes)

6. If time or interest allows, ask participants to change something again. If some participants have stayed together for the first two rounds, a facilitator may encourage a change in group composition. If the text set was more than five texts, I suggest including a third round. (Five to seven minutes)

7. Debrief the process.

Notes

- The facilitator can make paper copies of the texts or use electronic spaces and platforms. If using paper copies, number the pages. This small action greatly assists participants in easily referencing segments of various texts.

- During the text introduction, consider having materials (for example, highlighters or sticky notes) ready so that participants may mark what texts intrigue them.

- The text set may be 100 percent teacher choice or a modification. One foundational text may be required reading, and the rest of the reading time might be spent in self-chosen texts.

- For a day-long professional development session, it works well to offer an extended lunch such as thirty minutes to read and sixty minutes to eat to equal ninety minutes in all. The goal is not to read it all, just to *read*.

Application Examples

- Michael only has forty-five minutes with high school teachers during their planning. As an external consultant, he has never met these teachers before and is a bit nervous. His focus was chosen for him: literacy across the content areas. He chose to use Symbaloo (www.symbaloo.com), curating over fifty-eight links to video, audio, and print texts. He used the department faculty listing from the school's website to make sure he had some options for every teacher who would cycle through the session—even the teacher of Russian and the career technical teacher of granite technology! He instructed teachers this was a BYOH, bring-your-own-headphones session. After twenty-five minutes of listening, viewing, and reading, twenty meaningful minutes are spent in a Coffee Talk.

- Pam is a mathematics instructional coach at the district level. During a district professional learning day, many fifth-grade teachers from around the district are required to attend a full-day professional development session. As they are moving into the lunch break, Pam decides to extend their lunch break by thirty minutes to include sixty minutes to enjoy a duty-free lunch with colleagues and thirty minutes to read a text set she created about the geometry unit for the next marking period. One required reading is an unpacking of the fifth-grade mathematics standards. The rest of the text set includes a variety of other texts (part of an academic text about geometric misconceptions in elementary school, an exemplar lesson plan, a link to a video in which a model lesson is being taught, and a work sample from a student).

Questions and Assumptions

I first experienced the Questions and Assumptions (SRI, n.d.g) protocol in a professional development session. It was developed in the field by educators, and then I adapted it. A tacit assumption often occurs in schools that when adults receive text to read, the proper response is to nod in agreement. The Questions and Assumptions protocol challenges that cultural reality, instead encouraging readers to critically analyze a text. The ultimate irony: curriculum standards for students often ask them to question the author or identify bias, but adults don't always emulate that same expectation.

Purpose

Participants aim to uncover the assumptions authors make as well as their own.

Group Size

This protocol is suitable for any group size (modification for larger groups made near the end).

Pre-Protocol Preparation

Use large pieces of paper on the wall to house the questions and assumptions participants will identify. If the document being examined has logical sections or breaks, multiple pieces of paper separated by space can be helpful.

Sequence

1. Explain to participants their tasks as they read a chosen text: identify questions and possible assumptions.

2. Ask participants to make sure they have a pad of small sticky notes (2 inch × 2 inch) to record their questions and assumptions, one thought per sticky note. (Less than ten minutes)

3. After mining the texts, participants take their sticky notes and place them on the pieces of paper around the room.

4. When everyone has placed their sticky notes, the facilitator will pivot to another text-based discussion protocol (recommendations include Affinity Mapping [page 46] and Making Meaning [page 140]) to examine the posted questions and assumptions. Modifications for larger groups would take place within the next chosen protocol.

5. Debrief the process or processes. (Five minutes)

Notes

- I often list this protocol as *Q and A* on an agenda, then ask participants to guess the full name of this protocol. Of course, *questions and answers* is the likely response, which is part of the learning. We aren't acculturated to identify and talk about assumptions; instead, we want answers.

- As I explain the task, I contrast their jobs to summarizing or writing a tweet about the text. A hint that has proven helpful: if you are pausing while you are reading, or if your highlighter or pen hovers for a moment, that probably means a question or assumption is brewing.

- When I facilitate Q and A, I ask participants to each gather a hunk of sticky notes and tell them that if it doesn't make a sound when they drop it twelve inches from the table, they probably don't have enough. I also make every effort to have the same color of sticky notes for everyone. Unintentional coding and grouping can occur when colors are different. I remember once when a teacher commented that her administrator (the only administrator in the group) happened to be using the only harvest orange sticky note pad.

- This protocol is usually more successful when the facilitator offers a model at the beginning. You could use a term (for example, *restorative justice*) or an example from the text ("A question I have about that sentence is . . .") or a piece of student work ("What do you assume about this writer or about the instruction the writer received prior to writing this piece?") as a short minilesson.

- One word in my facilitation has been particularly helpful to participants: that is *interrogate*. We are not often asked to interrogate text, to push on it and the author's viewpoint. Giving participants a license to be critical is necessary in this protocol.

- Spelling doesn't count. I remember a participant who had her phone with her during Q and A. She was checking it so often, I grew worried she really needed to attend to the issue at hand and just take a break from us. After gently checking in with her, she showed me her screen: Dictionary.com. As a dyslexic, she didn't want to be embarrassed in the group and felt like she needed to check spellings. Since that time, I ask groups to concede their predisposition toward standard spelling, saying, "We will interact with your ideas, not your command of the English language."

Application Example

- Laura is helping her leadership team decide whether or not to apply to be a state STEM-certified school. She has the set of state certification standards and decided to use a Questions and Assumptions protocol to ground the team members in the document before personal opinions are brought to the table.

The Text Rendering Experience

The Text Rendering Experience (SRI, n.d.j) protocol was developed in the field by educators. I first experienced it at a national meeting of facilitators of protocols. I have since adapted the process. *Rendering* means to find the good stuff. That is what the Text Rendering protocol does—helps a group find the good stuff. Text Rendering is useful with a variety of texts including articles, book excerpts, procedural texts (for example, the new RTI process), and even electronic texts (such as by providing a transcript of a TED Talk while watching it). The simple directions for this protocol provide a helpful purpose and structure in reading a text, as well as an efficient focus for articulating the good stuff from each person in the group.

Purpose

Participants aim to collaboratively construct meaning, clarify, and expand their thinking about a text or document.

Group Size

Generally, fifteen or fewer is ideal. Within larger groups, smaller groups can form with multiple facilitators.

Sequence

1. Participants read the chosen text, marking one sentence, one phrase, and one word that they believe are the most significant for them or for the group. (Less than ten minutes)

2. Participants, in turn, read aloud their chosen *sentence*. Duplication is permitted—in fact, it may be important for the group if the same sentence is chosen multiple times.

3. Participants, in turn, read aloud their chosen *phrase*.

4. Participants, in turn, read aloud their chosen *word*.

5. The group discusses using one of the following prompts, or the facilitator poses a focusing question. (Less than ten minutes)

    a. What new insights have you gained about the text by looking at it in this way?

    b. What do you think this text is *essentially* about?

6. Debrief the process. (Five minutes)

Notes

- Asking participants what contexts they know for the word *render* is a helpful way to begin this protocol. These are the typical responses.

    ⇨ A cook renders bacon on a stove. When the bacon is removed, the healthy option is to discard what is left in the pan. However, the liquid that is left is quite flavorful. It could create a wonderful gravy or jazz up some peppers and onions.

    ⇨ An artist may render an image with a chosen medium. The artist isn't trying to *copy* the image but instead trying to capture the parts of the image the artist thinks are the most important.

    ⇨ A multimedia designer may use a video program to take several files—a video file, an audio file, a voice file, and some sound effects—to find the best in each of those files. The button in the program is called *rendering* as it creates a file that isn't too big to overwhelm people's personal viewing devices.

- You can also use Text Rendering with paired texts. In that case, I ask participants to read text 1 and choose their sentences, words, and phrases; then they read text 2 and choose their sentences, words, and phrases; and finally, participants only choose one sentence, phrase, and word from everything they have read.

- Participants tend to read quickly, not allowing enough time for others to find their chosen excerpt. When a group is reading out the sentences and phrases, it can be helpful to have the members follow a simply phrased process such as *location*, *pause*, *read* that forces them to slow down.

- A personal tenet of my facilitation practice is to combat misconceptions or missteps before they become a problem. In the Text Rendering protocol, it is common for individuals to read out their sentences or phrases, then launch into their explanations of why they made these specific choices. I might say exactly that: "After you read aloud your sentence or phrase, you can stop talking. Seriously. You can stop. We want to render the *text* at this point, not your *opinions*."

- I personally find it helpful to mark the text as participants read out their responses. Not only does it create focus for me, it may help in the discussion step. I think of it as examining likes on a social media post—which paragraph or section of the text had the most hits?

- Some facilitators talk about Text Rendering in creating a new text, particularly if a scribe writes down steps 3–4. This next text can be used for the discussion or even in future group experiences. Scribing phrases impacts the momentum of the protocol.

- I usually choose to have only step 4 recorded. This can be done in a few different ways, such as by asking individuals to write their words on an index card and post it, or text their words to create a word cloud. My favorite is treating this step like a poem. If twelve people are in a group, the poem would have twelve lines, one word per line. One person would begin, then whoever thinks his or her word goes next in the poem would speak the word. This would continue until the last word is spoken. Either one person could be scribing the words, or everyone could come forward one by one and write their word as they say it aloud.

- The Text Rendering protocol can work well in online environments. Asynchronously, the sentence, phrase, and word could all be posted, then a discussion can ensue.

- A facilitator might use step 5 to design a relevant question for the group or use the suggested prompts.

Application Examples

- Stacey, a middle school principal, frequently uses Text Rendering when her leadership team needs to read a text. The team enjoys having a familiar process to use across different kinds of texts (for example, in one meeting reading an article about higher-order questioning, while in the next meeting reading the district's stance on blended learning).

- Todd has been part of so many meetings where his team has unpacked curriculum standards. He uses Text Rendering to look at documents the team created in the past, both to refresh members' memories as well as provide new team members a structured way to look at historical team artifacts.

Three Levels of Text

The Southern Maine Partnership (2003) adapted a process called Rule of Three used by professional developer Camilla Greene. I further adapted it to its present form. Sometimes reading a text should prompt an action. If it is important for that action to be informed by others' opinions and thoughts, the Three Levels of Text protocol could be an excellent choice. The structure is also helpful for building prowess in protocols to seek perspective (chapter 4).

Purpose

Participants aim to deepen understandings about a text and identify a next action.

Group Size

Generally, groups of three or more are ideal; divide any larger group into triads or quads. The larger the individual group sizes, the longer the total time.

Sequence

1. Participants read a text and identify a text excerpt that has important implications for their work. They should be sure to choose a secondary text option in case another group member chooses the same portion. (Less than ten minutes)

2. Person A now speaks, uninterrupted, using his or her text to address all three of the following levels of text engagement. (Three minutes)

   a. *What?*—Reads and points to the chosen text excerpt

   b. *So What?*—Asks, "Why did you choose that excerpt? What is the importance or significance?"

   c. *Now What?*—Says, "What will you do next based on this text?"

3. Persons B and C face each other and discuss what they just heard while Person A listens and takes notes. (Two minutes)

4. Repeat steps 2–3 with Person B. (Three minutes plus two minutes)

5. Repeat steps 2–3 with Person C. (Three minutes plus two minutes)

6. Debrief the process. (Five minutes)

Notes

- It can be difficult for speakers to not look at the person who just spoke at the three levels. I frequently ask the person who just spoke to turn 90 degrees to the side. That gentle move helps the new speakers to not talk at someone who is not supposed to respond. It also helps the person who turned to just listen. This move in a protocol to build shared understanding lays important groundwork for educators to serve as presenters in the protocols listed in chapters 3–6.

- There is not a final word or spot where the person who first spoke at the three levels (Person A) can speak one more time. This is intentional, as it begins to build a disposition in educators in which they don't always need to have the last laugh, the last hurrah, the quick word spoken underneath their breath as they exit the room. As discussed in the introduction, protocols can transform how individuals work with each other, both in and out of the protocols themselves.

- If the group has used a protocol from chapter 4 (page 111), step 2 of this protocol aligns to the steps of description, interpretation, and evaluation. A facilitator may use that language to help the group be successful in differentiating the three ways of talking about their text.

- Group size can be flexible, but the process becomes extremely difficult to facilitate if the individual groups range in size.

Application Example

- JJ hopes a text he brought about accountable talk in mathematics classrooms will help his department see the benefit of the practice. At the department meeting, he divides everyone into triads, gives them time to read the text, and then facilitates the process. Before they leave, everyone fills out an exit ticket with their name and their chosen next step.

If the text-based protocols presented here intrigue you, visit **go.SolutionTree.com /leadership** to access four more.

1. **4 As:** Group members aim to explore a text through the lens of personal values and intentions. Any group size that can divide into groups of three to five is appropriate.

2. **Block Party:** Participants aim to build interest in a text. This protocol works well with large groups.

3. **The Final Word:** Participants aim to gain a deeper understanding of a text or a perspective. Groups of four or more are ideal, and larger groups can divide into triads or quads (the larger the group sizes, the more time it will take).

4. **Planting the Seed:** Participants aim to expand interpretations of a text or multiple texts. This protocol works well with larger groups.

Reflection Protocols

Teaching is a reflective practice, however, in the frenetic pace of schools, reflection is often relegated to the car on the way home (unless you have your own children), to your home when you get there (unless you have a second job, so when you get home you immediately crash in bed), to the treadmill (unless you need to read from a mandatory book study, so you bought the audiobook) . . . you get the picture. Groups become a place where reflection can take place, and the following protocols help achieve that goal.

Affinity Mapping

The original authors of the Affinity Mapping protocol are unknown, but Ross Peterson-Veatch (2006) adapted and wrote down the steps. I have since adapted it. It is quite common for a meeting to look like this: individual educators write ideas on small 2 × 2–inch sticky notes (one thought per note), then small groups gather at a large sheet of paper stuck to the wall and group their ideas. The constraints that the Affinity Mapping protocol offers create a much more efficient, effective, and equitable experience.

Purpose

Participants aim to find points of entry into a conversation.

Group Size

This protocol works quite well with large groups; with more than eight participants, set up multiple spots to have smaller groups work with their sticky notes.

Sequence

1. Offer the focusing question (for example, ask, "Why do we have a campus improvement plan, anyway?"), and ask participants to use their sticky notes to write one idea per sticky note. (Five to seven minutes or less)

2. Break into as many groups as needed to have three to six participants at each paper grouping.

3. Ask all participants to put their sticky notes on the paper in a randomized way.

4. Ask participants to group sticky notes together *without talking*. The categories may shift as your group thinks together, so participants can move sticky notes multiple times.

5. This step is optional. As groups stop moving sticky notes, they may wish to organize the sticky notes in straight rows and talk aloud together about what category names they might use.

6. In this next optional step, groups may report out, walk around to see each other's categories, or simply return to their seats and reflect on what their individual next steps might be regarding their learning.

7. Debrief the process. (Five minutes)

Notes

- Affinity Mapping differs from the Moving Sticky Notes Around a Big Piece of Paper protocol (fictitious) in three ways. The silence is the obvious first indicator. Participants often find it soothing and thought filled. That constraint also relieves some individuals from feeling obligated to explain every move they make. Secondly, all sticky notes are placed on the paper first. No single person's ideas seem more important or primary. Everyone's ideas get equal voice—in fact, participants might read each sticky note several times over the course of an Affinity Mapping protocol. Finally, once the sticky note is up on the paper, it belongs to anyone—it feels more anonymous. This adds to a feeling of equity, as there are not requirements about who can move which sticky notes.

- Two of the suggestions from the Questions and Assumptions protocol are also appropriate for Affinity Mapping. First, tell participants they do not need to worry about spelling every word correctly on their sticky notes. Explain that everyone wants to interact with their ideas regardless of how they are spelled. Secondly, provide the same color of sticky notes for everyone to prevent unintentional coding and ensure equity.

- Step 4 does not have a suggested time listed. I often tell participants their group will know when they are done when no one has moved a sticky note for sixty seconds.

- If multiple groups work, before assuming members need to see what the other groups did or to hear a report from other groups, ask yourself, "Does the group need this next step I am considering in order to move to our next learning?" If the answer isn't *yes*, it may be a perfect opportunity to waylay the seemingly obligatory share out or gallery walk.

Application Examples

- After reading a draft of a school improvement plan, members of a school leadership team use a text protocol (that is, Questions and Assumptions) as they are reading. Their principal, Rachelle, then uses Affinity Mapping to silently categorize their feedback and wonderings.

- A second-grade team needs to decide on an end-of-year field trip. Instead of spending an entire planning period having that conversation, Patti asks members to take as many sticky notes as they need to write down their ideas— one possible location per sticky note. After categorizing them using Affinity Mapping, they only rank order the top choices of locations, that is, those that had the most sticky notes.

- Billy, an elementary school principal, wants to know from the teacher's perspective how the school's implementation of problem-based learning is going. At a faculty meeting, he asks staff members to write down their thoughts, one per sticky note. He then divides up the faculty to categorize their responses. Before concluding, he asks each group to title each category, then takes digital pictures of each grouping to use with the professional learning team.

Chalk Talk

Marylyn Wentworth (n.d.a) adapted and codified the process of Chalk Talk, originally reported to have started in the Foxfire organization in the northern Georgia mountains with editor Hilton Smith. I further adapted it to its present form. Due to its popularity, as a participant, I have experienced many ill-identified Chalk Talks: basically, any time paper is on the wall and participants are silently walking around with a marker. In its true form, asking participants to walk around and write on several charts but not engage in conversation (that is, adding on, validating, questioning) does not meet the true purpose. The experience is designed to feel paradoxical, as the pace of conversations seems to slow down and produce more thoughtful responses, while the entire experience often takes less time than a whole-group conversation. In this context, the word *chalk* is a reminder of the age of many discussion protocols. Few chalkboards exist anymore; Marker Talk is the rendition generally implemented.

Purpose

Participants aim to have a silent conversation.

Group Size

The size of the paper or whiteboard dictates how large a group can effectively function in a Chalk Talk. For large groups, the same prompts can be replicated in multiple Chalk Talks around the room.

Sequence

1. As participants each choose a marker or two, explain that the purpose of Chalk Talk is to have a conversation on paper. Chalk Talk is highly literate; you are always reading or writing. The prompt in the middle of the Chalk Talk paper will guide the group.

2. Explain the constraints of Chalk Talk.

    a. Speak with the writing implement in your hand.

    b. Draft and redraft—sometimes our first iteration isn't our best.

    c. Ask and answer questions.

    d. Show connections with lines or use a coding system you design.

    e. Draw or sketch if that is best to communicate your idea.

    f. Let conventional spelling go—we will interact with your intent.

3. People will write when they are ready. Pauses are natural in Chalk Talk, so the facilitator will allow plenty of time before the Chalk Talk is ended.

4. In this optional step, the team can identify specific pieces of content from the Chalk Talk (for example, you may ask participants to prioritize using small garage sale dots, assigning an exit ticket to list important concepts, asking a small representative team to stay and think some more, or posing what you believe to be the salient points).

5. Debrief the process. (Five minutes)

Notes

- The facilitator in a Chalk Talk serves in a namesake role, to make *facile*—make easy—the process. If participants are not asking questions on the paper, the facilitator may model this behavior. If the participants are not visually making connections, this modeling can jumpstart others to follow suit.

- Put up more paper than you think you will need. I often add paper to a burgeoning Chalk Talk; very infrequently have I regretted how much paper I put up on the wall. Similarly, markers (that work!) are a necessity. I remember one Chalk Talk where my supply of usable markers was low. Rather than have one for everyone, I simply put a few near the Chalk Talk and asked participants to reach down and access a marker when they were ready. This epic fail had a rich debrief in which participants (some who had been in a Chalk Talk before) talked about how having a marker in their hand increased their feeling of accountability.

- A Chalk Talk can also use artifacts. Enlarging the print and affixing to the paper provide a helpful reference point as participants reflect in writing. Similarly, Chalk Talk can be particularly effective as the driving force in a text-based discussion.

- Some facilitators use multiple Chalk Talks at one time, with multiple prompts. My experience with this practice has been less than favorable; I see more Chalk Talk "wanderers," educators slowly walking around the room, opening and closing their marker caps with popping sounds. Accountability can feel lacking when individuals are not needed at a particular chart. If multiple charts are desired, a more effective way to do this would be for the facilitator to offer adults choices about where they would like to spend their entire time. Then the facilitator could provide a summary of each chart or schedule a break immediately after the Chalk Talks so interested participants (not all will be) can examine the other products.

- Sometimes Chalk Talks can be posted for a period of time. My colleague and I call them Perpetual Chalk Talks. It is difficult to manage the constraints (for example, no talking), so this option may be more appropriate if a group is already experienced with this protocol.

Application Examples

- Suzanne, a principal of a new early childhood center, uses Chalk Talk for her entire staff (eighty-five employees) to help draft the belief statements of the center. She sets up several Chalk Talks with various foci (for example, beliefs about families, beliefs about curricula, beliefs about the child), and staff members choose one location where they can best contribute. At the conclusion of the experience, each Chalk Talk elicits three to four volunteers to draft a set of statements for the leadership team to consider (Van Soelen, 2014).

- Hailey, a mathematics instructional coach, wants to show grade levels the various ways that others are teaching the mathematical process standards across the school, so she sets up a Chalk Talk in the planning room. Each time a grade-level team comes in for collaborative planning, it spends a few moments adding on to the Chalk Talk.

Continuum Dialogue

Marylyn Wentworth (n.d.b) developed the Continuum Dialogue protocol, and I adapted it to its present form. Physical movement isn't just for five-year-olds. Adults need it too—whether you're twenty-five or sixty-five! A group can use the Continuum Dialogue protocol with whatever content it needs to explore by expressing poles (extremes) using various prompts. Group members move their bodies to somewhere along the continuum to represent their opinions. Facilitators can use various ways to elicit responses about members' thinking. Use Continuum Dialogue to respond to a text, tackle a difficult issue, or get to know others.

Purpose

Participants aim to consider personal stances on issues and ideas while also seeing the stances of others.

Group Size

This protocol works best with groups of four or more; it can work with extremely large groups.

Sequence

1. The facilitator shows two physical spots in the room that represent extremes (poles on the continuum). This might be one long line or two ends of an arc.

2. Ask participants to consider a practice continuum.

   a. You have a short deadline for a project. What kind of environment do you best need to meet your goal (figure 2.1)? Move your body to a spot on the continuum that best describes your preference.

Dead quiet, no Pandora in the background; the dog's toenails on the hardwood floors will be too much		A bar at 4 p.m. on a Friday, a drink with a salted rim, music definitely playing

Figure 2.1: Practice continuum no. 1.

   b. Consider your desk or workspace (either at home or at work). Move your body to a spot on this continuum (figure 2.2).

Everything in its place. Colored folders with matching colored sticky notes . . . you get the picture.		You might know where to find something, but you would never ask someone else to find it.

Figure 2.2: Practice continuum no. 2.

3. Now that it is clear how the continuum works, provide a prompt related to your purpose for using this protocol and ask participants to move their bodies to the spot that best represents their stance or opinion.

4. Ask participants to look around at the data spread and describe what they see (for example, skew to the left, all the science teachers are over here, or there aren't any males on that side).

5. Ask participants to make groups of two to three and discuss why they are choosing to stand there. (Two to three minutes)

6. If desired, some participants could volunteer a headline or a hashtag representing the essence of the conversation they just had.

7. The topic and group might necessitate one or more of the following paths.

   a. Move to another prompt.

   b. Participants may ask each other about their placement on the continua.

   c. Participants may pose a continuum extreme for the group to consider.

8. Debrief the process. (Five minutes)

Notes

- Continuum Dialogue works best with extreme poles. For instance, a pole stating, "Very effective" will cause a different reaction from the group than one that says, "So good other schools come to visit us."

- At the practice continua, it can be effective to point out potential hiccups that can occur later in the process. If a facilitator sees that someone wants to stand somewhere but moves because someone is already standing in that spot, bring that to light. It is OK for individuals to clump in a Continuum Dialogue if that location represents their opinion. A facilitator may hear an educator jokingly tell a colleague where to stand (saying, for example, "Your desk is such a mess— move over there!"). This is a perfect opportunity to remind participants that all participants can decide on their own where to stand.

- Continuum Dialogue works beautifully with a text. The facilitator can make various concepts from the text into continua. The hashtags and headlines can act as formative data that the facilitator uses to decide where to head next in the text. Think of it as a little like a *Choose Your Own Adventure* book.

Application Examples

- Javier, a professional learning specialist, uses a text about the characteristics of a professional learning community to ask high school department chairs to render their thoughts about how well the school is emulating these characteristics in their departments, one characteristic at a time.

- After working diligently on a new biology unit, Kendall, the collaborative team leader, is concerned members do not have a shared belief that the final summative lab is rigorous enough. Unsure if a simple discussion will produce honesty, she uses Continuum Dialogue as a way for the four members to physically stand up and speak their individual truths.

- Michelle is a newly hired superintendent trying to get the lay of the land. She reads through the strategic plan, identifying district, school, and department initiatives. With a mixed group of district and school leaders, Continuum Dialogue becomes the visual way for her to assess how well the plan matches the perceived needs as articulated by individuals in this group.

Microlabs

The Microlabs (SRI, n.d.e) protocol was developed by Julian Weissglass (n.d.) for the National Coalition for Equity in Education based at the University of California, Santa Barbara. This highly constrained process was designed to demonstrate the power of truly equitable conversations. The prompts used toward those goals reflect that purpose. Educators in the field adapted it such that they use Microlabs in a host of situations with whatever content is germane to the group. I first experienced this process in a university classroom in 2001. I use Microlabs in three ways: (1) to open up a topic, (2) to check in on progress, or (3) to bring closure.

The setup of this protocol is important, and I have found certain language helps to make the constraints clear and purposeful. Thus, under some of the sequence steps, I include interjections called Language You Can Borrow. If you feel some of the words or phrases from these sections would be helpful in your facilitation, feel free to borrow them. This scaffolded support is also provided in chapters 3–6 for protocols that require more complex facilitation.

Purpose

Participants aim to reflect on a set of questions using an equitable framework for talking and listening.

Group Size

Any size would work, but groups of three or more are ideal; divide any larger group into triads or quads.

Sequence

1. Briefly explain *Microlabs*, a compound word meaning a short, active experience. Ask the group to divide into triads.

Language You Can Borrow: *As you develop your groups, sometimes when adults gather and receive directions, there is a bit of measurement error in the directions. For example, groups of three might mean 3 + or – 1 . . . today that is* not *the case. Groups of three actually means groups of three!*

2. Each group should decide who will be person A, person B, and person C.

3. Describe the process.

    a. The facilitator reads aloud or projects a question to the group. The group members spend the next minute in quiet, planning their eventual response.

    b. The facilitator identifies which letter will begin, and the identified person has one minute to respond to the question, uninterrupted.

    c. Once the first person completes the time, the facilitator identifies a new speaker using the letter (A, B, C), and a new minute commences. The same will happen for the final person in that round.

Language You Can Borrow: *Microlabs gives us a chance to individually reflect on a series of questions with equitable opportunity to also hear others as they make their private reflection more public. For this environment to occur, I will pose various constraints this protocol uses. We believe we have enough restraint to apply these constraints to ourselves, and with that exchange some things may pop that otherwise may not.*

Here's how Microlabs works. The first question will be read aloud, and then everyone will have one whole minute to decide what they are going to say. Many of you might find it helpful to write a few notes to yourself during this minute . . . to plan your response to the question. Won't that be awesome—an entire minute of quiet! After the minute is over, I will call out a letter, person A, B, or C. Then that person receives a whole minute to respond to the question. Now, one of two things will happen, the person who is speaking may fill the entire minute, and you will hear this sound when a minute is up (make the sound). *If you are speaking, please do your best to find a period . . . not a hyphen, a dash, or a semicolon. It may not be the best period in the world, but it can suffice. The other thing that could happen is the speaker may not fill the whole minute. The other group members can resist the tendency to help out their colleague. They don't need coaching, some questions, a charming anecdote . . . just sit there and listen. Perhaps the poet Langston Hughes (1968) can help all of us with these words he penned: "listen eloquently." Isn't that a lovely phrase? Almost an oxymoron. We think of eloquent speakers, not eloquent listeners.*

When there is quiet in the room, another person will be called, and he or she will have a minute to respond to the question. Each person always responds to the question, not to what the previous speaker just said. There is not any piggybacking in this experience—no farm animals of any kind.

Once the final speaker has spoken, we move into another question. There are three questions, and each round takes four minutes for a total of twelve minutes. Give a signal if you have a question about the process. (Pause for three seconds.) *Let's begin.*

4. Lead participants through each round, starting with a different person for each round, so each person has a chance to be the first speaker for a question.

5. Participants may have heard something in their interactions that is really important for them to remember; however, they were focusing on listening, not note taking. Offer time now for them to write any notes to self. (Thirty seconds)

6. Debrief the process. (Five minutes)

Notes

- Strategically crafted questions in Microlabs are as important as the constraints themselves. There are two methods for creating meaningful questions (usually three questions), as shown in figure 2.3. I have been collecting Microlabs questions for fourteen years. Please visit http://tinyurl.com/microlabquestions to see my compilation.

Method 1	Method 2
1. A strength area: + (the plus symbol means something going well or a positive) 2. An area for growth: △ (the delta symbol means something that needs a change) 3. Some call to action	1. Describe 2. Extend 3. Personalize
Sample questions: 1. Describe one moment in a group (perhaps a collaborative team) that felt really awesome. What was going on? What specific behaviors from individuals contributed to the awesomeness? 2. Describe one moment in your group experiences (perhaps in a collaborative team) that produced anxiety, fear, or anger. What specific behaviors from individuals contributed to that environment? 3. What might be the hardest thing to do or say, but you know it is the right thing to do or say in order to replicate the awesome moments? What is it going to take from you in order to muster the courage?	Sample questions: 1. Define empowerment. 2. What are the potential pitfalls and challenges of fostering an environment of employee empowerment? 3. What might specifically happen in your context if all individuals felt the level of empowerment you want for them?

Figure 2.3: Methods to write Microlabs questions.

- It is much simpler to facilitate Microlabs when all the groups are the same size. It is possible to use quads or groups of five, but the process becomes incrementally longer when the group sizes grow. As a facilitator, you might consider joining a group, but this protocol has several starts and stops, so it is often tricky to be a participant and a facilitator. If the number of participants is not easily divisible, another option is to ask for volunteers to be process observers, to sit and watch, collecting data on what they see and hear. This person would not walk around, as that move may impact participants' willingness to take risks.

- Dependent on the content and outcome, consider how groups will be made. Purposeful triads can be powerful in a Microlabs protocol due to the amount of listening. In a debrief, I sometimes ask participants to make a pie chart of how they spent their time during the protocol. After a moment of sketching, I unveil mine, shown as figure 2.4.

Time Spent

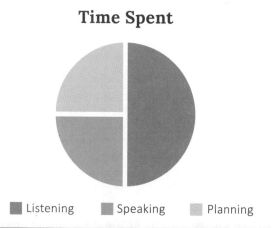

■ Listening ■ Speaking ■ Planning

Figure 2.4: Time spent in Microlabs.

- Microlabs can be an important experience as groups begin to develop. The notion of intentional listening can often make its way onto a set of group norms.

Application Examples

- Kelley is a newly hired assistant principal who was tasked to lead a summer meeting of teachers to help reduce office referrals. She is worried she doesn't have credibility or trust yet with the staff. She uses Microlabs to open the conversation about a potentially difficult topic.

- With a group of new teacher mentors, Dina, a central office professional developer, uses a set of Microlabs questions to encourage each person in the room to identify something new that they are feeling—helping to reduce the hierarchy often present between mentors and teachers new to the profession.

- A school staff needs to be more public about its assumptions and practices for grading student work. Janey, an instructional coach, designs a set of Microlabs questions to help create space for a topic that is often quite private. When educators hold tight to the constraints offered in a Microlabs protocol, they might say something they have never said before.

Success Analysis

Vivian Johnson (n.d.) developed the Success Analysis protocol. I further adapted it into its present form. As educators, we are prone to quickly move past our successes, not spending a requisite amount of time exploring what made them so successful. In the Success Analysis protocol, each person has a chance to articulate a success, then small groups explore each success, searching for common success factors across the stories. The participants can use the generation of these factors as touchstones for future work.

Purpose

Participants aim to articulate what causes success in an effort to replicate those actions more frequently.

Group Size

Any size would work. Generally, groups of three or more are best; divide any larger group into triads or quads.

Sequence

1. Display Burch's (Mind Tools, n.d.) concept of Conscious Competence (Van Soelen, 2016), as seen in figure 2.5, and ask participants to have a brief conversation with someone near them about their reactions to the model. It may be helpful to point out that the numbers in the model do not represent a sequence; they are labels only. Tell participants the Success Analysis protocol will help them move a part of their practice from quadrant 2 (Unconscious Competence) to quadrant 4 (Conscious Competence). (Two minutes)

	Incompetence	Competence
Unconscious	Quadrant 1: Unconscious Incompetence	Quadrant 2: Unconscious Competence
Conscious	Quadrant 3: Conscious Incompetence	Quadrant 4: Conscious Competence

Source: Mind Tools, n.d.; Van Soelen, 2016.

Figure 2.5: Conscious Competence model.

*Visit **go.SolutionTree.com/leadership** for a free reproducible version of this figure.*

2. Ask participants to write about a successful experience, being sure to answer the question, What made this different from others like it I have had? The success doesn't have to be large scale; sometimes analyzing seemingly small successes can be quite productive. (Five to ten minutes)

3. Ask participants to form triads (or quads if need be) and identify each person as person A, person B, or person C.

4. Person A tells a story of success, giving as much detail as possible while other group members take notes. (Less than five minutes)

5. Group members ask clarifying questions (defined as quickly asked, quickly answered) to fill in any gaps in their understanding of what happened. (Two to three minutes)

6. Person A now listens and takes notes while group members look at each other, discussing the successful situation. The goal is to analyze the success, attempting to identify other factors that may have positively impacted the situation. (Five to seven minutes)

7. Person A reflects on what may be helpful for future work. (Two minutes)

8. Repeat steps 4–7 with person B.

9. Group members consider the two stories told thus far and start to brainstorm a list of success factors that could be generalizable across stories. (Three minutes)

10. Repeat steps 4–7 with person C.

11. Group members now consider all stories, revising their list of success factors. (Three minutes)

12. In this optional step, use the success factors identified in each group, look for trends, and create a list unique to the group. (Less than ten minutes) Discuss what conditions would need to be in place for Conscious Competence to occur more often in their work.

13. Debrief the process. (Five minutes)

Notes

- It can be difficult for speakers to not look at the person who just shared a success story. I frequently ask the person who just spoke to turn 90 degrees to the side. That gentle move helps the new speakers to not talk at someone who is not supposed to respond. It also helps the person who has turned to just listen. This move in a protocol to build shared understanding lays important groundwork for educators to serve as presenters in protocols listed in chapters 3–6.

Application Examples

- Shawna is a principal mentor of several new principals. In a monthly meeting after their first one hundred days on the job, she uses Success Analysis to help them step back from their busy schedules to consider all the ways they were unconsciously competent.

- Rhonda is an intervention specialist at a school. After receiving the state assessment scores, Success Analysis became a way to articulate what practices seemed to make the difference for certain students in their successful results.

If you are finding that reflection protocols are meeting your needs, visit **go.SolutionTree .com/leadership** for one more option. The Creating Metaphors protocol prompts educators to explore their behaviors when they are at their best, then choose a metaphor to exemplify those efforts. It's flexible to use with a variety of group sizes and with those in different jobs in various contexts.

Equity and Diversity Protocols

Discussion protocols can be an effective tool for educators to explore issues of education equity and diversity. These processes ask the participants to focus inwardly on assumptions and beliefs. To improve their use of these protocols, facilitators may choose to engage in studying facilitation techniques to be more aware of their habits and to grow new skills. It is also important for facilitators to examine their own identities and how personal facilitation is often a mirror of tacit beliefs.

Several facilitators of color have insight to share about the use of protocols. Debbi Laidley, retired district office leader from Los Angeles, calls this *inner equity work* (D. Laidley, personal communication, August 4, 2020). Some people of color may feel a sense of rigidity from discussion protocols, interpreting them as another method of control. Laidley believes participants may blame the protocol in lieu of the person who is conducting it, differentiating the word *conducting* from *facilitating*. Thus what happens is the protocol (and even the larger practice of using protocols) is demonized. Instead, "true facilitators might have more flexibility, taking the reins off a bit as they see the need" (D. Laidley, personal communication, August 4, 2020).

Deirdre Williams, former executive director of SRI, agrees: "A protocol is only as liberating as the person facilitating it" (D. Williams, personal communication, August 13, 2020). If facilitators have not sufficiently explored their identity, "people of color will feel that tension," Williams explains. "If the facilitator isn't comfortable with the topic, they might believe the protocol is getting out of hand, thus using their power as a facilitator to shut it down" (D. Williams, personal communication, August 13, 2020).

This discussion is not intended to label discussion protocols as more appropriate or comfortable for White educators. Ileana Liberatore, Latina teacher educator from San Antonio, loves protocols:

> For me, it was a way to enter a conversation when I thought I couldn't. I started using them as a teacher and was put in tough positions with male Latino administrators. Machismo is real! Protocols let me say things I didn't know I could. (I. Liberatore, personal communication, August 9, 2020)

In his work as a coordinator for equity and inclusion in Atlanta, Oman Frame sees facilitation as unique to the group and their needs: "I don't know what blind spots I may have until the group helps me see them" (O. Frame, personal communication, August 10, 2020). By engaging openly with the group, admitting they don't know everything, and effectively using debriefs, facilitators can become more culturally sensitive as they use discussion protocols.

An effective resource for those interested in improving this aspect of their facilitation is *Guiding Teams to Excellence With Equity: Culturally Proficient Facilitation* by John Krownapple (2017).

Diversity Rounds

I first became aware of the Diversity Rounds protocol in conversations with other facilitators from around the country at a national meeting. The protocol had been in my book of protocols for over a decade, and I had never used it. Educators in the field developed the Diversity Rounds protocol, and I adapted it to its present form. Diversity is a multifaceted concept, often relegated to one or more criteria, for instance, race or gender. Diversity Rounds pushes on that narrow notion, encouraging educators to think more broadly about their identities and in what ways they are alike and different from others. This protocol helps educators personally define themselves in multiple ways and also builds more stamina in talking to others about these various criteria.

Purpose

Participants aim to become more aware of the multiple notions of diversity and describe their identities in various ways.

Group Size

This protocol works quite well with large groups.

Sequence

1. Ask participants to group themselves (two to four in a group), using the following question as a criterion: Where are you from? Individual answers to this question dictate the groups. For example, one person might say, "Atlanta," and another might say "Fulton County." Although these might be geographically the same place, they mean different things to the people who live there. (Less than three to five minutes)

2. When groups seem to be static, ask the small groups to discuss one or more of the following questions. (Four to five minutes)

   a. What does it mean to be _____?

   b. How much do you define yourself this way? How is your group unique or different from the other groups?

   c. One thing we would like the other groups to know about us is _____.

3. Before moving to a new criterion, ask each group to say one thing—a big idea or theme (one to two sentences).

4. Ask participants to regroup themselves based on the following question: What is your birth order in your family? (Less than three to five minutes)

5. Small groups discuss one or more of the same three previously offered questions.

6. Before moving to a new criterion, ask each group to say one thing—a big idea or theme (one to two sentences).

7. Continue the pattern (steps 4–6) with various other prompts as time allows.

   a. What's your work? And, if you are tempted to say you are a teacher, say something else. Think really hard how you would explain your work to someone else if you didn't have the traditional label for your work or your job.

   b. How do you define your race and ethnicity?

   c. How do you define or qualify your gender?

   d. What is one core belief on which you will not compromise?

8. Offer a final reflective question, starting with quiet writing time, then open up the conversation with questions such as the following: "How has (choose one of the criteria) affected you as an educator?" (Less than ten minutes)

9. Debrief the process. (Five minutes)

Notes

- As educators group themselves when different criteria are offered, the facilitator can look for two types of groupings, singletons or large groups. In the case of individuals standing by themselves, encourage them to talk to those in other groups to see where they might fit, without losing any sense of their own identity. Large groups (for example, we all were born in this state), would need to refine their notion of sameness in order to create smaller groups which do not exceed five people.

- A facilitator may choose a variety of organizing ideas (in steps 1, 4, and 7) for the group to use in regrouping themselves. It is important to start with criteria that may feel safer (for example, geography or where you are from) and moving to more sensitive topics.

- Some educators' experiences in these sorts of processes have not always been positive—the labels can feel like the very ones we are trying to reconsider. Remind participants that groupings are not right or wrong; they also are temporary and will change.

- I find it helpful to chart the various criteria you are using, as it helps participants in the final reflection.

Application Examples

- A cultural competence initiative uses Diversity Rounds as an opening experience to help participants grow more comfortable in discussing issues related to diversity.

- Staci, a White woman in a high school with a majority of students of color, seeks to improve the relationships teachers have with students. She chooses to use Diversity Rounds as a way for staff members to see how they might have some things in common with their students even when their skin color might not be the same.

- Eddie, a principal of a large middle school of 165 teachers, wants to build more connections across grade levels and content areas. He sees the teachers as silos, not being able to capitalize on the wide range of experiences on the large staff. The Diversity Rounds protocol helps shrink the world using meaningful prompts.

History of Your Hair

Having facilitated many of these protocols for two decades, I didn't experience the History of Your Hair protocol until my second decade. A co-facilitator was familiar with the process and suggested it might be a helpful way to introduce equity into the work of the group. My version of the protocol is listed here. The title sounds light and humorous, and the implementation can also feel that way. However, the discussion in the History of Your Hair protocol can reveal strong cultural and racial assumptions and biases, resulting in deeper understandings of factors outside of school that affect students and families of color and families who live in poverty.

Purpose

Participants aim to see hair choices as proxies for cultural decisions and inequities.

Group Size

Any size works for this protocol.

Pre-Protocol Preparation

Be sure to provide sticky notes, various sizes of paper, crayons, highlighters, colored pencils, and markers.

Sequence

1. Ask participants to consider how their hair has changed over the course of their lifetime. The following list may be helpful to facilitators as they build background knowledge regarding possible factors that informed hair choices. They could generate this list by asking participants to come up with questions or present questions (such as, What led you to change how your hair looked over the years?). (Five to seven minutes)

   a. Fashion or cultural

   b. Political

   c. Passage of time (for example, as we age . . .)

      d. Life changes (for example, becoming a parent)

      e. Activity level (for example, sports)

      f. External factors (for example, medical)

      g. Personal choice

      h. Technology

      i. Religion

      j. Weather or geography

      k. DNA or inherited characteristics

      l. Socioeconomics (for example, cost)

2. Participants now have time to create a product representing the history of their hair. Offer participants product options for their work time: jot list, drawings, flip-book using sticky notes, time line, or narrative or story. (Ten minutes)

3. Ask participants to partner up, each using up to five minutes to share their work product—the chronology of their hair. (Ten minutes)

4. As a whole-group reflection, ask, "What poignant moments or critical discoveries were present in your partner conversations?" (Five minutes)

5. Debrief the process. (Five minutes)

Notes

- In building the factor list in step 1, the composition of the group may play a critical role. For instance, groups that are primarily all one race and gender may not consider some of the factors present on the list. The facilitator can take this opportunity to explicitly offer these factors.

- Sometimes men (particularly White men) may claim they do not have any stories to tell about their hair. They might need coaching or prompting as to the *why* of the decisions they made (or were made for them) throughout the years and what those decisions may illuminate.

Application Example

- As part of a cultural competence district focus, Jana, a White woman, sees this protocol on a list of district-provided options. As she has never experienced it herself as a participant, she reads through the process and then decides to call a fellow principal, Jillian, who is Black. After talking through the process and some potential tricky places with Jillian, she feels more confident to lead it with her entire staff after school at a faculty meeting.

Paseo

The Paseo protocol was developed by Debbi Laidley, Debbie Bambino, Debbie McIntyre, Stevi Quate, and Juli Quinn (2001), and I adapted it. Various components of our identity help us understand why we do the things we do and why we think the way we think. Being explicit about these identity factors is significant. Paseo moves past the get-to-know-you games often present in faculty meetings, past the articulation of character or personality traits, and into the dimensions of ourselves that we cannot, have not, or will not change. Courageous spaces exist in Paseo, in part with the modeling of the facilitator combined with the protocol's constraints:

> The Paseo is a process that has been used in Mexico and the southwest United States as a way of getting acquainted quickly. Traditionally males and females of the community would line up in concentric circles, facing each other, and would make "un paseo," or pass by one another, holding eye contact and having brief opportunities to make connections. (Laidley et al., 2001)

Purpose

Participants aim to see the connections among beliefs, identity, and actions.

Group Size

Generally, groups of six or more are ideal; in large groups, use one large space that would accommodate either one large circle or multiple smaller circles.

Sequence

1. The facilitator can model the creation of an identity map. The refrain during the model is the following: *This map helps me see why I do the things I do and why I think the way I think.* (See the first bullet in the Notes section for this protocol; less than fifteen minutes)

2. Participants now have time to create their own identity map in whatever form they wish (visual, list, or narrative). (Ten to fifteen minutes)

3. Invite participants to take their identity maps and come to a larger open area to form two concentric circles. The same number of people should be on the outside facing in as the number on the inside facing out. An even number of people is required to create revolving partnerships.

4. Once the physical structure has been ensured, explain the process.

   a. The facilitator will tell the group that each time they are partnered, one person will be the speaker and the other the listener. After a requisite amount of time, the jobs will change. Have a designated sound to indicate the time, and introduce that sound before the first prompt.

b. The facilitator will offer a prompt (see the protocol notes for prompt options) to consider in examining your identity map. Every person will have one minute to ponder the prompt and plan a response.

c. Either ask the outside person or the inside person to speak, uninterrupted. The one to two minutes will belong to the first speaker. If the speaker doesn't fill the time, the listener continues his or her role until the time is up.

d. When participants hear the designated sound, participants switch roles. The listener becomes the speaker, and the speaker becomes the listener. Another one or two minutes ensue.

e. After each person has spoken once, both thank each other and listen for the next direction. The facilitator will either ask the inside circle *or* outside circle to shift one person either to the left or the right.

f. New partners greet each other and wait for a new prompt. Each prompt lasts approximately five minutes.

g. Facilitators can gauge the group to help decide when to close the protocol with the content debrief.

5. Conduct a content debrief. After the last partnership, invite participants to return to their chairs and prompt uninterrupted writing for ninety seconds, choosing one of these three prompts.

a. What did you *see* during the Paseo?

b. What did you *hear* during the Paseo?

c. What did you *feel* during the Paseo?

Ask participants, in order around the room, to read *one thing* from what they just wrote.

6. In this optional step, conduct a large-group or a small-group conversation that considers the question, What will you do differently as a result of this process?

7. Debrief the process. (Five minutes)

Notes

- In the model (step 1), I find it important to delineate *character traits* from *identity characteristics*. For instance, a participant brings up a character trait when he or she says, "I see the world as a glass half full," and brings up a trait of identity by saying, "My Dutch rural background prompted me to hold back negative emotions about people and places unless able to talk privately about those situations."

- The riskier the model, the more valuable the first drafts of the identity map become. My identity map is available at **go.SolutionTree.com/leadership**; I worked on it numerous times in facilitating this protocol and continue to revise it nearly every time I facilitate it.

- In choosing prompts, there are many options to consider. The original version of the protocol, developed in the 1990s, offers several prompts. Check **go .SolutionTree.com/leadership** for these prompts as well as additional ideas. Using prompts that ask participants to reference their maps is particularly helpful. Many prompts could begin with, "Take a look at your map and . . ."

- As participants begin creating their identity maps in step 2, I find it helpful to let them know their writing audience is themselves. Later in the process, they will talk from their map, but they do not need to post or visually display it for others.

- Participants may find it helpful to take their maps, something to write with, and something to write on when they go to the concentric circles. I have seen participants add to their maps as they are processing and listening.

- For large groups and in groups where it is important to mix participants more quickly, step 4e may ask participants to move multiple people to the right or left. Once, I was with a very large staff in the gymnasium, and I said multiple times, "Please move eight people to the right!"

- The protocol can be very effective in smaller groups, deepening the potential for them to take risks with each other. In larger groups, an individual might not partner with the same person more than once. In smaller groups, participants would keep revisiting each other—just with different prompts each time.

- As a facilitator decides when to bring Paseo to a close, they might look for signs of physical and mental fatigue. In my experience, an average number of rounds ranges from six to eight.

Application Examples

- Jennifer, director of student supports, wants assistant principals in the district to consider the choices they make regarding discretionary behavioral placements and how personal identity may be playing a role in these decisions.

- Marci wants her leadership team to move past management issues into the messy work of school culture and school improvement. Paseo helps lay the groundwork for deeper relationships where they might not always agree.

- An eighth-grade science team has been stuck in congeniality for years. The collaborative planning lead, Julie, wants her colleagues to engage more deeply with one another, so she uses Paseo with just herself and her three colleagues.

Student Profiles

Gene Thompson-Grove's original version of Student Profiles was revised by Connie Zimmerman Parrish and Susan Westcott Taylor (n.d.), and I further adapted it to its present form. A continuous through line of educator reflection involves seeing beyond ourselves— what we think we know about ourselves and how we involuntarily expect others to be like, sound like, and act like us. The Student Profiles protocol is a highly interactive way for educators to consider their own student behaviors when they were in high school (between the ages of fifteen and eighteen). Participants find those high school archetypes using a set of Student Profiles, which the facilitator can adapt for various student demographic contexts.

Purpose

Participants aim to identify the ways their experiences as adolescents impact the decisions they make as adult educators.

Group Size

Generally, groups of twelve or more are ideal.

Pre-Protocol Preparation

1. Create a wall that includes sticky notes, index cards, or pieces of paper with a number on each to represent a student profile (if the group is using twelve profiles, post twelve pieces of paper).

2. Create a poster with these two questions.

   a. What do educators need to know about students like you if they want you to learn at high levels?

   b. How does your student profile influence your teaching practice?

Sequence

1. Ask participants to read the Student Profiles (see **go.SolutionTree.com /leadership** for a reproducible list), looking for the specific profile that best captures who they were as students between the ages of fifteen and eighteen. If several seem to be true, they should choose the one that affected them the most or seems to be the most significant. (Five to seven minutes)

2. Ask participants to stand. *Without using the profile number*, the participants' job is to find others who chose the same profile. They can do so by asking questions as they walk around the room. Be sure to tell the group it is possible that only one person might choose a profile—that is just fine. Once participants find others whom they think would share the same profile, they stay with them, continuing to move around the room. The only way to know if there are others with your profile is to circulate around the room and talk to each person or each group. (Five to seven minutes)

3. When it appears the groups are stable, ask for one volunteer per group to come to the wall with the posted profile numbers. While their group watches, the volunteers remove the number they think their group represents. Some individuals may regroup based on the information this reveals. Some numbers will generally remain on the wall.

4. Ask participants to sit and create small groups (three to five people). If a profile has more than five people, subdivide. Similarly, if certain profiles only have one to two people, they could join together.

5. Offer time for participants to plan a response to this prompt. *Choose one specific story that illuminates what it was like for you to be this kind of learner between the ages of fifteen and eighteen.* (One minute)

6. Ask participants to individually respond to the question, uninterrupted. (Ten minutes, based on groups of five people with two minutes per person)

7. Talk openly in small groups about the two questions posed on the poster. Encourage groups to spend time with the first question, then move to the second question at the sound of an audible signal, if they haven't already done so. (Five plus five minutes; ten minutes total)

8. Bring the whole group together and ask the following questions. (Less than ten minutes)

    a. "What struck you as you listened to others?"

    b. "Who is not represented in our groups?" (Referencing the remaining posted profile numbers)

    c. "How might we find adults who are the grown-up versions for the profiles we are missing?"

9. Debrief the process. (Five minutes)

Notes

- The Student Profiles protocol makes an impact when the actual profiles match the population of the school. Using the eleven default profiles (Parrish & Taylor, n.d.) might match some schools, but usually revisions would make the experience far more authentic. Here are links to several different iterations as each sought to create a meaningful experience.

    ⇨ Alpharetta High School, Alpharetta, Georgia: http://bit.ly/3jqhILl

    ⇨ Garland Independent School District, Garland, Texas: http://bit.ly/36ISAdS

    ⇨ Lewisville Independent School District, Lewisville, Texas: http://bit.ly/3tvr6SE

    ⇨ Iowa Culture and Language Conference: http://bit.ly/3oPYmjN

- In step 1, I find it helpful to ask participants to find themselves in the profiles, but then keep reading. Having knowledge of all the profiles is helpful later in the process.

- During step 2, facilitators can ensure groups have checked in with other groups around the room. Sometimes when a group thinks it has completely formed, it stops looking for anyone else.

- In facilitating step 6, the facilitator can monitor time in a tight way (for example, every person has exactly two minutes, and silence should fill the time in case participants don't fill their time) or in a loose way (for example, offer an audible signal every two minutes in case groups haven't already moved on to the next speaker).

- If participants are interested in scribing ideas in step 7, have them do so. A final document created after that step could include helpful strategies when teachers eventually become stuck in working productively with a student who has a particular profile. However, if no one will be compiling and sharing the information following the protocol, asking educators to work on chart paper usually causes the leaders to lose credibility.

- Groups can become stumped with the question posed in step 8c. When looking at the profiles educator groups usually leave posted on the wall, many align to students who were less successful in traditional schools. Some of those individuals work in schools but are not in the teaching profession. Asking noncertified, classified staff to assist in strategy development for those profiles is a brilliant solution.

Application Examples

- Gary leads his entire middle school staff in considering what student profiles they represent, and more importantly, which profiles they do not intimately understand. At the end, they have created a resource list of strategies to match certain student profiles.

- Whitney, a Student Government Association (SGA) sponsor at a high school, uses Student Profiles with SGA to consider this question: Whose school is this, anyway? The students dig into the experience, identifying cultural shifts the school could make to be more inclusive to a variety of student perspectives.

Student Profiles also has a variation called Passion Profiles, available at **go.SolutionTree .com/leadership**, that focuses on adult archetypes as they work in schools. In the process, participants aim to see the ways that their why impacts their practice. It can be incredibly helpful for teams to see how individuals may have common goals but differing methods.

Community-Building Protocols

Community-building protocols can be great fun. They can bring a group of educators closer, but without a larger learning goal, the positive effect is short-lived. For instance, my wife is a middle school teacher and detests particular parts of faculty meetings. It isn't what you think—she just doesn't enjoy bridal shower–style games if the purpose is just to get to know people. Bridal shower games often feel perfunctory—in her estimation, they're just a prelude to the cake! The protocols listed in this section all have joy and laughter as outcomes. However, the larger goal is individual, group, and organizational reflection. It is in those moments when the playful nature of these processes becomes far more than a bridal shower game.

Compass Points

The Compass Points (SRI, n.d.b) protocol was developed in the mid-1990s and remains a popular choice. I first experienced this protocol in a professional development session in 2001. Educators often report similar outcomes when using other individual analysis tools, such as Myers-Briggs personality inventories and the True Colors inventories. Indeed, in its original form, Compass Points can feel comparable. My adaptation is more expansive. It identifies individual preferences and then leverages that information to focus on the group as an organism, a living being, which needs to be developed and nurtured, otherwise (like any living organism that ceases to develop or is not cared for) it dies.

Purpose

Participants aim to understand individuals' preferences in a group setting and how groups can acquire and use group vocabulary to assess themselves.

Group Size

Generally, groups of four or more are ideal, but the protocol can work well in large groups.

Pre-Protocol Preparation

- Place four signs on the four walls of a room, each one representing a point on a compass, *North*, *South*, *East*, and *West*. Prepare a slide or a handout similar to figure 2.6, containing the following information.

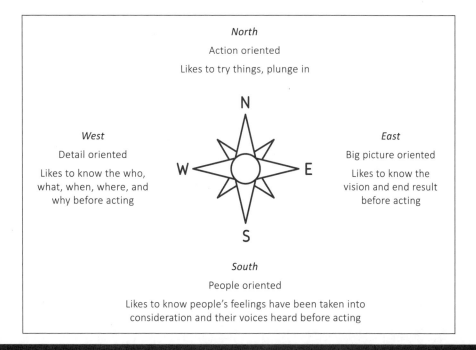

Figure 2.6: Compass Points cardinal directions.

*Visit **go.SolutionTree.com/leadership** for a free reproducible version of this figure.*

- Consider having some copies of the Compass Points Explanation Expanded (**go .SolutionTree.com/leadership**) available—enough copies for 25 percent of the number of participants usually works.

Sequence

1. Ask participants to examine the displayed or copied compass rose graphic and move to the wall that best corresponds to how they tend to work when they are in a group. Explain that this isn't meant to indicate who they are as a person overall—just how they tend to behave and act in groups.

2. Encourage the individuals in each direction to consider the following questions. (Ten minutes)

    a. What's it like being me when I am working from my direction?

    b. What's it like for everyone else when I am working from my direction?

3. Ask participants why groups usually don't look like this—all the same work preferences together. Raise an assumption many often have about the perfect, utopian, idyllic group, one that would have representation from each direction. Announce that today's experience will hopefully challenge that assumption because that thinking is faulty logic. If people assume the perfect group exists with representation from each corner, then they *long* for that grouping, rather than using their current group composition to be productive. In essence, they blame the person who created the group rather than building capacity in the group to be more effective and efficient. (One to two minutes)

4. Ask participants to draw three pie chart circles, perhaps on sticky notes or on a piece of paper. Draw three charts on large chart paper yourself to model for participants. Label the first pie chart *Actual*. Like composite rocks (more than one type of rock), as educators work in groups, they are more than one direction. Create a pie chart that represents how much of each direction is in your personal work pie chart. Remind participants again that the directions today refer to how you work in groups, not who you are as a holistic person. (Three to four minutes)

5. Ask participants how this information may be helpful to know about the people you work with frequently. If the group desires a specific application, one is available in the notes at the end of this protocol. (One to two minutes)

6. Working in our areas of strength can be helpful, but it also can be tiring to be seen in only one way. Groups can take advantage of individuals when they know each other's strengths. The second pie chart, labeled *Ideal*, is what participants wish their pie chart looked like. If they could snap their fingers and change how they work in groups, what would the pie chart look like? (Two to four minutes)

7. The first two pie charts focus on the self. The third pie chart, labeled *Group*, takes a broader view. Ask participants to choose a group of which they are a member. If they are in multiple groups, they might choose the group they least

enjoy. As they prepare to draw a pie chart of the *group*, pose the metaphor of a group being an organization. At the heart of any organization is an organism—a living, breathing thing. In creating their pie chart of the group, they can ask themselves questions like the following. How is the group working, quickly, like North? Not until all questions are answered, like West? (Four to five minutes)

8. Ask participants to consider all three pie charts together and answer this question with a partner near them: What are you learning about yourself and this specific group? (Two to three minutes)

9. One of the goals for this experience is to build group vocabulary. Participants can use the very same vocabulary they use to assess group work in this protocol as the group is working. Consider telling one or both of the following stories to show how groups have used this experience to impact their group experiences. (Two to three minutes)

    a. *Story 1*—A central office team was noting principals were having meetings after the meeting in the parking lot. They used Compass Points to build group vocabulary so individuals could advocate for what they needed *in the meeting* rather than using time in the parking lot after the meeting. Next time the superintendent asks in the meeting, "Any questions?" a principal chooses to use the language from the Compass Points protocol and asks, for example, "Could we have some time for West? Perhaps to just ask questions with some principals of our same grade levels?" Their *organism* needs more West—not necessarily the individuals who had substantial West sections on their pie charts.

    b. *Story 2*—A first-grade collaborative team plans in the team leader room each week. After discovering their team is made up primarily of people with East and South work styles, the members now say things like, "Can we be North for a few minutes right now? It's about time for the kids to come back from PE." On the wall is a compass rose with North and West circled—*for them*, not for the students. The team leader is relieved as she does not need to be a super-facilitator, trying to fill in for whatever pie piece the group needs. Instead, the group can use group vocabulary to surface the needs. These group redirections are about the organism, not about individuals, and are therefore less risky.

10. Debrief the process. (Five minutes)

Notes

- Consider placing the cardinal directions in geographically accurate locations on the wall. Someone in the room will definitely know which locations these are! Anything a facilitator can do to remove barriers from participants' learning is worth doing.

- For participants who will have difficulty choosing only one cardinal direction (they may stay in their seat, they may simply state they can't decide, or they might stand in a corner between two signs), hand them the expanded version of Compass Points (**go.SolutionTree.com/leadership**) to help them make a decision.

- If it would be helpful to build descriptive skills in a group, consider looking at group composition after step 1. Descriptive skills are helpful in many discussion protocols (see chapter 4, page 111). Participants might consider the group members as data and comment, "So, this is our data set—we are the data! So, look around. What do you see in our data? Not what do you think, but what do you see?" Gather a few inputs, making sure the responses are truly descriptive. If the group has difficulty being descriptive, asking for quick hand raising for aspects such as the following can be helpful—grade level or span taught, content specialty, years at a particular location, and gender. It can be helpful to point out (if it's true) that most descriptors position people in multiple corners. You might say, "Notice how not all the middle school teachers are standing in the east direction, nor are all the science folks near West. See how the administrators aren't all gathering in North, and the elementary school teachers are not all by South."

- Sometimes, groups may need help thinking about the impact of their directional behaviors. For instance, a group of educators standing in North may only identify the positives or strengths of their approach to group work and dynamics. Framing the second question as the *splash zone* can be a humorous entrance for groups to pivot to other impacts of their directional behavior. As a child, I remember going to see Shamu, an orca at SeaWorld. I wanted to sit in the front row, but my parents declined because it was labeled Splash Zone. In groups, every behavior we demonstrate, in essence, gets people wet. We splash all over each other, every day.

- After step 3, it can be helpful to ask groups to identify how the group they were just in demonstrated the very direction they were talking about. For instance, folks in the South group may have found chairs for each other to sit in, they may have ensured everyone spoke, and they may have told stories about their work. This small moment helps participants see the automaticity of these behaviors, even in temporary groups.

- In groups where individuals know each other well, there can be some playful banter ("Hey, Joey, I knew you'd be over there because you are so bossy!") that can be useful for the group's learning. Consider this prompt after step 3 when participants sit down, "As primarily [direction], people may think we _____, but what they really need to know is _____." This move can help to combat implicit or explicit stereotypes present in the room.

- In step 6, a specific application of this knowledge can be helpful, time permitting. An example of an application scenario could include language a facilitator might borrow, such as "Perhaps a leader has a short-term project for a group. Many leaders would intentionally create a diverse group with some North, South, East, and West participants, believing all perspectives are needed. In particular, imagine there is a very short time line to accomplish something.

What happens to each person's largest pie slices when they hear about the task and the time line? You may think everyone moves to North, trying to accomplish the task quickly. Instead, each person's largest slices tend to get even bigger. So, the person who calls the meeting thinks the best thing to do is call everyone together, but that may actually backfire! The group could all come together and accomplish absolutely nothing. Consider this workflow option instead of creating a diverse committee or workgroup that needs to meet and come to an agreement to accomplish the task at hand."

   a. *Step 1*—If we need a starting draft, ask some folks with North dominance to draft it out.

   b. *Step 2*—The draft might go to East next if the leader isn't sure we are on the right track. If that isn't a concern, the draft could go to West next to fill in all the details.

   c. *Step 3*—Send the draft to the reverse of wherever it went for step 2. If the document went to West, now send to East to make sure the big picture hasn't been lost with all the added details. If the document had been in East, send the document to West to make sure the details are added.

   d. *Step 4*—Folks with South dominance are process and people experts. They know how and when to communicate. Might this information be shared during a faculty meeting? If so, how? Grade-level or department meetings? By whom? When is the right time?

- If you ask participants to share their thinking in step 9, one of two situations generally emerges: in the first, a participant loves the group because the group pie chart looks just like that person's. The contrast is often true: participants may see now why they feel queasy when a particular group meets on a particular day because, in the second type of situation, the group's pie chart is directly opposite from their pie charts.

- After using this discussion protocol, a group of teacher leaders asked, "Where do the complainers go? What direction are they usually in?" Their working theory is that complainers could be in any corner, and the complaining can stem from the gap between what they expected and what they got. For instance, people with North dominance expected a "get 'er done" meeting and instead experienced many slow processes with East thinking. They fill the gap between what they expected and what they got with complaining. A leader might conference with a continual complainer and say, "Help me understand the gap between what you are expecting from this group (or meeting) and what you got."

- What might this experience mean for the it's-just-his-or-her-personality argument? When groups use more *we* pronouns in their assessment of their work, explicitly talking about their performance and behaviors using the Compass Points directions, they experience more efficiency and effectiveness. Individuals might still have the same personalities they always have, but participants tend to recognize and more aptly act on their impact on the group.

Application Examples

- Jennifer is a new principal and remembers the drama-filled moments on her team, some quite fresh in her memory. When she experiences Compass Points with other new principals as part of a university support initiative, she decides to use it with her entire staff. The timing is just right—November—when the honeymoon for many teams has definitely worn off, and groups need some time to assess not the students but themselves as groups.

- As part of a leadership pipeline initiative, Bertha facilitates the aspiring leader program. In one of the first sessions, Compass Points has become an important community-building experience, but far more valuable than other team-building experiences, which may be fun but don't have as much process learning.

- Jana's school has a great experience with Compass Points and has continued to use the language in various groups. As various individuals plan agendas, they now draw a small pie chart in the corner, giving a preview of how the agenda creator believes this meeting may feel to participants. For instance, a mandatory meeting for state assessment proctoring is focused around North and West (efficient and full of the necessary details), rather than East and South (talking about purpose or big picture and making sure everyone in the room participates).

Group Juggle

The Group Juggle (SRI, n.d.c) protocol was developed in the field by educators, and I adapted it to its present form. I first experienced it in a professional development session in 2001. The facilitators used the process to help us think about our natural behaviors when we are group members. A throwing and catching game (using soft items of various shapes and purposes) can be the source of deep learning about how groups function and communicate. A large space, where individuals can stand in a circle, is necessary for the Group Juggle protocol. This adaptation is specifically targeted toward creating group norms.

Purpose

Participants aim to provide a playful opportunity to reflect on group dynamics and collaborative skills.

Group Size

Generally, groups of six or more are ideal; any group larger than twenty-five may benefit from regrouping. However, if it is important for the group to stay together, then individuals will need to stand very close to one another to reduce the size of the circle.

Pre-Protocol Preparation

The facilitator should gather a variety of soft objects for juggling.

Sequence

1. Ask the group to form a circle and explain that there is a bag of items and each participant will touch each item one time.

    Language You Can Borrow: *This process is called Group Juggle. No one person needs to juggle alone—we all will do it together. Our job is for each person to touch* (important to just use that word) *each item in this bag. Sometimes in schools, when we are involved in a new initiative, we do it this way.* (Pass one item around the group, feigning excitement and cheering.) *However, I don't believe that's how adults want to work and learn. They need some skin in the game. So instead of passing items to each other, why don't we toss them to each other? Notice I said,* toss to, *not* hurl at, *so we should set some agreements before we start. Who has some ideas?*

2. Keep talking with the group until these five agreements of tossing (include others as you see fit) are set.

    a. Throw underhand.

    b. Throw with an arc (roundhouse softball pitches won't work).

    c. Say the name of the person you are throwing to.

    d. Ensure eye contact.

    e. Continue in a pattern (so you only have to know one name).

3. Conduct the first round with just one item, creating the pattern so everyone receives the item one time.

    Language You Can Borrow: *OK, _____, you are my partner. All right, I'm thinking through all of our agreements (name them under your breath), and . . .* [throw]. *Look how hard I worked for _____, and what did I get in return?* [Pause] *Nothing! Perhaps you now notice the norms are out of balance—they are all for the thrower and none for the receiver. That can happen in groups when we aren't throwing balls, too! For today, I pose we need to add one more agreement. After someone catches the ball, the person who threw it says thank you and the name in return. So we have six agreements moving forward. Now, _____, choose someone and keep these agreements going.*

4. Debrief the first round. Ask participants to assess how well the group lived up to the agreement.

    Language You Can Borrow: *Time to check in on our agreements. Take a moment, turn to someone, and see first if you can name all six agreements. Then chat about how well the group lived up to those commitments.* [Sixty seconds] *If the whole group needs to hear a reminder about one or more of them, this is the time to say it.*

5. Conduct the next round, adding one to three more items.

    Language You Can Borrow: *Wouldn't it be nice if we only ever had to juggle one item at a time in our work? That is not our profession, is it? So, I'll start with* *only one and then a few more will come. What won't change? (The six agreements won't change.)*

6. Debrief the second round. Ask participants to assess how well the group lived up to the agreements. Elicit any reminders for the group and any possible additions (avoid if at all possible—six is plenty). Ask participants to set a goal for the number of objects in this round.

7. Conduct the third round, adding more items.

8. Debrief the third round. Ask participants to again check in with their partner for any reminders the group needs or additions and deletions to the agreements.

9. Conduct the last round, using all items. As each item comes in, place it on the ground in order.

10. After a celebration of the last round, ask participants to turn away so they aren't looking at the items on the floor. Ask them to work with their partner to identify all items thrown . . . in order. As partners seem to be finished or admit defeat, let them know they can turn and visually check their answers.

11. Conduct a whole-group reflection by asking the following questions.

    a. "What did you notice about yourself and the group during the experience?"

    b. "Just because we can juggle many items doesn't mean we really should, does it? Did any of you remember every item, in order?"

    c. "What items were harder to throw or catch? Why might that be so?"

    d. "So, we had these agreements we used throughout the process. How did we develop them? How did we use them?"

    e. "Each of these items may be like initiatives we are asking classroom teachers to juggle at any one time. Try to make a metaphorical connection to some of these items by asking, 'We are asking teachers to do _____, and that is like the _____ (item juggled) because . . .' For example: 'We are asking teachers to differentiate instruction, and that is like the stuffed centipede because it has so many different segments.'"

12. Tell participants there is one last round. In this round, none of the agreements or constraints need to apply. This means no need to call out names, no need to gain eye contact prior to throwing, and so on. The facilitator does not need to convene this round—the threat of the round without constraints will generally make the need for meaningful norms quite clear.

    Language You Can Borrow: *As we close, let's just try this one more time, juggling every item but without any of the rules we agreed on. No need to call out names, throw underhand . . . those were probably just all unnecessary. OK, everybody ready?* Usually, participants will show signs of fear or dread, and some will remove themselves from the group. *Why is the thought of a round without our agreements such a problem for some of you? (Sixty seconds to discuss) Agreements—we might call them norms—or what is* normal *in a group, are critical to highly functioning* *teams. Today was about experiencing a very meaningful way to create norms that are essential rather than perfunctory.*

13. Debrief the process. (Five minutes)

Notes

- There is not a specific set of items to toss. Raiding children's toy boxes or a trip to a dollar store will usually suffice. The only criterion is this: make sure items are soft. I also find it helpful if the items are unique. For instance, having ten different colored spherical balls provides less of a meaningful debrief than three spheres, one football, two small stuffed animals, one plush dog toy (unused!), one beach ball, one baby toy, and one oversized pair of dice.

- In step 5, sometimes participants will offer an addition to the agreements which really is a strategy, not a constraint. For instance, a participant might caution others to be careful that when they step into the group they aren't in the trajectory of another object. My response might be something like this: "That sounds like that was a helpful strategy for you. I suspect we all might have helpful strategies to share. The goal of our agreements is to make clear what each person needs to do for the health of our group. Most strategies are personally chosen."

- Through trial and error, I have found around ten items seem to make the learning stick without unnecessarily extending the experience. I often try to have a duplicate of an item, and I throw it twice; for instance, in my ten items I might have two green balls. I throw one as item 1 and then one as item 10. This makes for a great reflection experience in step 9. If possible, you might keep the duplicate item and hide it to see who might notice. If someone does, you might say, "No, I guarantee all items on the floor were only tossed one time." As someone disagrees, I might walk toward the items and then place the tenth item back in line and say, "No, no, no, this first item is a green ball. This last item (add to the line) is a chartreuse sphere. In education we never do the same thing twice and call it two different things, right?"

Application Examples

- As part of an institute about leading collaborative teams, Louise uses Group Juggle with collaborative team chairs to help recognize the power of setting norms which are meaningful, useful, and practiced.

- Jordan believes his school is suffering from initiative fatigue. As a visual way to prioritize the three goals of the campus improvement plan, the group juggles three items. Multiple times during the year, the group uses Group Juggle again to check in on the three initiatives and to see if any other initiatives have snuck their way in.

Say, Say, Do

I remember first hearing about this protocol as a game a teacher at the American School in London played with her students. As Frances Hensley, one of my mentors in facilitating protocols, talked about the experience, it became clear it could be a meaningful experience for adults as well. The Say, Say, Do (SRI, n.d.h) protocol represents the recollection of the experience, and I adapted it to its present form. Taking risks and making mistakes in front of other adults can be a humbling experience. The Say, Say, Do protocol creates an environment where these errors are widespread and humorous. Prepare for much laughter and learning!

Purpose

Participants aim to reflect on individual approaches to a task of varying difficulty.

Group Size

Generally, groups of six or more are ideal.

Sequence

1. Ask participants to stand in a circle. Tell participants that when you give a direction, they should say exactly what you say and do it at the same time.

2. Round 1 is called *Say, Say, Do*. To begin round 1, start with one of four directions, such as *step left*, *step right*, *step in*, and *step out*. For instance, the facilitator might say, "Step *left*," and participants will step *left* as they also say, "Step *left*." The facilitator gives directions at a lively pace and usually mixes the four direction options. (Two to three minutes)

3. Round 2 is called *Say, Say, Do Opposite*. To begin round 2, tell the participants the four directions will stay the same, but their action needs to change. Whatever the facilitator says, participants should also say, but this time while doing the opposite. For instance, the facilitator might say, "Step *left*," and participants will say, "Step *left*," as they actually step *right*. Again, the facilitator gives directions at a lively pace and usually mixes the four direction options. (Two to three minutes)

4. Round 3 is called *Say, Say Opposite, Do*. Tell the participants there is one more change. Whatever the facilitator says, they are asked to say the opposite but do the requested action at the same time. For instance, the facilitator might say, "Step *left*," and participants will say, "Step *right*" as they actually step *left*. Again, the facilitator gives the directions at a lively pace and usually mixes the four direction options. (Two to three minutes)

5. Conduct a whole-group reflection by asking the following questions. (Less than ten minutes)

    a. "Which round was hardest? Easiest? Why?"

    b. "How does your brain feel?"

    c. "How does this apply to your work?"

    d. "What strategies did you use as the task became more complex?"

6. Debrief the process. (Five minutes)

Notes

- Educators with temporary or permanent physical conditions that would prohibit these movements might do so on the side of the space and show with their arms which direction they would move. For educators in wheelchairs, the experience works the same, except the facilitator might change *step* to *move*.

- Visit **go.SolutionTree.com/leadership** for a version of this protocol focused on leadership.

Application Example

- Carmen is a second-language acquisition specialist, seeking to give teachers a taste of what it might feel like for a student who is learning a new language. Say, Say, Do became a perfect protocol to better envision what struggles some students have in schools. During the debrief, teachers also made connections to students with dyslexia or other learning differences.

- Connie is the instructional coach at a high school and is increasingly having problems with members of the mathematics department. It almost seems they are intentionally trying to antagonize teachers and other departments. Instead of pulling out an article on teamwork, she decides to use the Say, Say, Do protocol. At the close of the experience, she suggests to the group members that they might find themselves in any of the three rounds each day at work. She asks a participant to say, "Step in" whenever she points toward him or her. "Sometimes our relationships with folks at work are like round 1 (points to colleague who says "step in" and you step in as you say step in). Other times work is like round 2 (points to colleague who says "step in" and you step out as you say step in). Finally, other times it is like round 3 (points to colleague who says "step in" and you step in as you say step out). One round feels disingenuous; one round feels defiant. In which round was there the most congruence and do you feel the most success? Now, what would it take for us to live more in round 1?"

Verbal Legos

The Momentous Institute (2015) developed Verbal Legos, and I include my adaptation of it here. Communication is always a behavior that educators can improve. The Verbal Legos protocol prompts participants to consider both sides of the interaction, that of the communicator and of the listener. This process can yield results benefitting classroom instruction with students and in collegial conversations among staff.

Purpose

Participants aim to consider communication clarity.

Group Size

Generally, groups of four or more are ideal, although it can work with any group size that is divisible by two, since participants will work in partnerships.

Pre-Protocol Preparation

For each set of partners, provide two bags of identical Legos—same number, same color, same shape.

Sequence

1. Hand out identical bags of Legos to partners. Each partner should verify with each other that the bags have the exact same pieces.

2. Partners sit back to back on the floor or in chairs, so they can't see each other.

3. Person A builds a structure out of the Legos in his or her bag. The person may or may not use all the pieces. (Less than three to four minutes)

4. Person A verbally describes to person B how to replicate the structure—without looking at person B or showing person B the structure he or she just created. Person B uses the other bag to attempt to build the structure that person A described. (Five to seven minutes)

5. When person B believes the structure is accurately assembled, the partners can compare their structures.

6. Switch roles and repeat the process. If timing works, a set of partners might choose to switch bags with another set of partners. Partners must always have identical bags.

7. Partners can talk together using the following prompts. (One to two minutes per question)

   a. How did you do? Was it easier or harder than you expected?

   b. What strategies did you use?

   c. When you were the speaker, how did you let your partner know what to do next?

   d. When you were the listener, what words did you listen for?

8. Conduct a whole-group reflection. (Five to seven minutes)

   a. Which was more difficult, listening or describing? How might your preference impact how you currently choose to communicate with your colleagues?

   b. Sometimes, participants may talk about either having or not having a shared language. If you had one, how did you develop it? When?

(Sometimes, when partners are double-checking the accuracy of their bags, they implicitly create new vocabulary.)

9. Debrief the process. (Five minutes)

Notes

- Watch carefully as groups work, taking notes of behaviors, particularly toward the second whole-group reflection prompt about shared language (step 8b).

Application Example

- In a professional development session about feedback, Lisa uses Verbal Legos to show feedback as an ever-present part of work. She asks this question: "How was feedback present in the interactions?" Too often, her colleagues believe feedback is only part of a supervisory or evaluative conversation, when, actually, it is ever present in their workdays.

Zones of Comfort, Risk, and Danger

The Zones of Comfort, Risk, and Danger (SRI, n.d.l) protocol was developed in the field by educators, and I adapted it to its present form. This protocol was one of my first foundational experiences learning about protocol use in 2001. Originally conceived as a paper-and-pencil process, this adaptation offers a more kinesthetic experience where participants can stand next to one another in a large circle. They spend time building shared understanding of three words, comfort, risk, and danger *in this context*. They then use this understanding to apply the learning in a variety of situations. The protocol offers a scaffolding of prompts, from less school-specific situations to more risky contexts.

Purpose

Participants aim to assess personal risk-taking tendencies to help groups spend more of their time in the risk zone.

Group Size

Generally, groups of four or more are ideal; this protocol works well with large groups.

Pre-Protocol Preparation

Using ropes, yarn, or masking tape, create three concentric circles on the floor, as seen in figure 2.7 (page 82). These circles should be big enough for participants to stand in.

Sequence

1. Introduce the names of the three zones and invite participants to move into the comfort zone.

Language You Can Borrow: *These are the zones of comfort, risk, and danger* [step into each one with each word spoken]. *I'm certain you know these three words, but we don't want to assume we share a common understanding of these words, or that we know what these words mean in this context. So, please engage in some imagery with me. As I read a description of this first word, comfort, please create a*

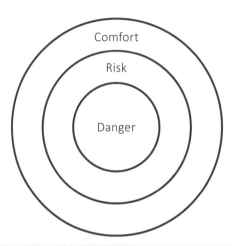

Figure 2.7: Zones of Comfort, Risk, and Danger physical setup.

picture in your mind of what that looks like for you. As soon as you have that clear picture, step into the comfort zone. I may still be talking; the person next to you may not have moved yet—that is all fine. The comfort zone is usually a place where we feel at ease, with no tension, have a good grip on our environment, and know how to navigate occasional rough spots with ease. It is a place to relax and renew yourself.

2. After everyone has stepped in, ask for two or three volunteers to describe what their image of comfort looks like.

   Language You Can Borrow: *So, this is the comfort zone and the key word is* relax.

3. Introduce the risk zone.

   Language You Can Borrow: *We will use the same process for the risk zone as we did for the comfort zone. As I read the description, please identify an image in your mind of this zone, and when you have it, step inside. The risk zone involves adapting to new circumstances. It is where most people are willing to take some risks, to not know everything, or sometimes to not know anything at all except that they want to learn and will take the risks necessary to do so. It is where people open up to other people with curiosity and interest, and where they will consider options or ideas they haven't thought of before. The risk zone is the most fertile place for learning.*

4. After everyone has stepped in, ask two or three volunteers to describe what their images of the risk zone look like. *So, that is the comfort zone, and the key word is* relax. *This is the risk zone, and the key word is* learning.

5. Introduce the danger zone.

Language You Can Borrow: *Now for the danger zone. At the end of this step, we won't ask anyone to share their image—there is a reason why! But once you have your image, please step inside. The danger zone is full of defenses, fears, red lights, and the desire for escape. It requires a great deal of energy and time to accomplish anything when you are in this zone. The best way to work when you find yourself there is to recognize it is a danger zone and figure out how to get out. So that is the comfort zone, and the key word is* relax. *That is the risk zone, and the key word is* learning. *This is the danger zone, and the key word is* escape. *Let's get out of this danger zone all the way to the outside! Now that we have some shared understandings about these zones, let's test them out.*

6. Give the first example situation, which is *cooking a meal for other people*, and ask participants to move to whatever zone matches their response to the idea of participating in this situation.

7. Invite participants to look around and see where their colleagues are standing. Now add to the context slightly, *cooking a meal for other people, and they will be eating at your home.* Keep adding tighter constraints, for instance, saying, "There are twenty people coming over, and they have never had your cooking before." The goal in this step is to increase the risk. Once many participants are congregated in the danger zone, consider asking, "Someone in the Danger Zone, if you couldn't change anything about what I have said, but could add something to make this less dangerous, what would it be?" As they change the context, the group reacts and moves to another zone, if applicable.

8. After several iterations involving cooking situations, ask the group to walk all the way out and start over with another concept (for example, swimming, singing, or driving). If an individual or multiple individuals continue to stall in the comfort zone, no matter the contextual changes, consider asking them, "What would it take to move you into risk if you could add something to this context—not change what I said?"

9. As additional contexts are added, look for a moment when the group is spread out—several in comfort all the way to several in danger. Raise the idea of a *risk gap*, which is when a topic has caused some to want to escape (and some maybe have), and others are not engaging in the topic at all. The gap feels inequitable and adversely affects the group. Ask participants, "What happens if this gap continues and is not effectively addressed?"

10. Work with one of the topics to move almost everyone to danger. Once there, ask them to turn to someone and identify what danger looks like for them in a group. After a few moments, make a short list of all the possibilities (for example, not speaking, angrily participating, abruptly leaving, playing on a phone or computer, and disagreeing over small issues). Ask participants, "Why don't we talk about these with our colleagues?"

11. After several non-school-related concepts, consider more school-centric ideas (for example, having a tough conversation with colleagues about grading; about how they are treating a student; about how they treat another colleague;

about how they don't follow through on their commitments to the team; about teaching five-year-olds, fifteen-year-olds, or fifty-five-year-olds; or about holding a contentious parent conference).

12. Debrief the process. (Five minutes)

Notes

- Discussion protocols create an environment of safety, but it's not how the word *safety* is often understood. I am talking about the safety to take risks, rather than the safety in a group where individuals stay (and want to stay) in the status quo (comfort). If *safety* equals *comfort*, then no risk taking would take place. I contend if groups aren't taking risks together, why are we meeting?

- The risk scenarios can be completely customized to the group. The examples in the protocol attempt to scaffold from comfort to higher levels of risk.

- A choice in step 7 is to identify how effective facilitators attempt to shape environments where participants can move out of danger. Similarly, in step 8, masterful facilitators also work to ensure each participant is solidly in the risk zone.

- At any point, a facilitator might ask participants to turn and explain why they are standing where they are standing. Another option would be to ask a volunteer or two to speak out loud about their thinking.

- Equity-based prompts are also potentially meaningful.
  - ⇨ Having a tough conversation with a colleague of a different _____ (for example, gender, race, nationality, or ethnicity)
  - ⇨ Addressing a microaggression with an entire staff
  - ⇨ Addressing a microaggression with one person individually

Application Examples

- When introducing protocols in other families (chapters 3–6), Jean uses the Zones protocol to introduce the expectation that each job in a protocol (presenter, participant, and facilitator) requires a presence in the risk zone.

- Deb, an instructional coach, wishes to see visually how individual teachers may assess themselves in specific teaching moves relative to their instructional framework (for example, differentiating by learner profile or pulling a small group for science).

- As department chair, Adam is seeing that social studies teachers need a clearer model of acting formatively in a classroom. They are currently calling every quiz *formative* just because it occurs before the summative. He wants to give them a clear model of what it means to act in a formative way. As he adjusts the prompts in zones, he identifies his formative moves. Then in the final reflection, he makes the connection to formative assessment.

Building community is a strong strategy for leaders. Beyond the many options in this section, check **go.SolutionTree.com/leadership** for eight more.

1. **Balloon Bounce:** Participants aim to consider behaviors in a group with multiple parameters or high stress. Groups of four are ideal; groups larger than eight can divide up.

2. **The Change Activity:** Participants aim to reflect on the contextual factors that impact sustainable change. Any size group can work.

3. **Connections:** Participants aim to provide a space for adults to mentally enter into a meeting or gathering. Groups of three are ideal; larger groups work but will need more time.

4. **Defy Gravity:** Participants aim to examine behaviors during change as constraints are added. This protocol works best with pairs.

5. **Football Spoons:** Participants aim to build connections to group dynamics and equity. Groups of three or more are ideal; larger groups can divide into subgroups of three to five.

6. **Hog Call:** Participants aim to simulate what it means to find each other in collaborative experiences. This is one for larger groups; sixteen or more is ideal.

7. **Say, Say, Do—Leadership Version:** Participants aim to reflect on what adult facilitation strategies are helpful or hindering as a task becomes more difficult. Groups of six or more are ideal.

8. **What's in Common?:** Participants aim to identify collegiality as the goal of educator teams. Groups of eight or more are ideal.

Build Shared Understanding in an E⁴ Way

It is intentional that this chapter about protocols to build shared understanding is the largest in this handbook. All groups have gaps in their shared understanding. If they didn't, the organism, the group itself, would cease to develop, which in biological terms means it dies. Educators who simply *do* protocols choose a protocol from this chapter simply because of its allure or fun factor or interesting title. Instead, *using* a protocol requires a more thoughtful approach to selection. Remember to apply E^4: be sure to consider whether the protocol will be effective and efficient while contributing to equity and excellence. A matrix in appendix D (page 243) can serve as a tool to consider a current challenge and consider a protocol that may help address it. The next chapter builds on the work of matching protocol to purpose, especially when an educator has a product that needs refining.

Protocols to Refine Products

Refining protocols are designed to check alignment between a document or practice and the intended goal or goals. An individual's beliefs and practices may be out of alignment. Someone may have written a document to accomplish *X*, *Y*, and *Z*, but it really doesn't meet those expressed outcomes. The protocols in this chapter can be particularly useful in two situations when an educator wants to compare a document or practice to a goal or set of goals.

1. When an educator is somewhat confident

2. When an educator is concerned

Chapter 2 (page 35) featured protocols to build shared understanding. A hallmark of these processes is that they have facilitators and participants but often do not have presenters—there is not one person who primarily owns the work or content of the session. Protocols to refine products are the first of four families where all three jobs are present—presenter, facilitator, and participants. No matter the job, these educators want feedback to be offered in effective and efficient ways.

I explain four protocols in this chapter. I summarize the first three—Gap Analysis, Collaborative Ghost Walk, and The Slice—with protocol notes and explain the final protocol, Tuning, in detail. Protocols such as Tuning are called *foundational protocols*. These processes are more complex, and therefore I offer expanded supports for facilitators.

Educators in both of the following situations would benefit greatly from a protocol to refine products.

SITUATION A

Rebecca has just been named the school leader at a K–5 elementary school. She prides herself on asking for feedback on almost everything. In her last post as principal, her staff gave her frank, sometimes brutally honest, feedback on documents and ideas. She has been having trouble finding that level of truth with her current staff.

The last time she sent out a draft plan to the school leadership team, it seemed their feedback fell into four categories.

1. Recommended grammar and usage changes ("Misplaced semicolon in the third row, second column." "I think Principal should be capitalized." "A few typos on the third page—perhaps you were in a hurry!")

2. Affirming statements ("Looks great!" "Love it." "This looks manageable.")

3. The emoji version of affirming statements (winking face, smiling face with halo, smirking face with starry eyes)

4. Radio silence—no responses at all

She knows she could call a meeting and ask for this feedback, too, but she's afraid she might just receive more of the same, just in person.

SITUATION B

After a successful stint as a school principal, Hayden now works in the central office. He is experiencing the realization that central office leadership is not the same as building leadership. A particular area of struggle has been receiving feedback. He is not at a dearth for it—it comes from every vantage point, all the time!

He honestly wants feedback—constructive feedback, that is. He feels like so much of what he receives is off the mark or seems to be perpetuating a particular, often personal, agenda. He's at a loss for how to help the schools he serves offer feedback that can be useful.

You may relate to Rebecca, Hayden, or both in the previous situations. In theory, educators should be excellent at giving feedback—after all, they do it all day long with students. Unfortunately, researchers of feedback with students would disagree, as students do receive frequent feedback, but a majority of it may not be classified as productive (Moss & Brookhart, 2019; Wiggins, 2012; Wiliam, 2011).

These same researchers have provided various frames for how to render students helpful feedback, and some promising practices have emerged for how to provide educators usable and actionable feedback, such as providing more descriptive, low-inference feedback based on classroom observations (Van Soelen, 2016). However, educators often struggle with giving productive feedback to each other on a document or an idea. Without some guidance or framework, it is not shocking when the received feedback misses the mark. Enter refining protocols.

The Protocols

In this family of structured conversations, the Tuning protocol is by far the most widely used. Although I will also briefly discuss a few others, a lion's share of this chapter is dedicated to the time-tested Tuning. I will, however, begin with Gap Analysis.

Gap Analysis

Daniel Baron (n.d.a) developed the Gap Analysis protocol, and I adapted it to its present form. The process this protocol uses is particularly useful when it is important for participants to be individually risky in their sharing of practices, as each participant takes a turn being the presenter. The protocol doesn't explicitly assess the organization as a whole; instead it focuses on individual members' practices.

Purpose

Participants aim to make a stronger connection between belief and practice.

Group Size

Any size group can work; divide into triads (or quads).

Sequence

1. Educators assess themselves against a document, writing about areas of alignment and non-alignment. (Five minutes)

2. In groups of three, the first person (presenter) talks about both personal areas of alignment and gaps. (Five minutes)

3. The rest of the group asks clarifying questions, and the presenter answers. (Three minutes)

4. As the presenter turns away to focus on listening and note taking, the remaining group members engage in a gap analysis—attempting to clearly describe what

it might look like if the presenter had a stronger alignment between belief and practice.

5. The presenter now turns back toward the group and offers a brief reflection of current thinking, sharing at least one idea as a next step. (Two minutes)

6. Repeat steps 2–5 so another member can become the presenter. (Twenty minutes)

7. Repeat steps 2–5 so the last group member can become the presenter. (Twenty minutes)

8. Debrief the process. (Five minutes)

Notes

- Since this discussion protocol has various steps and the steps repeat with jobs shifting (for example, this time a presenter is now a participant), displaying an anchor chart can be extremely helpful. Check **go.SolutionTree.com/leadership** for sample anchor charts for various protocols.

- For the protocol to be effective, the facilitator must ask, "What will we gap against?" Using *gap* as a verb, a facilitator needs to identify a document, standards, or a set of beliefs—anything that is currently static. If the facilitator asks participants to gap against their interpretation of something unwritten, it will be easy for the triads to wander away from the goal, thus severely decreasing the value of the shared experience.

- Educators are often quick to self-deprecate and focus on the negative. Leaders see this in post-observation conferences, teachers hear this from each other during collaborative team meetings, and students may even hear this in one-to-one conversations with their teachers. In Gap Analysis, it is essential that all participants acknowledge where they are *in* alignment and currently *out of* alignment with what they are gapping against. One way I have made this expectation clear is by asking participants to consider using a T-chart (figure 3.1) in the initial step.

In Alignment	Out of Alignment (Gaps)

Figure 3.1: T-chart for presenters in a Gap Analysis protocol.

*Visit **go.SolutionTree.com/leadership** for a free reproducible version of this figure.*

Application Example 1

Nelson is a professional development director in a large, urban district. Twenty-five educators in the department function similarly to instructional coaches, albeit with a different job title. The job title is quite relevant in this context, as Nelson inherited these educators from various offices and departments around the district. The potential for impact with these positions is high, but various factors have conspired against realizing the benefits. One pivotal piece of the puzzle is that although Nelson is the official evaluator of these positions, they essentially have direction coming from three locations, the professional development office, area superintendents, and the teaching and learning office.

At the beginning of year two of the reorganization and reconceptualization of the positions, Gap Analysis becomes an important measuring tool for these educators to self-assess against their new, carefully crafted job description. Following the protocol, which occurs in triads, Nelson will use a Chalk Talk (chapter 2, page 47) to look for trends across the contextual factors that may be contributing to the gaps.

Application Example 2

Billy is the principal of a K–5 school in a suburban area. As his school becomes more and more involved with data teams and collaborative structure, he is feeling pulled in many directions. In a leadership team meeting, as he shares his struggle, the assistant principal and grade-level leaders concur. The weight of leadership is palpable.

At the next professional learning day, with every staff member (including those classified as paraprofessionals and clerical), he uses a Gap Analysis with a text excerpt from Regie Routman (2000), a teacher and literacy author.

The text discusses the fear of being a "tall poppy" with colleagues and worrying about what they would think. Staff members meet in triads and bravely indicate a gap in their practice where they could assume more leadership—being a strong, tall poppy—but currently are falling short.

At the end of the sixty minutes (twenty minutes per person in the triad), each person writes a commitment on a sticky note, and one by one, comes up to a large paper on the wall and affirms the commitment verbally in front of the whole seventy-five-person staff.

Collaborative Ghost Walk

Debbie Bambino (n.d.b) developed the Collaborative Ghost Walk protocol. The intriguing title of this process has nothing to do with spirits or poltergeists! Instead, it poses the metaphor that the school is ghostly during the protocol's data-collection portion because students aren't present. This is not designed to be a classroom walkthrough or an episode of Instructional Rounds (City, Elmore, Fiarman, & Teitel, 2009). Instead, the goal is to find environmental evidence of the focus declared by an individual or a team.

Purpose

Participants aim to answer a targeted question using evidence collected by a team in classrooms without students.

Group Size

Any size can work for this protocol.

Sequence

1. The school host (presenter) poses the focus for feedback gathering. (Five to ten minutes)

2. Visitors (participants) brainstorm possible evidence expectations. (Five to ten minutes)

3. Visitors silently walk through designated classrooms, collecting evidence aligned to the focus. (Twenty minutes)

4. Visitors return to the initial space and report findings aligned to the expectations. The host (or team) listens and takes notes. (Ten minutes)

5. The host offers a reflection. (Five minutes)

6. Debrief the process. (Five minutes)

Notes

- Declaring the focus is key. It is helpful to talk through the intended focus with an external colleague. At times, assumptions about language may get in the way for the data collectors. For instance, a potential host who wants to collect evidence about rigor may not have the same understanding about rigor as the visitors.

- The process can be fruitful for both internal and external teams. The application example uses an external example. If you are using Collaborative Ghost Walk with a group of colleagues who all work at the same location, it would be prudent to spend more time in what constitutes evidence for the focus. It will be tempting for individuals who live and breathe in the school every day to make assumptions about what they see and articulate into descriptive evidence when they are probably interpreting or evaluating instead.

Application Example

Yvonne is a member of a group of principals who voluntarily meet each month to learn with one another (Van Soelen, 2019a, 2019b). They primarily use protocols from SRI to organize these ninety-minute gatherings. It is Yvonne's turn to host the group this month, so she uses it as an opportunity for her school to receive feedback on a particular schoolwide initiative, *meaningful anchor charts that students might find helpful and useful.*

Serving as the presenter in this protocol, Yvonne starts the Collaborative Ghost Walk by articulating her data collection focus. Usually, Collaborative Ghost Walk occurs on a day when students are not in the building; this time, Yvonne carefully orchestrates a schedule to ensure the principals were collecting data across two segments of the school day when students in various grade levels were engaged in special area learning (for example, physical education, music, and visual arts). After the second step, where Yvonne further explicates the focus area, each principal, armed with a clipboard, a unique schedule, and a school map, takes the next thirty minutes to gather observational data—only data related to the focus area.

At the conclusion of the experience, principals reconvene, take individual time to organize their observations, and begin the data debrief. Yvonne uses this opportunity to build capacity with other leaders in her building, asking assistant principals and instructional coaches to join in as they listen to information about the data.

As expected, some observations align with what the school team thinks, and that is good news! Other insights are surprising and leave the school team with new entry points.

The Slice

I first experienced The Slice (SRI, n.d.i) protocol at the university level, as instructors were examining what prospective teacher candidates were experiencing across each of the method classes, which entailed several departments. This process is a form of purposeful sampling. It acknowledges, with careful foresight and strategic thinking, that it is possible to assess a practice without collecting every bit of data across a school.

Purpose

Participants aim to gain insights and perspectives by looking at multiple pieces of work across classrooms or grade levels.

Group Size

The educators who convene The Slice intentionally choose data gatherers, usually through a purposeful sampling method; the interrogation of the slice student samples works best with a group of six to fifteen. Slice conveners might be central office leaders or school-level administrators.

Pre-Protocol Preparation

1. Decide on the slice focus.
2. Design the guiding question.
3. Decide on your sampling strategy.
4. Identify slice methods (for example, how many students, how many content areas).
5. Identify slice duration (that is, how long the student work will be collected).
6. Arrange logistics.
7. Decide on the slice interrogation method.

There are multiple ways for a group to interrogate the slice of collected student work. Several options are available through SRI (www.schoolreforminitiative.org/protocols). Regardless of the variation, generalized steps look like those in the Sequence section for this protocol.

Sequence

1. Review the focus of the data collection.
2. Look at individual work samples through the focus question or questions.
3. Generalize across work samples.
4. Identify possible recommendations.
5. Commit to next steps.
6. Debrief the process.

Notes

- The Slice protocol contains many options for customizing. One consideration is what I call horizontal versus vertical slicing. A horizontal slice collects the work of a student (or a set of students over a period of time). An example might be for a third-grade team to examine the work of several students for an entire day: a student served by gifted and talented programming, a student for whom English is the second language, a student who has an individualized education plan, and a student who receives no special services. A vertical slice collects multigrade work over a shorter time frame. See the subsequent example.

- Risk can be considerably higher if the participants gathering the data are also the educators who help produce the data. A facilitator will need to work carefully to hold participants to each step of the process, raising the risk and lowering any perceived defensiveness.

- Here are some examples of potential focus questions for a slice.

    ⇨ How do the work samples of different-gendered students compare?

    ⇨ How are individual students' learning styles reflected in the work samples?

    ⇨ What gaps might be present in our curriculum?

    ⇨ What evidence might exist of redundancy or unnecessary overlap in our curriculum?

Application Example

Peggy and Christine are school leaders at a high-performing elementary school. Many students score well on state and national assessments, other schools come to observe their collaborative planning process, and teacher retention is high. Many families work earnestly to live in the enrollment zone, and the demographic data demonstrate that 24 percent of students qualify for gifted and talented services. As state curriculum standards become more rigorous and schools start to be measured on individual student growth, not just student proficiency, Peggy, the principal, wants to ensure common understanding about a word many in her community use frequently in passing. The word is *rigor*.

The leadership team has used protocols for years, primarily to read shared texts. The Slice represents a deeper level of vulnerability than that available through the other protocols they use, as the teachers in the room will be the ones whose students have been selected for The Slice. A random sampling method selects the sixth, sixteenth, and twenty-sixth (if applicable) student of each teacher's roster on the leadership team. Peggy and Christine carefully prep teachers for what The Slice will entail but ask them—even beg them—to not plan differently for this data collection day. From 9–10 a.m., teachers ask each of these particular students to not submit their work as they usually might but instead place their work in a string backpack. They should include in the bag any materials they used for the work during that time frame.

At the end of the day, the leadership team comes together and literally empties out the bags. Using the focusing question, How is each student involved in rigorous experiences at our school? the team members dive in, attempting to waylay their assumptions about the work, the students, and most difficult, about one another. The external facilitator keeps bringing individuals back to the collected data, grounding the discussions in description.

Not all protocols are magical and have glorious results that yield blog posts or articles. In this case, the external facilitator leaves before the conclusion of The Slice, and the real emotions surface after his departure. Peggy and Christine realize they did not strategically scaffold risk for the leadership team. This experience is too much, too fast, and it takes several weeks to build back trust from the members.

Tuning

The Tuning protocol is one of the oldest discussion protocols in common practice in schools. Originally envisioned by Joseph McDonald to help high school students tune up their end-of-school exhibition projects in member schools of The Coalition of Essential Schools, the most commonly used version is a revision by David Allen (1998) and is now a staple in sessions of facilitative leadership teams, teams looking at student work, and collaborative teams. Unfortunately, the ubiquitous nature of the protocol has led it to be highly bastardized. For instance, some versions leave well-intentioned users unclear on the intent of the two types of feedback in a Tuning. Here I present my adaptation of the protocol. This is the first foundational protocol in this book, meaning it sees a lot of use; because of its importance I provide expanded support for facilitators. Each protocol step has explanation of the *why* and the *how*. The overall goal in providing these supports is to encourage the facilitator to have a deep understanding of not just the protocol but each and every step.

Misconceptions

There are two general confusion points in truly understanding and using the Tuning protocol that compel me to add a special section to address them. The first comes from the name itself. In sessions where I am using the Tuning protocol, I often ask participants to offer personal context where they have heard the word *tuning* used. The following three usually top the list.

1. **A musical instrument:** Tuning is a process of adjusting toward something. In an orchestra or band, the conductor asks the musicians to tune their instruments to an electronic pitch, or to an oboe if there is one. Why the oboe?

The bore (the hole through which the air flows) is the smallest of any musical instrument, therefore, the air moves rather quickly. What comes out of the end (the bell) is often a very bright, even nasal sound. Although it may not always be pleasing (particularly if the oboist is a fifth or sixth grader!), the pitch is very clear. All musicians in the ensemble will know the tuning note and can adjust their instruments accordingly.

2. **Getting a car tuned:** Usually, a driver gets some sort of signal a car needs a tune-up. This might be a sound, a warning indicator light on the dashboard, a bumpy ride, or the odometer indicating it has been five thousand miles. If a driver takes the car to a garage, the master mechanic may listen to the car run and diagnose the problem. However, the master mechanic doesn't do all the work on the car—that's what the apprentices are for!

3. **A stereo system:** Growing up with a wood-paneled station wagon, my music-producing device was not called a premium sound system or even a radio. It was dubbed a tuner. Also, in my family, the driver on any trip earned the right to decide what music we would listen to. If we started to hear static, he or she may abdicate the responsibility of adjusting the tuner button to the passenger, but with strict instructions for a preferred music genre. The goal is twofold for the driver if someone is allowed to touch the button: match the requested genre and make sure static is at a minimum. Tuning here is turning the dial just right to pick up the right station.

Any of the analogies found in table 3.1 help illuminate why a presenter brings work to be tuned.

Table 3.1: Tuning Analogies

Analogy	Clear Goal
Oboist	Tuning note
Master mechanic	Sound of a purring car
Driver	Music genre

Here's where the trickiness of working with groups kicks in. Many adults, particularly educators in schools, often believe they know better than a colleague. This belief may be tacitly present, not explicitly spoken. If the facilitation is weak and the group ends up not staying true to the Tuning goal, table 3.2 shows how the outcomes are not met.

When this happens, *individuals feel tuned,* rather than *the work product being tuned.* In Georgia and Texas, where I consult most, we joke this is a "Y'all give me feedback, ya hear?" protocol. To be clear, that protocol does not exist anywhere, definitely not in this book.

Table 3.2: Results of Weakly Facilitated Tuning Protocols

Analogy	Clear Goal	Unfortunate Group Response
Oboist	Tuning note	They don't like the tuning note, so they pick another note.
Master mechanic	Sound of a purring car	They choose to work on a part of the car not directed by the mechanic.
Driver	Music genre	They believe it would be best for the presenter to experience a new genre of music.

Instead, a well-facilitated Tuning protocol has constraints, the most obvious being the goal given by the presenter. *Without a goal or set of goals, the Tuning protocol cannot be effectively used.* The second misconception centers around the feedback delineations: warm and cool feedback.

When I ask participants what context they bring to the phrase *warm feedback*, here are the most common responses.

- The good

- The positive

- Happy—like a warm fuzzy

Thus the problem—those are all wrong. Instead, imagine you have a present for a small child. Instead of just giving the gift, you decide to hide it and ask the child to find it. As the child is walking through the house, as he gets closer, you say, "Getting warmer." Similarly, if the child walks in the wrong direction, you might say, "Getting cooler." This metaphor is apropos for a Tuning protocol: the presenter wants to know where she is aligned to the goal (warm) and where she may be far from the goal (cool).

The term *warm feedback* is broadly used, and therefore, broadly misunderstood. I've seen peer-observation classroom protocols organized around warm and cool feedback, a gallery walk using these two terms, and countless teachers in classrooms who ask students to give one another feedback in these categories. Not having shared understanding about these terms compromises the effectiveness of the Tuning protocol. Without clarity, the feedback can become so personal it is unproductive for the presenter.

One common (but problematic) sentence stem I frequently hear in a Tuning protocol is, "I like . . ." I find the stem to be dangerous because it is very easy for the participants to lose sight of the goal. They end up focusing on what they *like* for warm feedback and then suddenly lose courage when it turns to cool—I'm not sure I ever heard someone say, "I don't like . . . !" I usually post a reminder on anchor charts for Tuning, which looks like figure 3.2 (page 98).

Figure 3.2: Reminder on Tuning anchor chart.

Although this may sound a bit brash, the presenter doesn't really care if the participants *like* the document. What does the presenter really care about? The goal!

This gets at another important facet of using the Tuning protocol—the need to be mindful of different backgrounds and identities among the facilitator and the participants. In chapter 2 (page 35), you'll find some protocols related to equity and diversity. Facilitating those discussion protocols can be complex, and facilitators would benefit from studying their own identity and practice prior to their use.

Cultural differences can also emerge during protocols not explicitly focused on equity, diversity, and inclusion. Oman Frame from Atlanta recalls a White facilitator becoming nervous during the feedback step in a Tuning. "As a Black man, I want direct cool feedback in a Tuning. It is going to sound aggressive to someone from another culture, but to me, direct feedback shows you care" (O. Frame, personal communication, August 10, 2020).

Expanded Supports for Tuning

I find it helpful to create and display an anchor chart for this and other foundational protocols. Participants have told me the charts help hold their focus and increase the probability of their feedback being helpful. The anchor chart for the Tuning protocol could have the following information (figure 3.3).

Purpose: To align a product to a goal or set of goals	
1. **Presentation**	Less than fifteen minutes
2. **Clarifying Questions**	Five minutes
3. **Time to Examine Work**	Less than fifteen minutes
4. **Pause to Plan and Code**	Two minutes

5. **Warm and Cool Feedback**		Fifteen minutes
Warm Feedback Sentence Stems	**Cool Feedback Sentence Stems**	
It seems important . . . *I hope we keep . . .* *Considering the goal, I appreciate . . .* *One part that aligns well to the goal is . . .*	*One way to more closely align to the goal . . .* *In order to better _____, we could . . .* *We might . . .* *A possible misalignment . . .* *A potential disconnect . . .*	
6. **Presenter Reflection**		Five minutes
7. **Debrief**		Five minutes

Figure 3.3: Anchor chart for a Tuning protocol.

*Visit **go.SolutionTree.com/leadership** for a free reproducible version of this figure.*

Scaffolded Steps for Facilitators

Following is the sequence of steps for the Tuning protocol with accompanying explanations.

Step 1: Presentation (Less Than Fifteen Minutes)

It is helpful for participants if the facilitator gives a brief rundown of the steps before the presenter starts the protocol. Simply reading a printed anchor chart is not enough or valuable enough to spend time doing. Make sure what you do say prior to handing it over to the presenter adds value to the process. Additionally, your words are not designed to foreshadow or replace what the presenter is about to say. The group doesn't yet need to know the content of the document or the goal to which they will be tuning. A tangible task would be to time yourself rehearsing this opening. It shouldn't take longer than sixty seconds to give a preview of the steps.

Sometimes presenters feel like they need to give a *brief* summary of the work, even though the step has fifteen minutes carved out for the presentation. If the presenter stops talking (and usually looks at you!), you may wish to employ a few different strategies.

- Offer fifteen and twenty seconds of quiet for presenters to work through a mental checklist, making sure they communicated everything they wanted. When I create this space for the presenter, 95+ percent of the time, the presenter ends up saying more.

- You may know something about the work due to a previous conversation you had with the presenter. It may be helpful to prompt the presenter to speak about one or more of those topics if the presenter wishes.

Even with some of these strategies, the presentation may end up being shorter than anticipated. Some discussion protocols ask the participants to have the discipline and hold tight to the time frame, even sitting in silence if needed. That is not the case for Tuning. If a presentation only takes five minutes, that is fine—just be ready for the next step (clarifying questions) to perhaps extend past five minutes. The net result of the time spent for both steps combined will not extend the protocol.

Perhaps the most important move you must make as the facilitator is to ensure the group is clear about the goals the presenter wants them to tune toward. Remember, without a goal, participants cannot tune! If at the end of the Presentation step, the presenter has not explicitly named the goals, ask. If the presenter needs assistance, you might reference the preconference and name that goal, asking if it is still the most relevant.

A small but meaningful shift for some facilitators is to *not* over-prepare posters for a session in which they're using Tuning. For instance, some of my colleagues love having a poster ready with the presenter's goals already scribed using a colorful (perhaps odiferous) marker. This facilitative move is designed to produce efficiency, but it can inadvertently make the presenter feel limited. I have seen presenters change their goals at the end of their presentations because they gained clarity while talking, uninterrupted, during the first step. If we have the poster pre-prepared, presenters may not feel they have the liberty to alter goals.

After the presenter has completed the first step, post the goal for all to see (for example, write it on a poster or on a piece of paper and place it in the middle of a table), verbalizing it aloud. This move of clearly posting the goal may be the most consistent action participants have noted in my seventeen years of facilitating protocols—in particular, Tuning. They admit to losing sight of the goal once they start to have a flurry of their own opinions during and after the presentation. A laser-like focus on the goal will be a continued focus for the facilitator and the presenters throughout the process.

A group can handle tuning something to multiple goals; my experience has been that three is the limit. Even with three, the group may have difficulty holding each of those goals equitably in the feedback step. Recently, a teacher who writes model lesson plans for her school district told me they use the Tuning protocol for each plan. She looked somewhat weary as she mentioned it, so I asked how that experience went for her. She said it usually takes two hours for each Tuning protocol! At my visible shock, she explained they are using a checklist of fifteen look-fors. She has only been a participant in her colleague's sessions, but she was (understandably) nervous about when her lesson plan was going to be (in her words) "up on the chopping block" (P. Weiser, personal communication, June 26, 2019). In a situation with so many goals, I would venture a Tuning protocol may not be the best protocol match. Instead, perhaps post a set of charts around the room asking for two to three of the look-fors and use sticky notes to leave warm and cool feedback (using, of course, the accurate definitions of warm and cool).

Language You Can Borrow: *We are called in this process to point out where the work aligns well to the goal and where there might be gaps. That is the point of Tuning—to bridge the gap between the work and what* [presenter's name] *wishes it to be.*

My job as the facilitator is to guide us through the sequential steps in the order shown on the poster and on your handout. In just a moment, [presenter's name] *will have time to tell us the story of how this work came to be, and if implemented already, something about the results. After we hear from* [presenter's name]*, a time for clarifying questions will occur. Following that short time frame, the work will be passed out and we will have protected time to read it and prepare our comments. When we are ready to begin offering our feedback,* [presenter's name] *has the opportunity to release this piece of work to us. We will care for it, owning it as if it were our own. We will plan our feedback and talk about it as warm or cool. In that step, I will help us tease out the differences between those two notions. Also, in that step,* [presenter's name] *will listen in on the conversation, even turn to the side ninety degrees, so* [preferred pronoun] *ear is most attentive to our conversation. At the end of that step,* [presenter's name] *will have a few moments to verbalize the two or three things that are most present in* [preferred pronoun] *thinking. The last step of our protocol is to debrief the process of Tuning.*

What questions about Tuning do you need answered before we give it a go?

[Presenter's name]*, thank you for bringing your work today. We are honored to learn with and from you. In this step, fifteen minutes have been carved out for you to tell the story of this work. As we will be hearing much detail about your thinking, your preparation, and any implementation reflections, it will be necessary for participants to take notes. There will be much for us to remember.* [Presenter's name]*, what work have you brought today?*

Step 2: Clarifying Questions (Five Minutes)

Unfortunately, educators frequently use questions as a method of recommending. A colleague might ask, "Did you use the district item bank for the assessment?" which (whether or not it was intended) may sound like a recommendation or even an accusation. A broader question, such as, "What resources did you use to create the assessment questions?" feels less prescriptive.

Clarifying questions are designed for the asker to receive information. *Quickly asked, quickly answered* is the mantra I use. It is not the goal here for the presenter to think. If questions inadvertently cause the presenters to furrow their brows, lift their chins, look up to the right . . . some facilitators may choose to intercept the question and judge it to be out of alignment with the intent of the step. Although the facilitator may be correct in this judgment, the consequence of correcting a participant is risky—it could cause a decrease in participation from not only that participant but others as well.

Another way to manage a question which in your opinion is not clarifying is to watch the presenter. If the presenter chooses to start answering it (within a few seconds), then it may have been clarifying *to the presenter*. Remember, the goal of the facilitator is to make *facile*, make easy, the process for each person involved. It is far simpler to let the presenter be the arbiter of which questions feel clarifying or not.

Utilizing a *go-round* is a popular way to ensure voice equity. Start with one person, then after that person's participation, proceed to the left or right, going all the way around. Many discussion protocols use this method. However, consider its value for clarifying questions. It may inadvertently pressure participants to come up with a clarifying question when they really don't have one. Simply opening this up to the group popcorn style (with random participation) is more aligned to the step's intent. It also shows the group you want to be as authentic as possible—not forcing anyone to make up anything.

Language You Can Borrow: *Now, we each have a chance to ask any clarifying questions, so we more completely understand the context of this work. These sorts of questions are simple questions of fact. They might start with who, what, how many, where, or when. We will resist asking a question that is a disguised recommendation, such as "Did you ever think about using . . . ?" Some may think a question with a yes or no answer is automatically clarifying. Instead, think about your intent. A good rule of thumb for clarifying questions is that these questions are for you to understand the situation, not for the presenter to think deeply. That will happen later.*

What clarifying questions does the group have?

Step 3: Time to Examine Work (Less Than Fifteen Minutes)

Although not a hard and fast rule, usually the facilitator does not hand out the document to be examined until step 3. As my goal for you as a reader and potential (or current) facilitator is to be dangerous enough, it is important that you consider why that is. Some venture it is because educators will just stop listening if they receive a document too early. That may be true, but that is not a valid enough reason. Imagine colleagues asking you in step 1 why they can't see the document now, and you say, "Sorry—you probably will be a better listener if we wait." You are now engaged in telling the future—offering negative feedback on a potential future action. If your job is to make things more *facile*, this probably would not help.

Instead, consider the most important part about a Tuning—the goal! Most likely, if the document goes out (either from you or an overzealous presenter) right away, the group doesn't know the goal yet, so what would be the purpose of looking at the document? To use one of the previous analogies, it would be similar to someone adjusting the tuner dial on a car radio when we don't yet hear the static.

Although I use the written process as a general rule, sometimes the document may be complex in nature or so difficult to explain that it would benefit the presenter and the group if they saw it in step 1. If that is the case, it would be important to identify the goals early on, then distribute the document.

I ask participants to write their names on the document (unless electronic—continue reading if the document is shared through email or a shared drive) at this step. I believe it serves multiple purposes.

- Practically, it helps presenters if they have said something, but participants haven't quite written it down fully. They may be able to efficiently find it on one of the documents by looking for the speaker's name.

- Participants report having more accountability for their thoughts. Essentially, they have to *work* for the presenter and for the group when they annotate the document.

- I believe it adds to group ownership. Further moves can add to this sense of ownership, and adding your name to someone else's work is one small step toward that goal.

It is quite common for presenters to have an electronic copy of a document, or the work being tuned to be electronic in nature (for example, a website). In that case, I find it helpful to distribute sticky notes and ask participants to write all of their feedback on notes, even if the technology would offer electronic comments (such as Word Online or Google Docs). When participants leave electronic comments during this step, some members of the group have inadvertently moved to step 5 about warm and cool feedback without the prerequisite setup—be sure to see the importance of step 4.

This step is designed for participants to silently reflect and plan their feedback. Unlike many other collaborative experiences, there is not an expectation of consensus. Participants offer their best thinking, which eventually the presenter will consider. It can be tempting for a few individuals to quietly talk together, so it is important to have a response ready if the behavior continues. Focusing back on the goal of the step, rather than the behavior you may interpret as negative (the two talking colleagues may be excited about the work!), is the least obtrusive way to handle it.

Using figurative language examples (for example, tuning a musical instrument or giving a car a tune-up) can be a helpful way for each person to remember the overall intent of the Tuning or a specific move in a specific step. At this juncture, I find it helpful to refocus the group back on the goals. It is very common for groups to have already forgotten. Once the work is in their hands, their evaluative senses take over, and they often revert to evaluating the document against what *they want it to be* rather than against the goals laid out before them. In essence, they're tuning the radio station to whatever music they prefer. The Language You Can Borrow in the following section uses an analogy you might find helpful.

Watch participants regarding the timing of this step. Five minutes is probably too short, but fifteen minutes might be too long. When you think participants might have two to three minutes left in them, proceed to the next step.

Language You Can Borrow: *Now that we have heard the point of view from* [presenter's name] *and asked some questions, it is time to see the work!* [Presenter's name], *is it OK for us to write on this document?* [If yes] *We will also put our names on these documents, as it is highly probable that everything we write down may not be discussed. We will hand back all the work to you at the end of this experience, and you get to take it with you!*

Tuning is like the blinders horses have on their heads during a parade. These blinders keep them focused. We will not give whatever feedback we wish because that is a different conversation for a different day. Today we are building the discipline to offer feedback with the goals set in front of us—our blinders. You now have the next chunk of time to examine the document.

Step 4: Pause to Plan and Code (Two Minutes)

In the original Tuning protocol (Allen, 1998), this step was designed to be a pause for reflection. I have found providing two focused tasks during this reflection greatly increases the feedback quality in the next step.

It is perfectly plausible, dare I say *human*, for participants to have lost sight of the goals. This pause is an opportunity for them to look through their notes and code each piece of feedback. If there are multiple goals, the posted goals can be numbered for ease of coding. The most exciting thing about this step is that participants will find feedback that doesn't relate to any of the posted goals. The discipline to set that feedback aside is an example of a disposition that discussion protocols grow in educators.

Secondly, it is important to ask participants to code or mark their feedback *warm* and *cool*. Since this is one of the two most misunderstood concepts of a Tuning protocol, here is the juncture in the protocol when I usually clarify the concepts. Remember your sixty-second opener? You probably simply mentioned there would be feedback but didn't get into the differences between the two types. Now it is time. You might choose to use the analogy of hiding a present from a child. You might direct participants toward the anchor chart with the sentence stems. Perhaps you have another method—anything to help participants organize their feedback into the expected categories and avoid the misconception of warm fuzzies.

An important consequence is also that this step asks each participant to find warm feedback. Educators are often quick to judge and apt to find gaps in work. It is not always our nature or default to find the alignments in work. Interestingly enough, that behavior doesn't always come from the participants alone—presenters may even indicate they don't need or value the warm feedback.

I have been in meetings many times with several of the original authors and developers of protocols from the mid-1990s. I remember a story I heard at one of these about Nancy Mohr, a pioneer educator in the use of discussion protocols. Nancy was functioning as the presenter in a Tuning protocol and told them she didn't need any warm feedback—she would be fine. Perhaps time was short, or perhaps she was confident about the work. As the presenter, she sat and listened to all the cool feedback offered, found it quite helpful, and made changes. She later brought a revision to the group, which was dismayed. They wanted to know what had happened to *X*; they thought the *Y* section was important. Since Nancy didn't hear any warm feedback, she didn't know what to keep that aligned to her goal. There is a misconception that warm feedback is simply a prelude to the cool, but it is not. Warm feedback is not analogous to a nurse rubbing your upper shoulder *prior* to giving you a shot. The warm feedback has a critical function, all on its own.

Language You Can Borrow: *Very shortly, we will have the pleasure and challenge of taking this work up not only for* [presenter's name] *but for our own learning, too. This next step will be characterized by the warm and cool feedback we have to offer. A way to think about how to differentiate those terms is by thinking back to a childhood memory. Perhaps you hid something from someone—maybe a birthday present. As your friends walked around looking for the item, you may have called out* warmer *or* colder *to help them find the item or know when they were close to it. Our feedback will be organized around warm feedback, places in the work, or the experiences that are aligned with the goal of* [read goal aloud]. *What we say then is warm and very close to the goal. We aren't giving warm feedback as a warm fuzzy—it is more than that. If we skipped giving warm feedback,* [presenter's name] *might later inadvertently delete those experiences or steps, not knowing that they are worthwhile.*

On the converse, cool feedback is further from the goal. A space exists between the goal and the work. We will frame our cool feedback in ways to help [presenter's name] *think about the gap between* [preferred pronoun] *goal and what we see or think we see.*

As you look through your feedback, you might discover some things you wrote that don't align to any of our goals . . . just put those in your pocket! For instance, you find that pesky misuse of a semicolon or a typographical error. Congrats! Circle it and move on. If you can't connect it to one of the goals, you can still mark it so [presenter's name] *will know, but we won't spend time talking about those kinds of issues today.*

Take the next two minutes to look over your feedback and code certain comments as warm or cool and align them to one of the goals or identify some items to go in your pocket. There are sentence stems to help you frame this feedback on our anchor chart.

Step 5: Warm and Cool Feedback (Fifteen Minutes)

Several facilitators I know make a particular move at this point, asking presenters if it would be permissible for the group to take on their work. This respectful question asks the participants to borrow, to hold someone else's document and care for it as if it were their own. At this point, presenters might turn their chair ninety degrees, now facing the facilitator, so their ear is to the group. This physical shift has several benefits.

- Presenters can focus on listening and note-taking, as their ear is now directed to the group. They do not need to spend cognitive energy thinking about their nonverbal reactions (for example, furrowed eyebrows, raised eyebrows—basically anything with eyebrows). Presenters report the positive experience of having some space (intellectual and physical) between themselves and the work. It is relieving to give the work away even for fifteen minutes.

- The group can better own the work, instead of looking to the presenter for nonverbal feedback with each piece of offered feedback. Participants report having more courage to offer tough-to-hear feedback when the presenter is slightly turned.

If a facilitator chooses this method, a pronoun shift occurs with the group. The sentence stems on the anchor chart indicate the change of more *we* and *I*, rather than *she, they,* or the name of the presenter. This collective language can have broad impact; it helps the presenter be in a productively risky space because the group isn't just giving advice with fingers pointed. It also helps the group members really ponder their feedback. For instance, I vividly remember wanting to give some cool feedback, but then in using one of the stems, I needed to ask myself, "But would *I* really do what I'm recommending?" Reframing the pronouns internally requires another level of consideration.

With this method, at the end of the feedback step, the facilitator would invite the presenter back into the group, and the point of view switches—the group gives the work back to the presenter, and feedback has a clear stopping point.

A healthy tension for a facilitator to hold is whether or not to engage in go-rounds or open up the discussion popcorn style. In the step for clarifying questions, I encouraged facilitators to use the popcorn method due to the intent of the step. For warm and cool feedback, presenters have indicated they find it most helpful when a facilitator starts with a predictable method (go-rounds), then, if the size of the group allows, move to popcorn style. Presenters enjoy hearing a diversity of feedback at first. If you initially use popcorn, they report hearing the group perhaps getting stuck in one way of thinking. Since there isn't a spot to check in with a presenter (some protocols in later chapters include this feature), it is important to use facilitator moves that proactively help the group not get stuck. It also may be a function of group size. I tend to use more go-rounds in larger groups to better plan for voice equity.

I find it helpful to start with warm feedback—and not for the misconception of needing to hear what people like first. Instead, a presenter will want to hear the points of alignment to the goals before hearing possible gaps. Having the context of warm in order to hear the cool serves better understanding the feedback rather than softening the emotional stress of later feedback. Feedback, warm and cool, is about the work, not the person. When participants say things like, "First we want to tell Claudia what we like about the document . . . and then, we will let her have it!" they speak under the misconception that they must tune the person instead of the work. Each facilitator move is intentional toward combatting this unfortunate potential.

This is the first spot in this discussion protocol that uses sentence stems or prompts. Many discussion protocols use these scaffolds, but it is often unclear to participants why they are included. Once, a participant pushed back on this practice during a session, saying to me, "I don't like these sentence starters. I feel like an English to speakers of other languages student." Although there is probably more for that educator to unpack, it helped me become more consciously competent about why I find sentence starters so helpful.

In asking some teachers why sentence starters are helpful for second-language learners, they know it's a best practice, but don't always have a clear understanding of the why. I believe it is an access issue—without having the starter, the learners don't have equitable access to speak. I find it similar for discussion protocols. Without sentence starters to consider, I have not provided an equitable spot for each participant to begin. They need access—not to the English language, but to the *language of the protocol*.

A protocol police force does not exist—no one will arrest individuals or groups who don't use prompts and sentence stems! However, if I find the group isn't staying true to the step (offering goal-focused feedback), I usually start with what I can do.

- I might offer some feedback using one of the prompts in an explicit way.
- I might look at the poster where the goals are posted and use the number of the goal quite explicitly in my feedback.

If those moves don't help the group, then consider prompting the group to try on the behavior you just used.

- Ask the group to try the sentence starters for a few minutes.
- After an individual has given feedback, ask which of the goals that feedback is attached to.

Sometimes groups become quite adept at a particular protocol. A group of science specialists in Lewisville ISD, Texas, use the Tuning protocol quite frequently in their work. They tune lesson plans, project plans, professional development slide shows, websites, agendas, and a host of other products and documents. In a professional development session about improving their facilitation practice, we decided to generate a list of sentence stems to use for warm and cool feedback, as shown in figure 3.4. They reported a renewed belief in Tuning in addition to a generation of higher-quality feedback.

Warm Feedback	Cool Feedback
I hope we keep . . .	To better (<u>goal</u>), we could . . .
It seems important . . .	A potential disconnect . . .
A tight alignment to the goal . . .	A possible misalignment . . .
A part which aligns to the goal . . .	One way to better align to the goal . . .
There is evidence of goal number _____ when . . .	We could . . .
	What if we . . .
When we _____, it _____ . . .	When we _____, it _____ . . .
The goal is clear when . . .	A totally different way to (<u>goal</u>) is to . . .
The goal is evident when . . .	There is not evidence of _____ when . . .
Clarity exists with the goal . . .	

Figure 3.4: Other possible sentence stems.

Language You Can Borrow: [Presenter's name], *would it be OK for us to lift this work from your shoulders for a while?* [If yes] *It will be helpful for you and us if you would be willing to turn ninety degrees, so your ear is to the group. You can focus on listening and the group can focus on owning your work rather than talking at you, as you will not be verbally participating for a while.*

So, we now own this work—it is ours. In that spirit, the goal we have for this work is (read goals). In just a moment, someone will offer our first piece of warm feedback—we will start there, just like filling a bathtub up with water, starting with the warm faucet. We will then proceed to that person's right, moving around the group so everyone participates. Who will begin this round of warm feedback?

Later . . .

We now have the opportunity to deepen our conversation to include cool feedback—where might the gaps be in this work to help it reach the goal of (read goals)? So, in just a moment someone will start and then we will proceed to that person's left. So, time for more feedback, warm or cool. Both faucets are flowing. Who will begin?

Step 6: Presenter Reflection (Five Minutes)

Notice the name of this step: presenter *reflection*, not presenter *response*, nor presenter *defense*. If the protocol itself and the people within the structure all did their jobs artfully and skillfully, this step most likely shouldn't be problematic. However, our work as educators is personal. Thoughtfully leading into this step is important. Saying, "OK! That was hard! Joseph, turn on back, what are you thinking about all of our helpful feedback?" doesn't set up Joseph as a presenter very well.

Over the years, participants have shared that my metaphors have been helpful. They allow individuals to hold onto the intent of a step or a concept. At this step, the duck analogy is what I choose to use. Sometimes, presenters feel like a duck during the discussion step. They hear a piece of feedback, and write it down, but in the moment, it is sliding right off their backs. Other notions they heard were also intriguing, memorable, or even obvious—these pieces of feedback catch in their tail feathers.

This analogy helps presenters realize we do not expect, nor does the protocol have time for, a play-by-play rundown of everything said prior. Another means of helping presenters be ready to reflect to the group is encouraging their focus on their note taking during the feedback step. Presenters may have starred a few items, underlined something, perhaps their pen hovered a moment as they wrote something down—those could be the items they choose to share during the next step.

Even with a beautifully worded entrance by the facilitator, sometimes a presenter ends up offering a lengthy commentary on everyone's feedback. One facilitator move might be to acknowledge what the presenter has said by saying something like, "You heard a lot in this experience!" And use a quantifiable limit, saying, "Perhaps one more thing" to help find an endpoint.

Finally, if the group borrowed the work, don't forget to give it back! The work is physically collected as the presenters turn ninety degrees back to the group in order to share their thinking.

Language You Can Borrow: *So, as* [presenter's name] *turns back toward the group, we metaphorically hand this work back to* [preferred pronoun], *and physically hand back these pieces of paper as well.*

[Presenter's name], *you had an opportunity to listen in on a conversation that would not take place in this way without a Tuning protocol. We probably got some things wrong—it's not our work! This is a* reflection *for you, not a* response *or defense. Resist the urge to offer a play by play of every comment. Instead, you could think of yourself as a duck—some of what we said just went right off your back—not because you are unwilling to consider it, but perhaps we just didn't know enough in order to truly consider those ideas. However, other pieces of feedback really got you thinking—they got stuck in your tail feathers. So, what are the two or three big ideas or concepts with which you are walking away?*

Step 7: Debrief (Five Minutes)

A quick reminder about debriefing. Debriefing is discussing the process of learning for individuals and the groups, not reopening the content that was just discussed. See the introduction (page 1) for more detail as well as possible questions to use to frame a debrief.

Language You Can Borrow: *The debrief is a time to converse about the protocol itself and how we did, not about the content anymore. Remember, we gave that back to* [presenter's name]*! So, how did this go for us today?*

Application Example 1

Yazmine is a language acquisition specialist at an elementary school. Besides keeping all English learner services in compliance, the most exciting and rewarding part of her job is improving the instructional decisions teachers make for their second-language learners.

As she shares resources (which she hopes are helpful), she creates an online newsletter using an online tool called Smore (www.smore.com). One reason she uses this tool is to use the analytics in determining her impact. As she brings a sample newsletter to a group of other campus-based educators who don't work at her school, she wants to know what she can do to improve her analytics—not many of the teachers at her campus are spending much time in the Smore, and some don't open it at all.

She decides to use a Tuning protocol toward two goals: making the newsletter more (1) helpful and (2) concise. As Jennifer facilitates for Yazmine, the only difference she needs to navigate is the lack of a physical print document. Jennifer decides to remind the group members they aren't going to write on a document or leave virtual sticky notes—instead, she hands out yellow sticky notes that the members use to record their feedback. They still do the warm and cool feedback step aloud, but at the end of that step, instead of handing in the physical document, they hand in the sticky notes. Yazmine leaves excited, for she now knows which parts of the newsletter are more helpful than others as well as which parts are too wordy. She can now work smarter, not harder.

Application Example 2

Jaime is a top-notch teacher of biology to high school students. She works extremely hard and thoughtfully, trying to differentiate appropriately and skillfully. Recently, a lab on phenotype and genotype did not produce the results she hoped. Her exact words after the lab are, "I worked way too hard—they didn't."

At Jaime's school, each teacher is part of a cross-disciplinary group that meets several times during the year when students are not on campus. As part of her responsibility to the group, Jaime takes a turn bringing something on which she would like feedback. Kurt, a member of her group and a social studies teacher, took a summer course on facilitating discussion protocols and has stepped up to facilitate for Jaime. As Kurt readily admits he knows nothing about this topic, he mentions we are the perfect group because Jaime's students probably don't yet either!

Jaime and Kurt have a short preconference to talk about what her outcomes for the session might be. They choose a Tuning protocol, asking the group to look for spots in the lab where she may have done too much thinking for the students, as well as spots where she scaffolded them appropriately.

Jaime has been in the presenter seat before, and by the time Kurt asks her to turn to the side, Jaime already has. At various points during the feedback step, Jaime makes small, joyful noises, as she comes to some very important understandings about her thinking.

As Kurt asks Jaime to rejoin the group, Jaime interrupts Kurt with her excitement, saying, "Is this over now? I can't wait to get to work on revising this thing!"

Refine Your Work in an E⁴ Way

Each educator has work products that need revisions; the list of what these work products might be is virtually endless. Part of the challenge of using protocols in the refining family is to decide on a clear outcome or outcomes. For instance, saying, "to get feedback" is not a clear outcome! That hearkens back to the beginning of the chapter when we discussed the danger in replying to the email asking for the same. The Tuning protocol, in particular, *sings* only when the goals are clear to each group member.

To inspire you about the broad application, table 3.3 is a sampling of what various presenters have refined during my consulting practice.

Table 3.3: A Sampling of Products Refined

Group Composition	Artifact	Goals
Central office leaders	Professional learning framework	(1) Strategic plan alignment; (2) meaningfully differentiated for teachers
Teachers	Rubric	(1) Student-friendly language; (2) equitable grading practices
High school leadership team	Master schedule draft for next school year	School values and priorities
Instructional coaches	Presentation slides	Participant engagement
Principals	Teacher professional growth plan	(1) Manageable for teacher; (2) manageable for the principal
Higher education instructors	Grant proposal	Bias-free language
Instructional technologists	Website	Intuitiveness for users (parents)

Facilitators must know the nuances of why each step in a refining protocol is important. Only then can they make *facile* the process for each member of the group. In the next chapter, "Protocols to Seek Perspective," some protocol steps will be similar, but just as different family members from different parts of the world have eccentricities and unique qualities, so do protocols in different protocol families.

4

Protocols to Seek Perspective

Being passionate is a characteristic commonly attributed to educators. Although found through various contexts with differing intonations, passion can be both a blessing and a curse. In particular, being close—to an assignment I wrote, a test I developed, a student I nurtured—can prevent me from recognizing multiple perspectives and truths. The processes in this chapter use equitable methods to make sure a variety of perspectives get to the table. Protocols to seek perspective give educators a chance to step back and consider how their lenses impact what they see and hear, and therefore, think.

Chapter 3 features protocols to refine products. These processes require all three jobs in a protocol (participant, presenter, and facilitator), as well as a document (electronic or paper) to examine. The focus for this chapter, "Protocols to Seek Perspective," is to share those two features. What is particularly important and unique about this family is that participants examine these artifacts without any background or context. The goal is to gain a fresh, less subjective view of the document.

Not giving elaborate context to a work product can be difficult for presenters (Allen & Blythe, 2004). They can feel vulnerable and possibly judged by their colleagues. Similarly, not having all the details of an assignment, an assessment, or a student work sample is also complex for the participants. As members of an inquisitive profession, the desire to know is a job hazard. Without the parameters and details, educators sometimes flail, doubting that what they see and hear can be just as valuable (even more so) as what they actually *think*.

Both situations that follow would benefit greatly from one of the four foundational protocols you'll find in this chapter on protocols to seek perspective.

SITUATION A

"I'm just too close to it," Shannon says. She has been the principal at her high school for almost a decade. She worked hard the first few years to fill the logistical and managerial gaps and has subsequently poured her energy into her true love, instructional leadership. In her estimation, the master schedule is one of the primary artifacts that represents her values.

With so many changes and requirements (often beyond her control), she is concerned there has been some vision drift. She knows all the intricacies of the master schedule—why a course is offered where it is, why a certain department values each teacher having at least one on-level course— but the longer she stays at her school and natural teacher attrition occurs, there is less of a shared understanding.

The high school principals in her region gather once each month, and Shannon thinks it would be a perfect opportunity to gain their perspective.

SITUATION B

Rachelle has a pit in her stomach because it is Thursday—RTI day. As the response to intervention coordinator for her school, she feels guilty about what happens on this day. Although the schedule seems to work for teachers, and they do develop student plans, the overall culture and feel of the day are not positive.

It seems some of her staff gain a level of enjoyment from talking negatively about students. This isn't mean talk, rather it seems to be important to gather a laundry list of all the skills a student *cannot* do. Rachelle doesn't think the teachers even know they seem to have a deficit-first view of the students they are discussing; it seems to be innate.

At certain levels in the process, parents are not yet involved, and at others, they are invited but often cannot come to the meetings. More than once, Rachelle has been relieved the parents were not there to hear the discussion.

Next Thursday, Rachelle is determined to use a process or protocol that brings students' strengths to the table. She truly believes the teachers could use their same rich teaching strategy banks to develop even better plans.

Shannon and Rachelle are in prime positions to benefit from discussion protocols that seek perspective, but for different reasons. Shannon wants her colleagues to help *her* step back—to see the (master schedule) forest through the (individual courses) trees. Rachelle hopes her colleagues will lean away from their students' work samples, figuratively tipping their heads to the side in order to see their students and their work products from different points of view.

What Shannon and Rachelle want are responses that don't come naturally to educators. Frustration at not knowing is a natural instinct for educators, as is to question and desire context. Margaret Wheatley (2002) expands this group to include all humans when she suggests we all need to spend more time in the experience of not knowing.

Protocols in this family suspend knowing context until later in the sequence of steps. They choose to abstain from the all-too-common practice of playing twenty questions when educators collaborate. As naturally inquisitive beings, we seem to believe that when all of our questions are answered, we develop expertise and are able to fully understand.

Instead, participants in these protocols are asked to work *against the grain* (Cochran-Smith, 1991) because the presenter has already been working with mental models and in ways that are familiar to them. They truly are seeking different perspectives, and it takes discipline for their colleagues to provide what the presenter truly wants. There is some preparation work that facilitators and participants can do to have the best experience possible, which I'll discuss in the next section. After that, I move on to the protocols themselves, and then finally I take a quick look at how protocols in this family contribute to E[4] experiences.

Prep for Perspective: Three Ways of Looking

Educators often live their professional lives discerning right answers from wrong ones, distinguishing certain levels of understanding from others, and then acting on that information in formative and summative ways. "We weren't trained to admit we don't know. Most of us were taught to sound certain and confident, to state our opinion as if it were true. We haven't been rewarded for being confused" (Wheatley, 2002, p. 34). To waylay those learned behaviors (which can become automatic in educators) is difficult. For this reason, I suggest specifically addressing the issue of perspective before diving into this protocol family.

Prior to using one of the four main protocols in this family, I use the Three Ways of Looking minilesson. Some of this content originates in protocols that look at student work (Blythe, Allen, & Powell, 2008). As a facilitator, I might name this to a group as a minilesson or a skill-building experience. These moments are not protocols per se; instead they help participants experience critical learning before protocols actually begin.

Time

Set aside ten to fifteen minutes. As this is a minilesson and not a protocol, I suggest the overall time frame. As you assess the group and formatively use the data during the minilesson, you can adjust times.

Purpose

Participants aim to become aware of their default lenses.

Group Size

Since this is preparation work before getting into the actual protocols, any size group is appropriate.

Preparation

1. Have three small cards ready with the following information written on them.

    a. *First card*—"Description involves identifying in very literal terms what constitutes the piece of work being observed."

    b. *Second card*—"Interpretation involves assigning some meaning or intent to what is in the work."

    c. *Third card*—"Evaluation attaches value or personal preference to the work being examined."

    Alternatives to the cards would be to create a slide with the separate texts.

2. Bring an object for participants to look at (not touch). Ideas might include an illustration drawn by a student, a baby rattle, a meat tenderizer, or pliers. The only criterion for choosing the object is to consider how someone might move to interpretation or evaluation instead of simply describing. This minilesson example will use a student illustration.

Sequence

1. Explain the belief that no matter what we are looking at in the world, we are using one of three lenses. We might be looking at a piece of student writing, studying an art print at an exhibit, or watching a baseball game. Label a poster "Three Ways of Looking" and include the words *description*, *interpretation*, and *evaluation*.

2. Hand out each of the three small cards to different participants.

3. Ask a participant to read the description card aloud. When complete, ask the participant to read it again, this time charging others to identify what might be the key words in the definition. As participants determine the four key words, write them on the poster.

4. In this optional step, explore the four key words for description.

   a. *Identify*—Bloom's (1956) lowest level of thinking, black or white, there or not there

   b. *Literal*—Use the actual definition; don't use it in a joking sense, as when someone says, "We were *literally* killing ourselves laughing," which is the nonliteral use of the word.

   c. *Constituted*—Think less here about the social studies use of *constitute*, but instead a culinary use of the word. We decide to go to Jasmine's house for dinner. We walk in and take a whiff. We say, "Jasmine, that soup smells amazing! Is there oregano in there?" Jasmine shrugs her shoulders and says, "I'm not sure." We are probably far less confident eating her odiferous soup because she may not know the *constitution* of the soup.

   d. *Observed*—We need to see it (or hear it), otherwise we are using a lens beyond description.

5. Practice using description. Show the chosen object and ask participants to consider the key words and then describe with a partner. Tell participants if they think their partner ventured beyond description, they can use this prompt and say, "What do you *see* to make you think that?" (Note: for this minilesson, figure 4.1 represents the student artwork. The actual image has a yellow circle. The rest of the page is colored blue. The image is available in color at **go.SolutionTree.com/leadership** if the reader wishes to use it for the minilesson.)

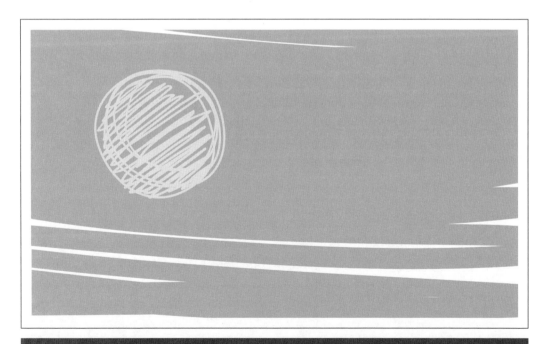

Figure 4.1: Minilesson object.

*Visit **go.SolutionTree.com/leadership** for a free reproducible version of this figure.*

6. Assess the group using thumbs up for true and thumbs down for false. Use three to five statements to check understanding of description. Use the student illustration in figure 4.1 as an example.

   a. *I see a circle.* (True)

   b. *I see the yellow circle is surrounded by blue.* (True)

   c. *I see a sun in the sky.* (False) Although most will place their thumbs down, knowing this isn't true, an occasional concrete-sequential thinker in the group will simply say, "But it is! It's a sun!" This lack of flexible thinking can start to be changed using discussion protocols that ask members to consider multiple perspectives.

   d. *I see it was done with marker.* (False) This response often divides the group or could completely trick every person. Ask, "What do you see to make you think that?" to which common responses include the following: horizontal strokes, same width of strokes, variations in color, and (my favorite) because it just is.

7. Description requires restraint but doesn't require a higher level of brain function. If the brain is actually *thinking*, then it probably isn't describing anymore—it is interpreting. Ask a participant to read the second card, interpretation, aloud. When complete, ask the participant to read it again, this time charging others to identify what might be the key words in the definition. As participants determine the three key words, write them on the poster.

8. In this optional step, explore the three key words for interpretation.

   a. *Assigning*—This verb implies a relationship between the person and the object. Assigning cannot happen without it.

   b. *Meaning*—Meaning making is unique to a person. Their constructions may be similar, but the very act of asking if they are similar makes it beyond description. There is no need to ask in description.

   c. *Intent*—This word implies more than description.

9. Ask partners to talk together about what interpretations someone might make about the object in question. For the illustration, the prompt might be the following words: "The student was trying to . . ."

10. Ask for an honest assessment from participants by saying, "When your partner said something about the object, what was your gut response? What did you think you needed to do with that information?" Many educators will admit they wanted to either agree or disagree; in fact, some may have even gently disagreed with each other about the interpretations they were making. The goal of this interpretive step is not to agree on *one* shared interpretation. Instead, the diversity in thought of the group creates multiple interpretations, which help us better understand the variety of ways students think.

11. Sometimes people describe what they see, and other times their brains move to interpretation; the last way of looking at something is to evaluate. Ask

a participant to read the evaluation card aloud. When complete, ask the participant to read it again, this time charging others to identify what might be the key words in the definition. As participants determine the three key words, write them on the poster.

12. In this optional step, explore the three key words for evaluation.

 a. *Attaching*—This verb is more aggressive than *assign*. We place value *onto* something.

 b. *Value*—Although it makes perfect linguistic sense, *value* at the root of *evaluation* might not be something we have thought about before. It assumes a judgment.

 c. *Personal preference*—Not just preference, but personal preference. Evaluation cannot happen without a personal response.

13. Ask the group which lens educators might tend to use as a default. Most answer with *evaluation*. Educators are paid to evaluate materials, student responses, and student work. They then bring those tendencies into collaborative time and collegial relationships. Consider sharing a sequence with the group about the three ways of looking in reverse order. The facilitator could share the following story, if desired.

 Imagine you and a friend are stuck at the airport. Your phones are charging, so you engage in the pastime of people watching. As your eyes fixate on someone walking by, you motion to your friend to also look. Which of the three lenses are you probably using? Although being rude is not one of the lenses, evaluation is probably the answer. You are placing value or personal preference on what you see—how a person is walking, what they are wearing, how they might be acting.

 Your friend feels uncomfortable and tells you to stop. Instead, you continue, this time pointing out to your friend what the situation might be: Perhaps they just got back from the islands for a vacation. *You moved from evaluation to interpretation.*

 Finally, your friend elbows you in your side, commanding you to stop embarrassing the both of you. Of course, you don't—instead, even pointing this time: Don't you see those huge hats?

 In this (fictitious) example, evaluation was first, moving to interpretation, and finally ending with description. The actual evidence (data) wasn't brought forth until the person in the example was pressured or forced into bringing it forth.

14. Many discussion protocols require educators to collaborate differently than typical activities do. Go back to the poster and circle the first letter of each of the three lenses: D, I, E. DIE is an unfortunate but memorable acronym that helps many groups stay focused on the intent of each step and the benefit of using the sequence with fidelity.

15. This step is optional. Since evaluation is the default behavior of most educators, practicing with description one more time may be helpful. Identify a water bottle in the room and ask participants to just describe it, referring

to the anchor chart for the key words regarding description (*identify*, *literal*, *constituted*, *observed*).

    a. *I see a label.* (True)

    b. *I see a lid.* (True)

    c. *I see a plastic bottle.* (False) Some may believe this is true; their brains moved too fast past description. Consider using the prompt, "What do you see to make you think that?" to help them.

    d. *I see water.* (False) Anyone who's been in a high school classroom can tell you: just because some clear liquid is in a water bottle doesn't make it water! (This one is optional.)

Art educators reading this text may be connecting this learning to Edmund Burke Feldman's (1987) model for fine art critique. Table 4.1 shows an alignment of the two models.

Table 4.1: Feldman and Van Soelen Models Compared

Fine Art Critique (Feldman, 1987)	DIE (Van Soelen, 2016)
Description	Description
Analysis	Interpretation
Interpretation	Interpretation
Evaluation	Evaluation

Some educators have resisted using this minilesson or spending time skill building with their colleagues before using one of the four foundational protocols in this family. They appreciate the protocol anchor charts I provide and argue the sentence stems are scaffolded enough. Let's test that out with dialogue from a grade-level team using the ATLAS: Looking at Data protocol (page 128) from this family. Figure 4.2 offers the results.

Protocol Step	Suggested Sentence Stems	Results
Description	I see . . . I notice . . .	*I see our students really need some help with regrouping.*

Figure 4.2: Describing without really understanding.

Notice the stem is not magical—it does not produce a response that matches the intent of description (key words: *identify*, *literal*, *constituted*, *observed*). The result in figure 4.2 is more evaluative. It puts value or personal preference on what they thought the group should do next.

Figure 4.3 shows a similar result when trying to interpret.

Protocol Step	Suggested Sentence Stems	Results
Interpretation	What might be under this . . . A potential root cause . . . A possible assumption . . . The data suggest . . .	The data suggest our students really need some help with regrouping.

Figure 4.3: Interpreting without really understanding.

Alas, once again, the prompt does not exert any magical powers. The results are evaluative—suggesting an action.

Participants are logically confused or annoyed when they are finally asked to suggest an action, as clearly shown in figure 4.4.

Protocol Step	Suggested Sentence Stems	Results
Evaluation	An implication for . . . might be	An implication for tomorrow might be our students really need some help with regrouping. (Haven't I already said this?)

Figure 4.4: Evaluating when previous steps fell flat.

It is not surprising when this team balks at using discussion protocols. Perhaps a well-intentioned instructional coach learns about this discussion protocol but does not have a deep enough understanding to facilitate it well, which includes ensuring participants show fidelity to each step. The teachers feel like they are jumping through hoops to get to the same result—thus feeling ineffective and inefficient. In my experience, that is the quickest way to lose credibility with teachers.

This notion of DIE is broadly applicable in leadership and teaching. It is a particularly strong way to approach classroom observations and teacher evaluation. For growth-supporting examples in the skill of writing effective classroom observations, consult *Crafting the Feedback Teachers Need and Deserve: A Guide for Leaders* (Van Soelen, 2016).

There is generally little disagreement when a group demonstrates fidelity to the description step; after all, it is just the facts. However, when educators start to interpret what those facts might mean, we tend to prematurely evaluate their responses. Educator teams often assume agreement, not consensus, as their default goal, which makes the interpretation step tricky to facilitate.

Picture a geometry team examining student samples of a word problem. The group members described well. They noticed where the student used a particular algorithm, made a computational error, and created a model. When it comes to interpretation (see the following example), they start to veer from the intent of the *I* in DIE:

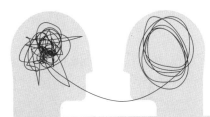

Jessica:	I think the student was getting confused about why she needed to use cosine.
David:	I disagree. See where she drew this secant? I think she knew that part really well.
Monica:	Honestly, I think she looked back at question 3 and just used the same formula again.
David:	No, that doesn't make sense . . .

The minilesson, Three Ways of Looking, explicitly states one person's view is not enough; instead, groups benefit from multiple interpretations. Using the student illustration from the minilesson (figure 4.1, page 115), as a reader, stop reading for a moment and try to complete this sentence stem with at least four different responses: *The student was* . . .

Now, consider your responses and categorize them using the two columns in figure 4.5.

Approached From Aesthetics	Approached From Skills
• The student was trying to show a moon in a sky. • The student was drawing a reflection in the water. • The student was showing a tennis ball on a court. • The student was zooming in on the eye of an animal.	• The student was trying to fill the page with color. • The student was having difficulty making sure the marker had an even consistency. • The student wanted to use blue up to the edge of the yellow circle but couldn't do it perfectly. • The student doesn't know how to use a marker near the edges of paper.

Figure 4.5: Description categories.

By each person uniquely approaching the stem, *The student was . . .* , the group ends with a more robust understanding of the student work. If a group had stopped to discuss each potential interpretation, not only would the members miss out on learning, the speed and energy of the group's work would significantly diminish.

The Language You Can Borrow portions in this chapter include three strategies to help groups in this regard. First, being explicit when explaining multiple interpretations is a helpful first step. Somewhere along the way, group facilitators in schools either got the message or developed the message themselves that the goal for every group is to agree (more on this notion in the introduction, page 1). Therefore, countless hours of educator collaboration are spent wrestling down the *one interpretation* of question 6 on the mathematics assessment that was so problematic for students, or the *one interpretation* of why this student is having such difficulty matching letters to sounds. Instead, protocols are built on the notion of multiple interpretations—thinking more broadly and learning how to work productively in the space of not knowing (Wheatley, 2002). "When so many interpretations are available, I can't understand why we would be satisfied with superficial conversations where we pretend to agree with one another" (Wheatley, 2002, p. 35).

Second, consider using go-rounds as participation in this step. Go-rounds can be implemented by facilitators for various reasons. In this case, go-rounds help to alleviate individuals jumping in to evaluate previous interpretations.

Third, pronoun shifts require more extensive explanation. If you read the Expanded Supports for Tuning in chapter 3 (page 98), I recommend asking presenters if the group might borrow their documents as they give feedback. As participants speak, they shift their point of view, using different pronouns. In two of the foundational protocols in this protocol family, the interpretation step asks participants to use a student's point of view.

In figure 4.6, consider how the interpretations previously offered about the student illustration would now sound if spoken from a student point of view.

Approached From Aesthetics	Approached From Skills
• I was trying to show a moon in a sky. • I was drawing a reflection in the water. • I was showing a tennis ball on a court. • I was zooming in on the eye of an animal.	• I was trying to fill the page with color. • I was having difficulty making sure the marker had an even consistency. • I wanted to use blue right up to the edge of the yellow circle but couldn't do it. • I don't know how to use a marker near the edges of paper.

Figure 4.6: Description categories—Student point of view.

The subtle shift in figure 4.6 allows participants to hear and acknowledge multiple perspectives their students consistently demonstrate. I find educators are less apt to correct a colleague's interpretation if spoken with a student's point of view. More discussion about this shift occurs in appendix A.

If a group has difficulty understanding why raising multiple perspectives is important for their collaboration and learning, consider using "The Danger of a Single Story," a TED Talk by Chimamanda Ngozi Adichie (2009). This Nigerian author eloquently speaks of her own experiences falling into the trap of having a single story of a person or group of people. Additionally, she offers compelling commentary on the impact that behavior from others has had on her.

The Protocols

The book's introduction (page 1) explores the concept that educators have jobs to do in discussion protocols. It takes *work* to collaborate in these ways, and the jobs may look different in the various protocol families.

Each of the four foundational protocols you'll find in this chapter includes the jobs of facilitator and participant. Unlike the protocols in previous chapters, each of these discussion protocols can work with or without a presenter. With no presenter, the group may demonstrate collective ownership over the student work, the data, the assessment, or the document being examined.

In pursuing the family metaphor, we could describe the four foundational protocols in this family as cousins. They might not have the same last name, reside in the same part of the country or world, or look alike. However, they have some of the same DNA—building blocks that make them similar. DIE is a substantial chromosome in that DNA.

Each of the four discussion protocols uses DIE or a variant to foster a sense of curiosity about the artifact the participants examine. Instead of starting with explanations about the work (called *presentations* in protocols that refine in chapter 3, page 87), the facilitator offers very minimal context as participants delve into the artifact.

If presenters believe a protocol in this family would help them meet their purpose, the artifact itself will create an alignment to which a foundational protocol could best provide the structure for the conversation. Figure 4.7 identifies four different types of artifacts and the corresponding protocol choice from this family. The following sections detail these protocols.

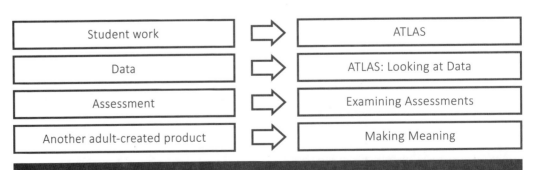

Figure 4.7: Choosing protocols to seek perspective.

ATLAS

The ATLAS protocol was developed by Eric Buchovecky (1996) and revised by Gene Thompson-Grove (2000). I present my adapted version here. This deceptively simple process still breathes life despite the closing of its founding agency, the Authentic Teaching and Learning for All Students (ATLAS) initiative from the 1990s. Often used with one piece of student work, a teacher who is stuck comes to the group—not sure what to do next to support this student's learning. Like all protocols in this family, the participants receive no context up front about the *student* (although they do get limited context about the work), as specific information may color or bias what colleagues see in the student's work. This lack of context is sometimes frustrating in the age of standards-driven alignment. However, this protocol must keep some mystique in order for the presenter to truly reap new perspectives about the student and the work.

Expanded Supports for ATLAS

Figure 4.8 shows the anchor chart you can post for the ATLAS protocol.

Purpose: To determine next steps for a particular student	
Sequence:	
1. **One- to Two-Sentence Context**	Less than one minute
2. **Look**	Four to eight minutes
3. **Describe** *I see . . . I notice . . .*	Six to ten minutes
4. **Interpret** *I'm working on . . . I'm trying . . .* *I understand . . . I don't understand . . .*	Six to ten minutes
5. **Evaluate Our Learning** *An implication for . . . might be . . .*	Six to ten minutes
6. (Optional) **Presenter Reflection**	Five minutes
7. **Debrief**	Five minutes

Figure 4.8: ATLAS anchor chart.

*Visit **go.SolutionTree.com/leadership** for a free reproducible version of this figure.*

Scaffolded Steps for Facilitators

An ATLAS protocol is designed for one teacher, the presenter, to gain insight into one student. However, the process can also work without a presenter, as an opportunity for a group to study a piece of student work and apply learning to members' own practice. In those cases, modify steps 1 and 6. In step 1, rather than a presenter providing limited context (one to two sentences) for the work, it might come from the person who brought it (for example, the instructional coach, assistant principal, or collaborative team leader). In step 6, considering the purpose of this iteration is for individual teacher reflection and application, the facilitator may ask each teacher to speak once to explain how examining this piece of student work will impact practice.

Step 1: One- to Two-Sentence Context (Less Than One Minute)

As noted earlier in the chapter, educators often have difficulty not wanting to know everything. As members of a profession that values knowledge, educators feel comfortable asking many questions and extensively explaining situations and phenomena.

In an ATLAS, removing most of the context is critical to the protocol's success. A presenter brings a sample of student work because this person is unsure what to do next. Before coming to a group, the probability is high the presenter has engaged in a number of prerequisite activities such as trying various known strategies, consulting experts in person (for example, other colleagues), and consulting experts through print resources (such as books, articles, and websites). Therefore, it must be something *in the work* that is a stumbling block to moving forward. Often examining the actual work is not involved in the activities the teacher has already tried.

Removing much of the context equips the presenting teacher with new eyes and ears to see and hear the work of the student. The expression, "Can't see the forest for the trees," is apropos here. Educators can know their students and their work products so well it is difficult to step back to gain another perspective.

It is important for the presenting teacher to plan what to say in step 1. The presenter's words here cannot be erased or unheard by the participants. For instance, read through the student writing sample called Sheep Dogs, in figure 4.9.

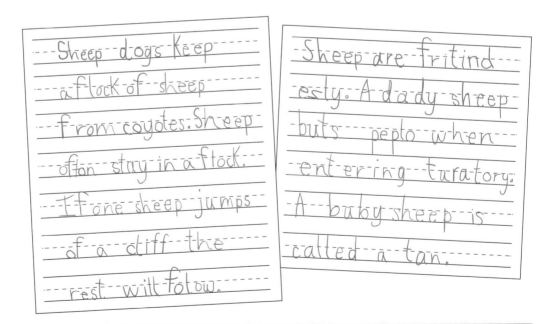

Figure 4.9: Student writing sample.

The presenting teacher is asked to talk about the *assignment*, not the *student*. Read through the two different one- to two-sentence contexts in figure 4.10 and feel your perspective start to narrow with version 2.

Version 1	Version 2
In this assignment, students were asked to read two different texts about an animal and then write an informational piece. They had two work periods to create this draft (without any conferencing with me as their teacher).	In this assignment, students were asked to read two different texts about an animal and then write an informational piece. This student is gifted—can you believe he is only five years old? He did such a great job.

Figure 4.10: Two versions of a one- to two-sentence context.

Once educators hear the age of the student and any associated labels (like *he* and *gifted*), their minds focus on a set of strategies and ideas that they believe may be appropriate for a male, academically talented five-year-old. The problem is this teacher is stuck; she has probably tried a whole host of ideas with this student already—the precise reason why she is asking her colleagues to help her! A poorly worded one- to two-sentence context can inadvertently close the minds of those she has gone to for support in the form of new ideas.

Language You Can Borrow: *So, here's how this protocol might go. As you can see, we will start by looking at the student work, then describing. When it is time to interpret, we will do so assuming the voice and perspective of the student. When it is time to evaluate, we will* not *evaluate the work nor the student who created it; instead, we will evaluate our next steps, both to support this student's learning and in our own practice. The last step calls us to talk about how this process went for us today. What questions do you have that you need to resolve before we begin?*

Thanks to [presenter's name] for bringing this piece of student work today. [Presenter's name] wants to gain a fresh perspective on this student and the work, which is why we are using ATLAS. Although [presenter's name] may have extensive history and experience with the student, we are not going to start there in this conversation, for if we do, it will be much harder for us to offer a fresh, objective view. However, we have one minute for a one- to two-sentence opening statement. [Presenter's name] will only tell us about the assignment and context of this student work, not anything specific about the student.

Step 2: Look (Four to Eight Minutes)

Appendix A (page 215) offers insight into this step.

Step 3: Describe (Six to Ten Minutes)

Appendix A (page 216) offers insight into this step.

Step 4: Interpret (Six to Ten Minutes)

The goal for this step when examining student work is to consider what the originator of the work might be thinking, the author, the artist, the musician . . . the student. The original version of this protocol (Buchovecky, 1996) asks educators to consider the question, From the student's perspective, what is the student working on? This question asks educators to consider the work from a student lens, rather than an adult lens.

When facilitating this step (and other discussion protocols in this family focused on seeking perspectives), I find it helpful to shift the point of view to raise more vantage points and perspectives. Asking educators to borrow the student's voice, using *I*, can make a palpable difference.

Instead of saying, "I think the student was trying to . . ." a prompt might sound like "I was trying to . . ." Instead of saying, "I don't believe the student understands how to . . . ," a participant could say, "I am confused by . . ." Asking participants to speak in first person as if they are the originator of the work seems to create more empathy and a deeper level of interpretation, which only serves to benefit the presenter who is seeking more understanding about the work, and therefore the student who created it.

Some groups may find it hokey to speak this way, so I may take time to explain why I am asking them to do so. (I might say, for instance, "I'm sorry this may feel a bit inauthentic right now, but let's keep giving it a try, then we can talk about it during the debrief.") When I take the time to do that, I find the presenter often mentions during the debrief the helpfulness of the interpretation step. Those moments are indeed glorious—I don't have to defend the protocol steps, as their colleagues proclaim it worthwhile themselves.

Language You Can Borrow: *Time to start interpretation. This step asks us to assume, to borrow, the voice of the student. It may feel artificial at first, but* [presenter's name] *will be hearing your words in the intonation and voice pitch of the student. It can be incredibly powerful. So instead of saying,* the student, *we will say,* I.

We have a few choices of how we might each participate—the anchor chart has several options. Remember, the I *here is the actual student who created this work. Who will begin?*

Step 5: Evaluate Our Learning (Six to Ten Minutes)

The four foundational protocols in this family usually have all three jobs (presenter, facilitator, and participants), but all can work without a presenter. If you are using ATLAS that way, this step is designed for teachers to generate their own potential actions with their own students. For those occasions, it seems important for all teachers to end with tangible actions to which they can commit. Consider then ending with each person speaking once with the prompt, "I commit to . . ."

Language You Can Borrow: Some of the language in appendix A (page 217) may also be helpful here.

We have come to the E of the DIE, that is, to evaluation. We are not *going to evaluate this student nor* [presenter's name] *who may have assigned it! I'm guessing* [preferred pronoun] *has already done plenty of evaluation—placing value or personal preference on this work—which is what led to our ATLAS today. Instead, we will evaluate our* next steps, *which might include specific actions to take in helping this student reach the next learning goals.*

In this step, we might take turns talking without going around the circle. You might build on what someone else says or raise something new. Just keep in mind the norms that we have set in place.

So, our discussion now is around this question, What are the implications of this work? What might we do next with our student? Note the sentence stem on the chart . . .

Step 6: Presenter Reflection (Five Minutes)

Appendix A (page 218) offers insight into this step.

Step 7: Debrief (Five Minutes)

A quick reminder about debriefing. Debriefing is discussing the process of learning for individuals and the groups, not reopening the content that the participants just discussed. See the introduction (page 1) for more detail as well as possible questions to use to frame a debrief.

Language You Can Borrow: *The debrief is a time to converse about the protocol itself and how we did, not about the content anymore. Remember, we gave it back to* [presenter's name]*! So, how did that go for us today?*

Application Example 1

As a prekindergarten teacher, Jenna consistently helps her students make connections between what stories they tell orally and the pictures they draw. For many students, this is an easy process as the connections are logical. This is not the case with Aubry.

Aubry's thinking is an enigma to Jenna. Even after repeated conferences with Aubry, Jenna is often unable to connect Aubry's drawings and storytelling. In an effort to understand what she might be missing, Jenna decides to record audio of Aubry talking about her picture. This audio file and the drawing are what Jenna brings to her collaborative team.

Since there is a static document (the picture) as well as an audio document, Karla, the facilitator, offers time for the participants to first listen to the audio file (twice—it is only sixty-five seconds long), and then two minutes to study the drawing.

During the description step, Jenna pauses. One of her colleagues just described a repeated phrase in Aubry's oral description. Jenna had never noticed it, and now she wants to go back to her classroom and listen to Aubry communicate with her friends at recess, in the free play area, and with the paraeducator—is it consistent?

The interpretation step brings more learning for Jenna, as the participants in the ATLAS protocol use *I* so Jenna can hear what else Aubry might be saying about her drawing, her storytelling, and the connection between the two. Finally, the group offers a few possible next steps for Jenna to consider. Jenna writes the ideas down to consider them later, but right now she has identified her next step.

When Karla asks Jenna to turn back to the group, Jenna's eyes are wide with excitement. She says, "Y'all, this was great! I thought I knew Aubry so well—and I still do—but now I think I know her in another way, which was really unexpected."

Application Example 2

Laticia is positive her tenth-grade student, Mackenzie, knows her stuff. All of Mackenzie's summative grades are outstanding. In the conversations Laticia has with her, all concepts seem to be lined up. But then, Mackenzie hands in a lab report that has some issues.

At first, Laticia thinks it may be a writing gap. She can completely relate—in graduate school, she did so much writing but felt like the professor took so many points off for writing problems when her ideas were sound. That doesn't seem to be the case for Mackenzie.

The reports have the required sections, like materials and hypothesis. Somehow, it is unclear when Mackenzie tries to articulate what she has learned through the lab. Even Laticia, who knows the labs intimately, can't seem to make heads or tails out of it. Laticia has checked with Mackenzie's language arts teacher and other adults who know Mackenzie, but they cannot relate to this seemingly unique situation.

The ATLAS protocol provides an opportunity for other colleagues in the science department to offer insight. Each department meeting contains a space where one person brings a challenge in their classroom—Laticia knows this is going to be hers.

As she hands out a copy of Mackenzie's lab report to each of her science colleagues, Laticia looks at her notes. Laticia and Theresa, the facilitator, had a long conversation the day before about how much to tell the group about Mackenzie. Their department had used the Tuning protocol (chapter 3, page 95) multiple times, so Laticia knows how to present a rich context of the situation. A Tuning protocol might have been a perfect fit if Laticia wanted Mackenzie's work to reach the lab report standard. However, Theresa had pointed out Laticia's *true* goal: it is to better understand Mackenzie's thinking when she writes lab reports.

The ATLAS protocol does not disappoint. Colleagues notice some cause-and-effect thinking gaps that help Laticia a great deal. In fact, as Laticia turns back to the group, her first words are "This student gets As on all the summatives, but you wouldn't know it by looking at this lab report. I'm not even thinking about lab reports anymore—I'm thinking about the rigor on my assessments. I wonder if this student, and probably others, are really good at memorizing . . ."

ATLAS: Looking at Data

This variation of the original ATLAS (Student Work) protocol, the concept of which was developed by Eric Buchovecky (1996) and revised by Dianne Leahy (2004) is effective with quantitative and qualitative data alike. It goes against the grain of most education conversations, which often start with our off-the-cuff opinions, are followed by our thinking about why our idea will work, and (if pushed by others) finish off with evidence. ATLAS: Looking at Data asks participants to ground the conversation with evidence (description) before moving on to any other cognitive function. I present my own adapted version here.

Expanded Supports for ATLAS

Figure 4.11 shows the anchor chart you can post for the ATLAS: Looking at Data protocol.

Purpose: To create specific actions informed by a data set	
Sequence:	
1. **Look**	Four to eight minutes
2. **Describe** *I see . . . I notice . . .*	Eight to ten minutes
3. **Interpret** *What might be going on . . . A potential root cause . . .* *A possible assumption . . . The data suggest . . .*	Eight to ten minutes
4. **Evaluate Our Learning** *An implication for . . . might be . . .*	Ten to twelve minutes
5. (Optional) **Presenter Reflection**	Five minutes
6. **Debrief**	Five minutes

Figure 4.11: ATLAS—Looking at Data anchor chart.

Visit go.SolutionTree.com/leadership for a free reproducible version of this figure.

Scaffolded Steps for Facilitators

In most cases, the ATLAS: Looking at Data protocol is used to examine collective data. A principal might bring copies of state assessment data to the very teachers who prepared those students. A third-grade team might examine its students' scores on the most recent summative mathematics assessment. In those cases, step 5 is eliminated, causing step 4 to feel like action planning. If a presenter uses ATLAS: Looking at Data with a group removed from the data, step 5 stays intact.

Step 1: Look (Four to Eight Minutes)

Appendix A (page 215) offers insight into this step.

The nature of the work sample will inform what participants do during this step. For instance, if the data are in hard copy form, participants might use multiple colors of highlighters and pens to annotate. If the data are available electronically, taking notes on sticky notes, paper, or in a word processing program would be necessary.

When this data-based variation of ATLAS was designed (Leahy, 2004), it is probable each participant was looking at the same data set. With the preponderance of data over a decade later, ATLAS: Looking at Data can also be effective when all participants may be looking at their own data set (representing scores of their own students).

Language You Can Borrow: *So, here's how this protocol might go. As you can see, we will start with some protected time to examine our data, then we will describe what we see. When it is time to interpret, the goal is to lift a layer* below *the data, without offering potential ideas. At the evaluation step, we will place value and personal preference on ideas we may individually or collectively pursue. The last step calls us to talk about how this process went for us today. What questions do you have that you need to resolve before we begin?*

We now have four to eight quiet minutes to examine the data, taking notes.

Step 2: Describe (Eight to Ten Minutes)

Appendix A (page 216) offers insight into this step.

Other data processes often include very specific questions to answer (for example, Which standard had the lowest average score? What wrong answer choices in the selected response did students most commonly choose?). I find teacher teams often use these questions as a task to complete—more compliance based than using data to inform next steps. In ATLAS: Looking at Data, all participants describe, but what they choose to describe is as varied as they are from one another, thus enhancing the depth to which they can analyze the data.

As a facilitator, it can be tricky to know how to respond when participants venture beyond description during this round. Notice how the Language You Can Borrow for this step approaches this potential complexity.

Step 3: Interpret (Eight to Ten Minutes)

The original version of this protocol includes the question, What do the data suggest? Even the very word *suggest* leans toward being suggestive! You can probably hear a colleague saying something like "The data suggest we need to reteach double-digit multiplication with regrouping." This is clearly an idea that participants could pursue in the next step, evaluating (putting value or personal preference on) next steps. You may notice a sentence stem with this language is listed *last* on the anchor chart.

Instead, the goal of this step is to skim off the data and see what is underneath. Imagine moving a box in the garage and a many-legged critter skitters away. You see the box—it is the description. You cannot discuss the black unidentified bug until someone helps it become seen.

A danger in this step is when teams wish to have dialogue about each interpretation. It is a natural tendency in teams to narrow the focus in on *the one* possible misconception in a concept, on *the one* assumption students may have been making in the essay prompt, or on *the one* interpretation students may have made when they read question 9. Educators inherently know there are as many interpretations as students they teach, but when teacher teams collaborate, multiple interpretations are often not welcome. In ATLAS: Looking at Data, the multiple interpretations enrich the conversation and greatly inform what actions the participants develop in the next step.

Teams who engage in root cause analysis would find much value in this step. Schools who use tools such as The Five Whys or a fishbone diagram (Visual Paradigm, n.d.) could insert those known structures into this step.

Language You Can Borrow: *Time to start the second round, interpretation. Here is an opportunity to explore the data from various points of view. We have a few choices listed on the* *anchor chart of how we might each participate. Interpretive statements are often debatable. Please don't let that make you nervous to offer your thinking. Who will begin?*

Step 4: Evaluate Our Learning (Ten to Twelve Minutes)

Some of the language in appendix A (page 217) may be helpful here.

It is more probable that the group has shared the data. In those cases, the ideas generated in this step are for the group members themselves. Adding a small bit of structure to this step has proved fruitful. Figure 4.12 shows a team's T-chart built after examining a common formative assessment. As an idea is spoken, a note-taker asks where the idea should be recorded. If each member of the group agrees the idea is worth implementing, and every person is committing to that implementation, the note taker records it in the We column. If the idea does not have a group commitment, it appears in the Me column, with the respective names of those who will implement it attached.

Me	We
Use *The Important Book* with a small group (Desiree, Joey).	Use the two-paragraph text about hermit crabs to reassess main idea.
Use Julie's newspaper headline lesson (Kirsten).	Create a learning station during literacy block Friday re: main idea.

Figure 4.12: Sample me and we chart.

The me and we chart builds accountability in the group for the idea generation that is taking place. Rarely are obscure or poorly grounded ideas spoken when the chart is used. Additionally, the chart can serve as a launching point for the next meeting with participants saying, for instance, "Let's take a look at the me and we chart. Desiree and Joey, why don't you start—how did *The Important Book* work out in your cotaught class?"

Language You Can Borrow: *We have come to the E of DIE—evaluation. We are going to put value or personal preference on our potential next steps, which we will record on our me and we chart.*

In this step, we might take turns talking without going around the circle. You might build on what someone else says or raise something new. Just keep in mind the norms that we have set in place. Note the sentence stem on the chart.

Step 5: Debrief (Five Minutes)

A quick reminder about debriefing. Debriefing is discussing the process of learning for individuals and the groups, not reopening the content that the participants just discussed. See the introduction (page 1) for more detail and for possible questions to use to frame a debrief.

Language You Can Borrow: *The debrief is a time to converse about the protocol itself and how we did, not about the content anymore. So, how did that go for us today?*

Application Example 1

It's a year of firsts for the honors chemistry collaborative team. This is the first year there have been so many student sections that a separate collaborative team was warranted. This is the first year to build common formative assessments together. And, today, this is the first time the team members are sharing item analyses from their last common summative assessment.

Andy, the honors chemistry collaborative team leader, anticipates this is going to be risky, so choosing a protocol is an important step. He believes ATLAS: Looking at Data fits who the members are as scientists; the description step seems like it calls on the same observing skills they might use in an experiment.

The team agrees to meet over lunch, downloading their data from their assessment program into a Google Sheet, so each of the three teachers can place scores next to one another to compare question by question.

Andy was right—it *is* risky. The risk comes out in his colleagues wanting to jump ahead in the protocol, starting to assign actions (evaluating) before it is time. He perseveres, consistently asking, "What did you see to make you think that?" And before he knows it, his colleagues are laughing with him when he says it.

"Will we get better at this?" one of them laments, with a smile.

The results are worthwhile, as the team develops next steps that are both personally and collectively informed by the data. More importantly, the platform for risk taking is built, as well as a process that can be replicated for any data set.

Application Example 2

"These parent surveys are a nightmare to go through," says Sherri to herself as the printer continues to spew more and more paper. As part of the district's strategic planning process, multiple surveys had been launched, targeting various stakeholder groups. In the next executive cabinet meeting, the associate superintendent wants time to be spent looking at these parent results.

The quantitative questions have been nicely aggregated into several graphs and charts. The qualitative, open-ended responses are producing the paper volume.

The cabinet knows ATLAS: Looking at Data, having used the protocol many times to analyze student achievement data, staff attendance data, and curriculum usage data. This would be the first time to use the process for qualitative data.

Sherri decides to divide the data up among the eight members of the cabinet, making sure that two different people will read each data set. This way, she knows the participants can accomplish the work *in the meeting*, rather than asking already busy people to prepare for their next time together.

As Sherri thinks through the facilitation, she wonders about how to make sure members can transfer their descriptive skills from quantitative to qualitative data. She decides to use a Shel Silverstein poem about an upcoming holiday. After projecting the poem on a screen, Sherri asks her colleagues to describe what they see—using the same skills of counting and quantifying they would use if the data looked differently.

Sherri's three minutes of practice pay off. After time to read and mark their data sets, the description step begins without a hitch. It is working well to have the data divided among many readers, as the aggregate picture is very similar across the group.

The superintendent is unable to be at the cabinet that day, and the work is still being accomplished. After everyone leaves the room, Sherri stays to clean up the note-taking document she created during the evaluate step. These ideas are well founded in the data and would serve the district well as they can now triangulate these results with other survey groups.

Examining Assessments

Gene Thompson-Grove (n.d.c) developed the Examining Assessments protocol, and I adapted it to its present form. Assessment work is just plain tricky. Decades ago, individual teachers would either create their own individual assessments or use a printed assessment from a textbook series. Now, various assessment types (such as diagnostic, formative, and summative) exist, created by various individuals or entities (for example, collaborative teams, the district curriculum office, or testing companies). Using the same three ways of looking (that is, descriptive, interpretive, and evaluative), combined with two other steps, Examining Assessments offer a powerful process to use prior to the beginning of an instructional unit. This process is particularly helpful in articulating what the assessment truly assesses. One unique way to do this in the third step is to actually *take* the assessment, then use that experience, borrowing the voice of a student who would be taking the assessment (that is, speaking like a fourth grader or a tenth grader).

Expanded Supports for Examining Assessments

Figure 4.13 shows the anchor chart you can post for the Examining Assessments protocol.

Purpose: To experience and better understand an assessment in order to revise or plan for instruction	
Sequence:	
1. **Look**	Four to eight minutes
2. **Describe** *I see . . . I notice . . .*	Six to eight minutes
3. **Try**	Six to eight minutes
4. **Interpret—Student** *I'm working on . . . I'm trying . . .* *I understand . . . I don't understand . . .*	Four to six minutes

Figure 4.13: Examining Assessments anchor chart.   continued →

5. **Interpret—Educator**	Four to six minutes
If this assessment was successfully completed by a student, it would show the student knows . . . *understands . . . is able to do* . . . (KUD)	
6. **Evaluate Our Learning**	Six to eight minutes
An implication for . . . might be . . .	
7. (Optional) **Presenter Reflection**	Five minutes
8. **Debrief**	Five minutes

Visit **go.SolutionTree.com/leadership** *for a free reproducible version of this figure.*

Scaffolded Steps for Facilitators

This protocol is most useful at the onset of a learning unit, since the focus is either to revise the final assessment or plan aligned instruction so students can reach the learning targets. Toward that end, it can be quite useful to spend time examining the standards prior to this protocol. Unpacking or unwrapping the standards is one way for a team to ensure each person has a deep understanding of the content. Any products developed in those processes are highly useful during the Examining Assessments protocol, particularly step 5.

Step 1: Look (Four to Eight Minutes)

Appendix A (page 215) offers insight into this step.

Step 2: Describe (Six to Eight Minutes)

Assessment creators are usually humans (except computers that auto-generate unit assessments in textbook series), therefore, there will be mistakes. Typographical errors can become diversionary for some participants. Some may find the misplaced comma, the incorrect homophone, or even a dispossessed apostrophe and use the description round to articulate these errors. These colleagues may be doing this with good intentions. Perhaps they are excellent at finding these standard English errors and enjoy serving that function for the group. Other times participants may be pronouncing typographical and formatting errors (for example, this area is double spaced instead of single spaced) because they see this feedback as safe. If they talk about content rather than visual stimuli, the risk level rises. As a facilitator, I may or may not know someone's intent. I generally handle it the same way. After the first time such an error is mentioned in the group, I might say something like the following, "Yes, I see that, too! Since our time is short, let's mark any formatting or typographical feedback on the assessments themselves. We can make sure not to lose those changes by writing them on our copies."

Step 3: Try (Six to Eight Minutes)

Participants are often struck by the insight this step yields. In the frenetic pace of teaching, it is all too common for assessments to be made without anyone actually trying them out. The potential of this step is not realized from simply carving out time for teachers to try out the assessment. The step is only valuable if educators find the right mindset from which to approach the assessment.

One way to help colleagues understand this step is to talk about audience. Ask, "Who is the audience for this assessment? Which students?" A second idea is to use the idea of pitch, for instance, How is this assessment pitched? Toward a fourth grader? Toward a seventh grader in an honors class? Both of these notions set the stage to ask educators to assume *those voices* as they try the assessment. Shifting the perspective from adult to a particular age of student makes all the difference.

The original protocol lists this step as, *complete the assessment*. When this assessment was originally developed in the late 1990s or early 2000s, teachers may have been using it in an after-school session or during a day without students in the building. Now, the Examining Assessments protocol can be effectively used during a job-embedded planning time with the times recommended on the anchor chart.

Logistically, completing some assessments in the time allotment could be problematic. Dividing the assessment among participants is one strategic move. When I choose this option, it might involve asking certain colleagues to start the assessment at a certain question or page number. Sometimes, individuals might work backward through the assessment, starting on the last problem. Without some strategy, I find educators try to work through the assessment quickly in order to finish it, rather than assume the perspective of the student to whom this assessment is pitched.

For certain assessments, you may need materials and equipment. For instance, a calculator may be permitted for students, thus, make sure those are available for the adults in this protocol. Similarly, if resources are *not* allowed, make that clear as well. If looking up words on Dictionary.com is not permitted on an English exam, then ask participants to keep their phones and computers off to the side for this step.

Language You Can Borrow: *It's time to try out this assessment. You may try any section you wish and start anywhere. The goal of this step is to understand what it may have been like for the student age group who will take this assessment. So, please don't be competitive like an adult might be! Get your mind into the space of a* [insert age of student here]*-year-old. What might be going through the minds of students in that age group as they are taking this assessment? The goal is not to finish the assessment but to try it. Please begin.*

Step 4: Interpret—Student (Four to Six Minutes)

In the original version of this protocol (Thompson-Grove, n.d.c), the interpretive actions are placed in one step. However, I noticed facilitators would not engage in the group in both parts, interpreting from the student and educator points of view. When the interpretation steps are separated, the functions and goals are clearer. The goal for interpreting from the student perspective is to get into the mind of a student who would actually be completing this assessment. The previous step gives the space and time for participants to be ready to engage in this interpretation.

In regard to asking adults to put themselves in the shoes of students, I find it helpful to shift the point of view in order to raise more vantage points and perspectives. Asking educators to borrow the student's voice, using *I*, can make a palpable difference.

Instead of saying, "On 4, I think the student was trying to . . ." a prompt might sound like "On 4, I was trying to . . ." Instead of "I don't believe on question 3 the student would know how to . . ." a participant could say, "I am confused on question 3 by . . ." Asking participants to speak in first person, as if they are the actual students, creates more empathy for both the student and the creator of the assessment.

Some groups may find it hokey to speak this way, so I may take time to explain why I am asking them to do so, saying, "I'm sorry this may feel a bit inauthentic right now, but let's keep giving it a try, then we can talk about it during the debrief." When I take the time to do that, I find someone will mention during the debrief the helpfulness of shifting perspective and point of view. Those moments are indeed glorious—I don't have to defend the protocol steps, as their colleagues proclaimed it worthwhile themselves.

Language You Can Borrow: *Time to start the second round, interpretation. This step occurs in two parts, first assuming, or borrowing, the voice of students. This shouldn't be hard considering how you just spent the last several minutes! It is important for us to articulate what skills, behaviors, insights, and emotions this assessment brought forth in you.*

We have a few choices for how we might each participate—the anchor chart has several options. Remember, the I *here is the actual student attempting this assessment. Who will begin?*

Step 5: Interpret—Educator (Four to Six Minutes)

In previous steps, working around a circle of educators in a predictable order (a go-round) makes the most sense. Those steps are not intended to include dialogue. Step 5 wants educators to discuss, disagree, and eventually build consensus on what this assessment truly assesses. I remember a fourth-grade teacher who said at this step, "Can't we just skip this step? The top of the assessment says RL.4." Just because an assessment purports to be aligned to a standard doesn't make it true. Using curriculum resource documents (either those provided to teachers or those teachers may have created when exploring the curriculum standards) is highly recommended in this step.

Additionally, assessments are not assessing a standard—they are really assessing a *student* and that student's demonstration and understanding of a standard. Since students are holistic (we can't just say to a student, "I'm just going to assess the mathematical part of you right now. Please put the other parts away"), it is helpful for educators to consider a holistic audience for the assessment.

In this step, an educator may articulate that a particular science assessment assesses stamina. Another colleague may claim that the same assessment assesses the student's ability to answer five different types of questions. A third may notice regional or colloquial language used in the assessment questions that may cause certain students some difficulty.

Language You Can Borrow: *So, now back to our own educator voices. The second phase of the interpretation step calls us to wonder what a* successful *assessment might tell us about what this assessment really assesses. The prompt here is long but quite intentional: If this assessment was successfully completed by a student, what would it show about what a student knows, understands, or is able to do? The anchor chart might have a new acronym for you in this step: KUD. We don't have to take these three (K, U, D) in sequence—it is up to us.*

Also, we will probably not work around the group in a predictable order. I suspect we will engage in dialogue with each other, probably disagreeing along the way—that is expected and good. Who hasn't begun a round yet and is willing now?

Step 6: Evaluate Our Learning (Six to Eight Minutes)

The developer of the Examining Assessments protocol may have never dreamed of schools that are highly assessment driven. Regardless, the steps transfer beautifully to various types of assessment usage (diagnostic, formative, and so on). Additionally, the process works with assessments that can be changed (for example, teacher created) and those that often cannot (for example, curriculum-based assessments, district benchmarks, state-released questions, or Advanced Placement test questions).

There tend to be four scenarios for which this protocol is useful.

1. Someone in the room created an assessment, and this group needs to provide direct feedback to the author.

2. Someone in the room helped create the assessment, but it cannot be changed (for example, district benchmarks).

3. An unattributed assessment is used to provide a platform for each person to learn about assessment. Who wrote this? Did any of us?

4. Someone outside the room created the assessment, and the teachers in this room need to teach students to be prepared for the rigor of that assessment (for example, district benchmarks).

The sentence stem on the anchor chart for step 6 stays the same regardless of what kind of assessment a group is examining. However, the outcomes change as this protocol can be used for two different purposes: (1) revision and (2) instruction. Figure 4.14 offers a method to see the *yes* and *no* conditions required to match to the four scenarios with corresponding guidance for step 6.

Scenario	Author Present	Revision Possible	Implications for . . .
1	Y	Y	Revision
2	N	Y	
3	Y	N	Instruction
4	N	N	

Figure 4.14: Options for step 6 in the Examining Assessments protocol.

In the first two scenarios, the group wishes to revise the assessment. Perhaps it hasn't been finalized or copied yet for students. If the author is present, that person serves as the presenter, listening in step 6 as the group makes recommendations for changes. Scenario 2 yields revision, but the author is not present. The group might be using an assessment someone outside the group created. In this case, the entire group offers ideas for revision, and one group member takes notes, indicating ownership for the revision process moving forward. It might sound like this, "An implication for question 4 might be . . ."

For assessments that cannot be altered, this discussion protocol can be as fulfilling as it is when the assessments can be altered. A team may be looking at a curriculum-based district benchmark at the beginning of an instructional unit in order to know what its students need to know, understand, and be able to do at the end of the unit. During step 6, it would be fruitless and unproductive to recommend revisions; instead, the group would focus on instructional strategies and plans that would yield better student outcomes. It might sound like this, "An implication to prepare students for question 6 could be . . ."

In scenarios 1 and 3, a presenter has offered an assessment for the group to consider. In those cases, several facilitators I know make a particular move at this point, asking presenters if it would be permissible for the group to take on their work. This respectful question asks the participants to borrow, to hold someone else's work and care for it as if it were their own. At this point, presenters might turn their chair ninety degrees, now facing the facilitator, so their ear is to the group. This physical shift has several benefits.

- Presenters can focus on listening and note-taking, as their ear is now directed to the group. They do not need to spend cognitive energy thinking about their nonverbal reactions (for example, furrowed or raised eyebrows—basically anything with eyebrows). Presenters report the positive experience of having some space (intellectual and physical) between themselves and the work. It is relieving to give the work away even for ten minutes.

- The group can better own the work, instead of looking to the presenter for nonverbal feedback as each piece of feedback is offered. Participants report having more courage to offer tough-to-hear feedback when the presenter is slightly turned.

If a facilitator chooses this method, a pronoun shift occurs with the group. The sentence stems on the anchor chart indicate the change. The shift is to *we* and *I*, rather than *she*, *they*, or the name of the presenter. This collective language helps the presenter be in a productively risky space because the group isn't just giving advice with fingers pointed. It also helps the group members really ponder their feedback.

With this method, at the end of the feedback step, the facilitator would invite the presenter back into the group, and the point of view switches—the group gives the work back to the presenter, and feedback has a clear stopping point.

Language You Can Borrow: *We are not going to evaluate the assessment or the teachers who created it; rather, we will evaluate our next steps. We might take turns talking without going around the circle. You might build on what someone else says or raise something new. Just keep in mind the norms that we have set in place.*

> (If there is a presenter) *[Presenter's name], you have described and interpreted with us, but in this step, I think it would be more helpful if we took on this assessment as if it were ours. Would it be OK for us to now lift this product from your shoulders for a while?* (If yes) *It will be helpful for you and us if you would be willing to turn ninety degrees, so your ear is to the group. You can focus on listening and the group can focus on owning your work rather than talking at you, as you will not be verbally participating for a while.*

So, our discussion now is around this question: What are the implications of this work? You might use the prompt on our anchor chart: An implication for _____ might be _____.

Step 7: (Optional) Presenter Reflection (Five Minutes)

Appendix A (page 218) offers insight into this step.

Step 8: Debrief (Five Minutes)

A quick reminder about debriefing. Debriefing is discussing the process of learning for individuals and the groups, not reopening the content the participants just discussed. See the introduction (page 1) for more detail as well as possible questions to use to frame a debrief.

Language You Can Borrow: *The debrief is a time to converse about the protocol itself and how we did, not about the content anymore. Remember, we gave it back to* [presenter's name]*! So, how did that go for us today?*

Application Example 1

Marlene is part of the district team that looked at the new English language arts standards this past summer. Although there was certainly some overlap to what they had used in the past, the standard about author's point of view was markedly different. Students now need to talk about why the author made specific decisions about point of view. In the past, the fifth-grade team taught various points of view (for example, first person and third person omniscient) and asked students to identify them in text excerpts.

As the next narrative unit draws near, Marlene is thinking it would be prudent to examine the district benchmark for the second quarter, which would include questions aligned to the new standards. In the past, whenever an assessment draft went out, team members tacitly agreed to read it, but Marlene has plenty of anecdotal evidence indicating that does not always happen—usually after teachers actually give the assessment and claim certain questions were, in their words, "unfair" or "not in the unit."

Marlene decides to serve as the facilitator for the session and doesn't have a presenter because the assessment wasn't authored by anyone in the group. The benchmark assessment was designed to assess the next two instructional units, but Marlene just wants to focus on the upcoming unit. So, she highlights certain questions and asks her colleagues to focus on those particular questions.

Step 3 takes longer than Marlene had anticipated because there are multiple passages to read; however, she knows step 6 might not take as long since they aren't revising the assessment. Step 6 ends up being shorter, and yet the dialogue is quite meaningful. Team members notice the difference in some of the questions compared to previous years, in particular, the attention to the revised standard about author's point of view. Participants make three specific suggestions to alter the new unit, one to actually *remove* something, which is joyous to each of the teachers.

In the debrief, another team member, Andy, asks Marlene, "Can we do this for all our assessments?"

Application Example 2

As Diana pulls out her fourth-grade geometry unit binder, she sees a sticky note that reads "Revise summative!" As she flips through the data sheets from last year's students, she remembers their postmortem conversation after the summative assessment. There seemed to be issues with the assessment, students' performance, or a combination of the two.

Last year, Diana made all the mathematics assessments since they were departmentalized. This year, every fourth-grade teacher teaches each subject, so the team decided to take turns being in charge of assessments in each content area.

It is Frank's turn to revise this geometry assessment, so Diana emails him to make sure he has the needed file. When they meet on Thursday, he has made a copy for each person, and Diana is ready with the Examining Assessments protocol.

This is the first time they will use this protocol with a mathematics assessment, so Diana makes sure to remind them to have the mindset of a ten- or eleven-year-old in step 3. "It is easy to solve these problems like adults, but that doesn't help Frank make any necessary revisions," she says.

Diana even surprises herself as she is working through the assessment. "I created this," she finds herself saying in her head, "and I am confused!" Both interpreting steps prove helpful for the group in identifying problematic areas. When it comes time to revise, Frank turns to the side, and Diana and Nadia, the third member of the team, have plenty to talk about. Before they know it, Diana's timer goes off to remind Frank to turn back toward the group.

After Frank lists what revisions he plans to make, the team sets a date when he will email the next draft. Email seems to make sense for the next step since they had such a thorough conversation using this discussion protocol.

The Making Meaning Protocol

Daniel Baron (n.d.b) developed the Making Meaning protocol, and I adapted it to its present form. Protocols to seek perspective restrict participants from knowing context and background when examining pieces of work in schools. ATLAS uses a student work sample, ATLAS: Looking at Data uses quantitative or qualitative data, and Examining Assessments uses assessments in print or electronic form. The Making Meaning protocol uses other adult-created products where the presenter wants to step back and rely on the perspectives of others. The product participants examine may be authored by the presenter or not.

Figure 4.15 shows the anchor chart you can post for the Making Meaning protocol.

Purpose: To hear colleagues process a document devoid of context	
Sequence:	
1. **Look**	Five to seven minutes
2. **Describe** *I see . . . I notice . . .*	Five to seven minutes
3. **Interpret—Ask Questions** *A question this raises for me . . .*	Four to six minutes
4. **Interpret—Speculate** *What's significant for me . . . Why this text exists is to . . .* *What this author is trying to do in this text is . . .*	Four to six minutes
5. **Evaluate Our Learning** *An implication for . . . might be . . .*	Six to eight minutes
6. (Optional) **Presenter Reflection**	Five minutes
7. **Debrief**	Five minutes

Figure 4.15: Making Meaning anchor chart.

Visit **go.SolutionTree.com/leadership** for a free reproducible version of this figure.

Scaffolded Steps for Facilitators

As with each of the foundational protocols in this family, DIE is the framework for the sequence of steps.

Step 1: Look (Five to Seven Minutes)

Appendix A (page 215) offers insight into this step.

Step 2: Describe (Five to Seven Minutes)

Appendix A (page 216) offers insight into this step.

Step 3: Interpret—Ask Questions (Four to Six Minutes)

The ATLAS protocol, which served as the muse for each of the derivations in this protocol family, uses DIE so that one step aligns to each of the three letters in the acronym. In the Making Meaning protocol, the interpretation step has been divided into two smaller steps, similar to those in the Examining Assessments protocol.

Some groups may struggle with the prompt in this round, giving responses such as "A question this raises for me is if this will be emailed to teachers" that are truly inquisitive rather than suggestive. Although the intention behind the response may be inquisitive, it could be construed as suggestive, implying *you better not email this.* Generalizing the question (changing its scope) is a helpful revision. A better question to ask in this case would be, "A question this raises for me is how will teachers receive this information?"

If a facilitator anticipates difficulty in this step, skill building prior to the protocol's onset is appropriate. A few moments of learning might lead to offering a more narrow question example and asking participants to change the scope.

If the presenter was the one to write or develop the document the group is examining, this step would be the first of many in this protocol where the presenter listens instead of speaks. I have found when presenters turn their chair ninety degrees, now facing the facilitator, there are several benefits.

- Presenters can focus on listening and note-taking, as their ear is now directed to the group. They do not need to spend cognitive energy thinking about their nonverbal reactions (for example, furrowed or raised eyebrows—basically anything with eyebrows). Presenters report the positive experience of having some space (intellectual and physical) between themselves and the work. It is relieving to give the work away even for ten minutes.

- Participants don't inadvertently expect a presenter to act contrary to the protocol. For instance, in this step about asking questions, if a participant is looking directly into the eyes of a presenter and raises a question, social and cultural habits may win out, and the presenter will offer an obligatory response.

If the author of the document is not part of the group, the presenter may stay as an active participant in this step.

Language You Can Borrow: *Time to start the next phase, interpretation. In this Making Meaning protocol, we will interpret twice, in two different ways.*

> *(If the presenter is the author of the document)* [Presenter's name], in this step, I think it would be more helpful if you listened more than spoke. To facilitate your listening and our fidelity to the protocol, perhaps you could turn ninety degrees, so your ear is to the group.

In this first of two interpretive steps, we will consider what questions this document raises for us. We could raise questions about the document itself, the author who created it, the circumstances under which the document was written, or something else. The questions will not be answered by [presenter's name] *or anyone else. Our job here is to simply list the questions. You might begin speaking using some of the words from our anchor chart such as the following: A question this raises for me . . . Who will begin?*

Step 4: Interpret—Speculate (Four to Six Minutes)

This step asks participants to take a significant interpretive leap, to get into the mind of the author and ascertain purpose and intent. If the presenter is not the author of the document, both participants and the presenter can speak in this step. As with many protocols that have interpretive steps, the goal is to raise many and multiple interpretations, rather than to agree on *the* interpretation.

Language You Can Borrow: *In this step, we use our interpretive skills to speculate about what the author may have been thinking and feeling during the development of this document.*

We have a few choices of how we might each participate. You might start with one of the prompts on the anchor chart. Who will begin?

Step 5: Evaluate Our Learning (Six to Eight Minutes)

In the other foundational protocols in this family, this step gives space for educators to offer ideas for the presenter to consider. Although this might happen in the Making Meaning protocol, this step also can be reflective for the participants. They may use the suggested sentence stem to draw parallels from the document to their own work in schools and for schools.

Language You Can Borrow: *We are not going to evaluate the document nor the author who created it. Our discussion is around this question: What are the implications of this work? You may think about the implications or impacts it might have in your own role, or you might think about* [presenter's name] *and the role* [preferred pronoun] *serves. You might use the prompt on our anchor chart: An implication for _____ might be _____.*

Step 6: (Optional) Presenter Reflection (Five Minutes)

Appendix A (page 218) offers insight into this step.

Step 7: Debrief (Five Minutes)

A quick reminder about debriefing. Debriefing is discussing the process of learning for individuals and the groups, not reopening the content the participants just discussed. See the introduction (page 1) for more detail as well as possible questions to use to frame a debrief.

Language You Can Borrow: *The debrief is a time to converse about the protocol itself and how we did, not about the content anymore. Remember, we gave it back to* [presenter's name]*! So, how did that go for us today?*

Application Example 1

Liz, a middle school principal, has been reading professional literature about how to write classroom observational feedback. Now she is questioning her approach and would like other principals to weigh in.

The district has set up a time each month when other middle school principals learn together. After talking to Kayla, the assistant superintendent, Liz is all set. She will bring a narrative she wrote for a teacher, and Kayla will facilitate the Making Meaning protocol.

At first, her colleagues have difficulty describing. Kayla works hard, several times using the prompt, "What do you *see* to make you think that?" Three principals in a row venture beyond description, and Kayla senses some frustration, so she decides to hold a facilitative time out. Holding her hand up like a basketball coach requesting a time out, Kayla reminds the group members they know how to do this, saying, "We have used ATLAS: Looking at Data before. Use that mindset, just looking for words rather than numbers. You got this!"

Kayla offers another two minutes for principals to go back into the text to re-enter the description round. The pause pays off, and the description really helps the group simply identify the words for what they are, rather than what they were interpreting them to be.

After a solid description round, both interpretation rounds are extremely helpful for Liz. She hadn't been thinking about what meaning the audience of this feedback, the teacher, might think at certain places in her narrative.

The evaluate step is probably the most rewarding for Liz. As she listens to her colleagues talk about what actions they are planning to take in their own feedback writing, she mentally checks off the list she had already started in the margin of her notebook. Forty-five minutes before, she had no idea her inquiry would become an important point of learning for each of her colleagues.

Application Example 2

As the public relations executive in the district, Sherri is often lobbied for feedback on documents and communications, but she rarely gets feedback herself on her own work. When Tim, the professional development director, announces there will be groups meeting at the beginning of each monthly administrative staff meeting, she is intrigued.

After the meeting, she asks Tim for more details, and she grows excited. A group of six to eight administrators will meet every month, taking turns bringing a product that needs some feedback. Sherri immediately volunteers to be the first person to bring something. She has worked hard on a brochure about the district. With the new open-enrollment policies in her state, marketing the school district has become increasingly important.

The next month, Sherri is ready. Anthony, an IT professional from another department, attended facilitation training last summer, so he helps Sherri choose a protocol and will facilitate the group.

It is hard for Sherri to not say too much at the beginning—it's her job to communicate, after all! However, she had listened to Anthony when they met prior to today when he said her feedback would be better if she could restrain herself.

He is right. Sherri isn't expecting the group to find any problematic semicolons or dangling modifiers, and they don't. What they do offer are the initial perspectives of readers who haven't spent hours on the layout, the pictures, and the text. Step 4 is the most helpful for her as she hears the group gently debate whether or not the flyer was more informative or persuasive.

As Sherri thanks the group at the end of her presenter reflection, she is already thinking about what she might bring next when her turn rolls around again.

Seeking Perspective in an E⁴ Way

The book's introduction makes clear that a match between a presenter's purpose and the protocol is critical. Now that you've read about refining protocols in chapter 3 and protocols that seek perspective in chapter 4, it is important to consider how to choose the right protocol for your purpose. What will be the most effective and efficient, while ensuring equity and excellence?

In the second example of the Making Meaning protocol, Sherri wants her colleagues to look at her work without the context and background she has in her head. However, Sherri could have a different purpose. She could have a specific goal in mind for the brochure and want her colleagues to look for evidence of where she met that goal and places where she does not yet meet it. The Making Meaning protocol would not help her meet her goal. Tuning (page 95) is a better choice.

Diana chooses an Examining Assessment for her geometry assessment. It is an effective match for her because it helps each member of the team consider the standards. The process also includes a step in which they place themselves in the mind of a fourth-grade student. If Diana wants to ensure each question is strongly aligned to the curriculum standards, a Tuning protocol is more appropriate. In that case, the group would use laser focus to identify the potential gap.

There isn't a *wrong* protocol in a situation, just ones that are more aptly matched than others. Some readers of this text may be avid protocol users and enjoy the efficiency. Perhaps these chapters are encouraging how to embrace more effectiveness within protocol use while also ensuring equity and excellence. If you used the expanded supports in chapter 4 because you were using one of the foundational protocols in this chapter, consider reading the introduction to learn more about matching protocols to a presenter's intended purpose.

The last two chapters include protocols in which artifacts are necessary. It is impossible to use a Tuning protocol without a product to examine or ATLAS: Looking at Data without a data set. The protocols in the next two chapters *may* include artifacts, but do not *need* them. Chapter 5 introduces how to wrestle with situations that don't seem solvable—the very definition of a dilemma of practice.

5

Protocols to Explore and Manage Dilemmas

Chapter 4 featured protocols to seek perspective. In that protocol family, it is critical for participants to attempt objectivity, whether they are looking at student work, data, an assessment, or another document. For the protocols featured in this chapter, "Protocols to Explore and Manage Dilemmas," context is key. The presenters who bring forth their dilemmas want the participants to deeply understand their situations, so they are better able to identify possible blind spots and potential biases. This sort of help is different from the assistance offered in chapter 6, "Protocols to Generate Ideas." As educators use the protocols in this family, they may better understand their contexts, find ways to cope with their frustrations, and use the space to consider other ways to manage their dilemmas.

Dilemmas are fraught with tensions and complexities. Discussion protocols create space to effectively work with the dilemma, so educators bringing them can take steps to feel more excellent about their work. Both situations that follow would benefit greatly from one of the four foundational protocols this chapter describes.

SITUATION A

Charles is just plain stuck. He is an experienced middle school teacher, usually able to capture the attention of thirteen-year-olds with the mysteries of introductory physics and chemistry. However, he has a particular student in third period, Justin, whom he just can't figure out. Justin's list of complicating factors is long—from instructional to behavioral to familial. Charles has had very positive experiences with students like Justin, but he hasn't been able to break through to Justin yet.

The multitiered system of support (MTSS) committee at school has already held meetings for Justin. Charles has attended some but hasn't really found them to be helpful for his daily work with Justin. A Tier 2 intervention is in place during a morning schoolwide intervention time, but no specific strategies or interventions are in place for science class.

Charles has brought this up to his multidisciplinary team that meets every other week. Unfortunately, the response wasn't super helpful either. The team offered strategies he has already tried, and charts and data collection mechanisms that seemed far too unwieldy. What he really wants is some help better understanding Justin, whose background is quite different than that of Charles. Charles is not sure who can help him and how they might go about doing exactly that.

SITUATION B

Babetta has a strong record in building consensus with others—it helped catapult her all the way to being named superintendent in a small urban district one year ago. She comes to the district with deep knowledge and experience in special education and support services. In fact, the district has been named a "District in Need of Assistance" by the state education department, mostly for its gaps in student performance between students with disabilities and those without.

Some of the necessary changes have not been difficult to implement—a new form here, a different way to contact parents there. However, Babetta is puzzled about how to help the middle school with what she perceives as a persistently resistant climate. Staff members did not push back on any of the changes thus far, but what she has been trying to talk with them about next has not been going so well. Being a small community, she is worried if she doesn't build a stronger strategy with that campus, board members may soon become involved.

When she asks central office leadership team members for help, she isn't sure if their posed strategies will get at the root of the issue. She is wondering if she needs to have some different kind of help—perhaps gaining some insight into what might be under the surface of this situation and being less focused on her next actions.

Before we jump into the protocols, I want to spend a little more time on dilemmas and how to distinguish them from problems.

Dilemma Versus Problem

Ask a group of educators for synonyms for the word *dilemma,* and the word *problem* will surely emerge. Students have problems, teachers have problems, and administrators have problems. In fact, the very premise of school in colonial North America, built from and for an uneducated public, could have been defined as a problem.

A few principal colleagues I know love this interview prompt: "Talk about a problem you had in a previous job and what you personally did to solve it." They are trying to ascertain that candidate's penchant for being a problem solver. Profile documents are becoming increasingly popular—profile of a graduate, profile of a teacher, profile of a leader. Problem solver is a common attribute in those documents. Entire student support team processes, like RTI and MTSS, are built around the careful and narrow identification of a problem. Then a group of educators meets and uses a problem-solving process.

When educators choose to identify something as a problem, the natural response is to seek a solution. How that looks might be different to each person, but these actions tend to be quite universal.

- Implement a remedy that has worked in a similar situation.

- Search online for possible next steps.

- Ask for advice from others whom we respect with similar jobs.

- Gather with others in our school or department and brainstorm.

Often with genuine problems, these work swimmingly! A conversation between a current principal and her retired principal mentor yields a fruitful result. A blog post from the American Association of School Administrators causes you to reflect on a previous situation, just with a tweak of the solution. However, the discussion protocols in this chapter have been specifically designed to address dilemmas, not problems. The synonymity we assume exists does not apply in this context.

Here are two metaphors to help you think about dilemmas.

In the first metaphor, dilemmas are a puzzle. Imagine I have a puzzle with all the pieces in a box, and I have asked you to assemble it. However, time is quite short today, so I ask you for your strategies upfront. In return, I will let you know if I think those strategies will probably work. After all, I don't want you to waste any time—efficiency and effectiveness are key. Here is what I might say in response to your three ideas.

1. **Find all the edges:** "Thank you for that strategy. Unfortunately, that strategy may not work very well for you. The puzzle does not have a typical quadrilateral shape. The edges are quite unpredictable—none of the pieces have straight lines."

2. **Look at the picture:** "Regrettably, the picture is long gone. It was ripped off by a few students years ago."

3. **Group all the colors:** "This sounds so promising, and it probably works really well on some puzzles. Perhaps the title of this puzzle, *Panther at Night*, will help you understand why it probably won't work here."

You probably are quite frustrated! Isn't that just like a dilemma? You have assumed a situation is a problem, so you approach it with your previous experience and several strategies in hand. The results, however, are not to your liking.

In the second metaphor, a dilemma is a tangled ball of yarn. Imagine Grandma has asked you to go to the guest bedroom and reach into the closet and bring her the yarn on the floor. You are somewhat resistant as you know the cats spend a great deal of time in that room, but you oblige. Reaching down with both hands and arms, you collect the yarn on the floor. It is a tangled mess. Perhaps it is smelly due to the cats. The colors are all mixed together. The cats' clawing has resulted in many yarn ends sticking up. You pull one end, and it feels like a clown's handkerchief—more, and more, and more coming. Pulling another end makes a different end disappear, leaving you with a very small piece of yarn. Finally, pulling another end creates the most dastardly result, making the yarn mass even tighter. The dilemma is clear (although some of you would just treat that as a problem, wielding scissors!).

Approaching a situation as a dilemma rather than as a problem changes your perception of the situation and, therefore, changes what you might need. In the earlier list of how people tend to approach problems, the goal was to seek solutions. In a dilemma, the goal is to *explore* the dilemma from many angles and perspectives and then learn how to *manage* the dilemma. The name of this family of protocols is not problem resolution. Instead, it is exploring and managing dilemmas.

This notion of exploring and managing dilemmas is not brand new, as many people have experienced challenges that helped them untangle tricky situations.

- In a data protocol, they look for root causes.
- In a coaching conversation, they identify possible assumptions.

Discussion protocols include these important steps to help presenters reach their goals but also to aid the participants in approaching the situation as a dilemma rather than immediately jumping to potential solutions. Let's look further at some characteristics of dilemmas and then think about the best way to arrive at what's called a dilemma question.

Dilemma Characteristics

In developing the following Consultancy protocol (page 153), Faith Dunne, Paula Evans, and Gene Thompson-Grove (n.d.) use a set of criteria to help participants define a dilemma. My organization of these criteria is in a checklist form. In order for a situation to be considered a dilemma, all boxes in figure 5.1 must be checked.

Dilemma Criteria

☐ You think about it often. This criterion makes the presenter pause and consider if this situation rises to the level of a dilemma. Is this a passing annoyance, or does this situation keep you up at night? Perhaps when your son says, "Did you see me catch that fly ball?" you feel guilty because you didn't. You were in the stands, your eyes were looking toward right field, but your mind was on the dilemma.

☐ The dilemma is not getting better. In terms of a line graph, the visual is horizontal (staying the same), or going down (getting worse).

☐ Your actions can impact the dilemma. The key here is to see yourself as a part of the dilemma. It is tempting to describe the dilemma in terms of someone else. For instance, imagine I said, "My dilemma is I can't get my wife to keep up with the laundry." If you're having a strong reaction to this fictitious situation, you likely believe I should play a vital role in the laundry at our house (which I do). If someone is unwilling to see the self as part of the dilemma, this criterion is not met.

☐ This is a three-part criterion.

⇨ The dilemma is important to you. Groups don't want to spend their hard-earned time talking and thinking about a dilemma if you feel you could take it or leave it.

⇨ You're willing to work on it. There are situations in my life I am willing to say out loud: I like complaining about X; however, I'm unwilling to do anything about it.

⇨ You've tried something. This means you have actively worked on the dilemma. It means you have done more than talk out loud in the shower. An action doesn't necessarily mean you enacted a step with the dilemma itself—it could mean you talked to some other colleagues, seeking advice. That means you tried something.

Figure 5.1: Dilemma criteria.

These criteria are all-inclusive. You must be four for four with the checkboxes. If just one of these criteria is lacking, the situation is not a dilemma, and using one of the discussion protocols in this chapter may not be an effective use of time and energy.

The Dilemma Question

A key to presenters getting what they need using a dilemma-based protocol is an effective dilemma question. Sometimes called the focusing question, it ensures the group stays at the heart of what the presenter wants, rather than pursuing the sometimes-alluring ground of where the group wants to go.

The introduction articulated the importance of a preconference, a conversation between the presenter and facilitator to determine which protocol will match the presenter's purpose. The "Preconference Key Words and Actions" (appendix B, page 237) is a reminder that drafting a dilemma question also happens in that preconference. I find it usually takes a few question drafts to find the heart of a dilemma.

The following represent a few examples of dilemma questions from teachers.

- How do I bring calm, peace, and order to my end-of-day routine?

- How do I productively engage an incessant parent?

- How might I combat negativity on my collaborative team without alienating myself from the group?

The following represent a few examples of dilemma questions from school-based leaders.

- "How might I best approach a situation I see as urgent but that no one else does?"

- "What might I do to build teacher leadership when the culture is *us versus them*?"

- "Why is it that a few members of my staff have negatively impacted so many others despite my very best attempts to mitigate their influence?"

The following represent a few examples of dilemma questions from central office leaders.

- How do I balance time for schools to implement initiatives and me checking in with them?

- What can I do to acknowledge that I don't teach students every day in a way that doesn't damage my credibility?

- What might be at the heart of a particular school's reticence to try _____?

Drafting a dilemma question is worth the time and energy. As groups wrestle with situations that don't seem to have clear answers, they may wander from the stated dilemma question. The facilitator can use the dilemma question to hold the group accountable to the presenter's focus.

The Protocols

The four foundational protocols in this chapter have several similarities but are unique enough to demand careful consideration. Figure 5.2 offers a quick explanation of what a presenter might be feeling or desiring and how that might translate into a dilemma-based protocol selection. Consultancy is often chosen when the presenter needs better thinking—not, generally, better ideas. The protocols, Issaquah and Descriptive Consultancy, are quite similar and fall into a coaching-to-action category. Finally, the Peeling the Onion protocol is a hybrid of the other three protocols. At the close of this chapter, I offer an expanded version of this figure, including various features of the four foundational protocols.

Protocol	One-Word *Why*
Consultancy	Depth
Descriptive Consultancy	Ideas
Issaquah	Coaching
Peeling the Onion	Fog

Figure 5.2: Choosing a dilemma-based protocol.

Dilemma-based protocols may or may not have an artifact. The important question, when deciding whether or not to use an artifact, is this: Does the group *need* to see a document to understand the dilemma and address the dilemma question? Educators are often quite adept at providing paper! However, there is not a 100 percent direct correlation between providing papers and offering relevant, essential artifacts.

I note ideal group size in all the protocols in this chapter. However, these are not hard-and-fast rules, as group size is not the most effective criterion to use in choosing a protocol. For example, the original version of Issaquah, developed in the late 1990s (Mohr, Bambino, & Baron, n.d.), lists fifteen to fifty people as a group size. This can lead a facilitator to assume Issaquah is the default choice for any group of this size. However, the facilitator could adapt the same facilitation moves and decisions required to facilitate Issaquah with a large group to any dilemma-based protocol. A general recommendation about modifying protocols for large groups is included in appendix C (page 239).

Consultancy

This protocol was developed by Faith Dunne, Paula Evans, and Gene Thompson-Grove (n.d.) as part of their work at the Coalition of Essential Schools and the Annenberg Institute for School Reform. I present my adapted version. With the word *consult* as the root, this protocol views consultants in this context. Consultants who do their jobs well do not give clients all the answers; instead, they build their thinking skills so when they gradually exit, the clients know how to move forward even in unfamiliar situations. In Consultancy, the participants serve as thinkers rather than solvers. A presenter may leave without a tangible next step, but instead a more thorough and nuanced understanding of the dilemma.

Expanded Supports for Consultancy

The anchor chart for the Consultancy protocol in figure 5.3 could include the following information.

Purpose: To help a presenter *think* about a concrete, named dilemma	
Sequence:	
1. **Presentation**	Less than fifteen minutes
2. **Clarifying Questions**	Five minutes
3. **Probing Questions**	Fifteen minutes
4. **Discussion**	Fifteen minutes
5. **Presenter Reflection**	Five minutes
6. **Debrief**	Five minutes

Figure 5.3: Consultancy anchor chart.

*Visit **go.SolutionTree.com/leadership** for a free reproducible version of this figure.*

Scaffolded Steps for Facilitators

In Consultancy, the participants use the steps to create thinking space because that is the ultimate gift of Consultancy, better thinking. Depth is an apropos one-word descriptor. If the consultants aren't helping the presenter think deeply, they are not risking enough. It also acknowledges that better thinking does not always emerge from providing ideas to one another. In those moments, educators often find themselves using their cognitive energy judging the quality and efficacy of the idea, rather than further examining and understanding the dilemma.

The Consultancy protocol has powerful learning opportunities. Its effective use is not, however, a foregone conclusion. Comprehensive understanding of each step is needed for effective facilitation.

Step 1: Presentation (Less Than Fifteen Minutes)

Appendix A (page 219) offers insight into this step.

In addition to the possible language choices in appendix A, the following Language You Can Borrow could be helpful choices for a facilitator to use in a Consultancy.

Language You Can Borrow:

- *Like the word* consultancy, *our presenter is seeking some consulting from us—and good consultants help people think; they don't just tell them what to do.*

- *Our goal today is to help* [presenter's name] *better understand* [preferred pronoun] *dilemma.*

Step 2: Clarifying Questions (Five Minutes)

Appendix A (page 221) offers insight into this step.

Step 3: Probing Questions (Fifteen Minutes)

Probing questions are a critical step in using the Consultancy protocol. This step also appears in the Issaquah protocol. Thus, the white space learning for both protocols and most of the Language You Can Borrow have been consolidated into appendix A (page 219).

In addition to the possible language choices in appendix A, the following Language You Can Borrow could offer helpful choices for a facilitator to use in a Consultancy.

Language You Can Borrow:

It's about time to have our gift-giving session with [presenter's name]. *We may not be able to metaphorically open all the gifts you just wrote, so please prioritize: if you only get to ask one question, what will that be? How about two?*

[Fifteen seconds]

Now, we will be able to ask our carefully crafted questions. Pass in your sticky note and pause as [presenter's name] *lifts back the paper to read it, and then listen to the response. We won't have a back-and-forth discussion about the gift; instead, we just get to consider the response. Who will begin? After we hear the first question, we will proceed to the left, one question at a time.*

[Ten minutes]

Our time for this step has ended, but you can still hand in any questions you didn't ask. They are still potential fodder for [presenter's name]'*s thinking.*

Step 4: Discussion (Fifteen Minutes)

The facilitator has an important decision to make at this step. The discussion protocol lists six possible questions to frame the dilemma.

1. What did we hear?
2. What didn't we hear that might be relevant?
3. What assumptions seem to be operating?
4. What questions does the dilemma raise for us?
5. What do we think about the dilemma?
6. What might we do or try if faced with a similar dilemma? What have we done in similar situations?

The protocol does not recommend a certain way to frame this step. Some facilitators may not pose these questions at all; others may take the possible questions one at a time. It is human nature to maintain a problem-solving posture—a tendency to immediately offer advice. Group members worked hard during the Probing Questions step to avoid recommending; if specific ideas are what the presenter wants, a different dilemma-based protocol might be a better choice (that is, Descriptive Consultancy or Issaquah).

The next example of Language You Can Borrow represents the way I choose to facilitate this step of Consultancy. My decision is based on the following.

- A dilemma is like being in a personal tornado. The noise is so significant that presenters might not really know what they said. The first prompt, "What did you hear?" ensures the presenter has a very literal hearing of the dilemma.

- The original developer of this protocol, Gene Thompson-Grove, no longer uses the last of the six prompts: "What might we do or try if faced with a similar dilemma? What have we done in similar situations?" (G. Thompson-Grove, personal communication, December 30, 2020). If the true goal of a Consultancy is to *think*, then focusing on solutions treats the situation like a *problem*, not a *dilemma*. There are other protocols for situations that only need ideas (see chapter 6, page 177). Gene also advises, "The presenter knows far better than the consultants the complexities involved" (McDonald et al., 2013, p. 32). By using the approach listed in the Language You Can Borrow, that prompt can be minimized or even eliminated.

- Identifying possible assumptions is often a difficult disposition for individuals to grow and a tough space for groups to stay in. Explicitly addressing the question, What assumptions seem to be operating? rather than waiting for an organic opening is more aligned to one of the reasons the presenter chose Consultancy, better *thinking*. It is naturally uncomfortable to engage in this kind of conjecture, but the benefits for the presenter are worth it.

A healthy tension for a facilitator to hold is whether or not to engage in go-rounds or open up the discussion popcorn style. In the step for clarifying questions, I encourage facilitators to use the open method due to the intent of the step. For this section, it may be apropos to start with rounds on the first several prompts. If desired, a back-and-forth conversation could occur toward the end of the time for this step. Presenters enjoy hearing a diversity of feedback at first. Facilitators who use the popcorn method initially report hearing the group perhaps getting stuck in one way of thinking. Since there isn't a spot to check in with a presenter in Consultancy, it is important to use facilitator moves that proactively help the group not get stuck. It also may be a function of group size. I tend to use more go-rounds in larger groups to better plan for voice equity.

Language You Can Borrow: At this point, you might ask presenters to turn so their ear is to the group. See appendix A (page 219) for more details about this empathetic facilitation move. The following are unique language choices for Consultancy.

To begin this step, we will use the first two guiding questions: What did we hear? And what didn't we hear which might be relevant? We will start this stem in go-rounds, where one person says one thing, then the person next to him or her speaks, and so on. This helps us ensure equity as [presenter's name] is seeking many perspectives in order to better explore and manage this dilemma. So who will begin using either of the first two questions?

[About one-third of the total time for this step (five minutes) is exhausted.]

We can continue to speak about what we heard or didn't hear, and let's add another option: What assumptions may be at work? Sometimes it feels clumsy or uncomfortable to initially talk about assumptions, so if you'd like a sentence stem to use, one of these may be helpful: An assumption I hold . . . or An assumption I hear . . . So, let's continue in rounds, adding this option.

[About two-thirds of the total time for this step (ten minutes) is exhausted.]

We can add any of the prompts now: what we have heard, what we may not have heard, assumptions, new questions we now have, and even potentially some ideas to consider. We have been taking turns using rounds; now let's take turns in a more organic way. Feel free to discuss openly, building on each other's ideas.

Step 5: Presenter Reflection (Five Minutes)

This step occurs in all four of the foundational protocols in this chapter. Appendix A (page 231) offers insight into this step.

Step 6: Debrief (Five Minutes)

A quick reminder about debriefing. Debriefing is discussing the process of learning for individuals and the groups, not reopening the content that was just discussed. See the introduction (page 1) for more detail as well as possible questions to use to frame a debrief.

Language You Can Borrow: *The debrief is a time to converse about the protocol itself and how we did, not about the content anymore. Remember, we gave it back to* [presenter's name]*! So, how did that go for us today?*

Application Example 1

Vic is one of those teachers who is a sponge for learning. He reads voraciously. He even signed himself up to go to the American Educational Research Association conference because he wants to know what the most recent research says about early childhood education. Now, as an instructional coach, he is not experiencing much success with one prekindergarten teacher named Daphne. After multiple coaching cycles resulting in fidelity to a nationally recognized coaching model, Daphne's practice is still inconsistent. He has spent way too many nights tossing and turning about this situation.

The instructional coaches in Vic's district gather once a month for a day of learning, organized by the associate superintendent. The coaches co-construct the agenda, using many discussion protocols for individual and shared work. Vic volunteers to bring his situation—which, after a preconference with another instructional coach, Joel, he sees as a dilemma—to his peers for them to help him see what he isn't seeing.

Vic isn't short on ideas. In fact, he took a Gallup StrengthsFinder assessment, and ideation is one of his top five. Joel and Vic believe Consultancy may be the best fit for his needs, as this protocol won't provide many more ideas; instead, it will provide Vic with more root cause analysis.

Throughout the discussion protocol, Vic has several moments that are uncomfortable—in particular, the time spent around assumptions. Vic perseveres through the tension, resisting the urge to respond to the group, knowing if he does, the conversation they are having would never occur.

When Joel invites him back to the group to reflect, Vic is a bit overwhelmed. He doesn't have his next steps yet, nor does he need them. Instead, his thinking is significantly moved, realizing his method of approaching Daphne was colored by some of his previous experiences. His commitment to moving forward is to surface that bias, acknowledging it in his coaching.

Application Example 2

Claudia is a family engagement specialist at a high-needs school in an urban district. Her 90/90/90 school, as the principal reminds the staff, is certainly challenging, and she enjoys (almost) every minute of it. It has successfully partnered with a local health organization, which now sponsors a clinic on site. Cultural events are well attended, the most recent being the fifth-grade steel drum band performance celebrating Cinco de Mayo.

Unfortunately, sessions on parenting have been, at best, a bust. Others have assured her the marketing is logical and timely. The topics seem to be aligned to what teachers see as needs. Free food is always a draw. The parenting sessions are an important part of the school improvement plan, and she is feeling pressure to make sure participation is high. In fact, she wonders just a bit about her job security if this doesn't change.

The student and family engagement team meets every month, as per the Title I plan, so Claudia places this item on the agenda. Danielle, the assistant principal, agreed to facilitate for her. In their preconference, Claudia initially says she just needs more ideas, but Danielle keeps paraphrasing Claudia's words. Eventually Claudia realizes this may be more than just a deficit of ideas. Although she believes she knows this school community intimately, as she lives within its attendance zone, perhaps she has been blinded by something else? They choose a Consultancy protocol.

Many team members are community partners (for example, the clinic liaison, a tutoring coordinator from a local church, and the after-school organizer), and Danielle strategically plans for members who not only haven't used a Consultancy protocol but may have never been part of any discussion protocols before.

Danielle's opening takes more time than she had expected, as she gives more detail about each step, making sure she is clear about each person's job as they progress. A few times, some of the community members want to step in, but Danielle gently asks them to hold their thinking for a bit.

Danielle scaffolds the probing questions, giving time to write, share with a partner, and then offer to Claudia. Although she forgot to copy the *Pocket Guide to Probing Questions* (see appendix C, page 240), they quickly turn on technology and project the sentence stem ideas. The questions are clearly probing as Claudia often tips her head, looking up to the ceiling before doing some of her thinking aloud.

When it comes time for the discussion step, Danielle says, "Claudia, may we take this dilemma from you for a few moments?" to which Claudia replies, "Yes, please!" The group has a much-deserved laugh and then immediately reverts to the serious processing Claudia needs.

A short time later, Claudia swivels her chair back to the group, noticeably relieved. Smiling, she gives a heartfelt thanks to the group, and even before Danielle can say anything, starts to offer her reflections.

Danielle begins the debrief with, "So, how did that go?" The group clearly notes how the disciplined conversation yielded a fruitful result. In fact, the conversation was much richer than if she had asked for more ideas about how to increase the parent participation in sessions. Another member poses the idea that future agendas could be streamlined to allow time for this kind of collaboration to occur more often.

Descriptive Consultancy

Descriptive Consultancy is a unique variation of the Consultancy protocol originally developed by Nancy Mohr (McDonald et al., 2013) and revised by Connie Zimmerman Parrish and Susan Westcott Taylor (2013). The original Consultancy asks participants to avoid developing or posing any specific next actions for the presenter to consider. Descriptive Consultancy, on the other hand, has a dedicated step for brainstorming ideas, but only after the participants have a robust understanding of the dilemma, both using the words of the presenter and their own words. *Ideas* is the one-word descriptor for Descriptive Consultancy. I present here my own adaptation.

Expanded Supports for Descriptive Consultancy

Figure 5.4 shows the anchor chart you can post for the Descriptive Consultancy protocol.

Purpose: To ensure a robust understanding of the dilemma before offering ideas	
Sequence:	
1. **Presentation**	Less than ten minutes
2. **Clarifying Questions**	Five minutes
3. **Description: What?** *I heard . . .*	Four to six minutes
4. **Interpretation: So What?** *An assumption here might be . . .* *What could be under this . . .* *What might be going on . . .* *A possible root cause . . .* *Something I'm thinking . . .*	Four to six minutes

Figure 5.4: Descriptive Consultancy anchor chart.
continued →

5. **Presenter Check-In**	Two minutes
6. **Evaluation of Next Steps: Now What?** *What if we . . .* *We might . . .*	Five to seven minutes
7. **Presenter Reflection**	Five minutes
8. **Debrief**	Five minutes

Visit **go.SolutionTree.com/leadership** *for a free reproducible version of this figure.*

Scaffolded Steps for Facilitators

These multiple levels are analogous to DIE, explained in detail in chapter 4, "Protocols to Seek Perspective" (page 113). Steps 3, 4, and 6 correlate to description, interpretation, and evaluation.

Step 1: Presentation (Less Than Ten Minutes)

Appendix A (page 219) offers insight into this step.

Language You Can Borrow: In addition to the possible language choices in appendix A, the following could be helpful choices for a facilitator to use in a Descriptive Consultancy.

- *After we ask clarifying questions, we enter the first step, description. We will read from our notes so our presenter can make sure [preferred pronoun] communicated the dilemma clearly. Next, we will engage in probably the most important step, interpretation. This will be helpful for our presenter to truly think about this dilemma, hopefully in a new way.*

- *We might be wrong at some point during the interpretation—if so, we don't need to be worried because step 5, Presenter Check-In, exists. Our presenter will let us know if we are far afield. At that point we can borrow the work from [preferred pronoun] and offer specific ideas. We call that step evaluating next steps. Then, [preferred pronoun] can turn to the side so [preferred pronoun] ear is to the group, listening but not feeling like it's necessary to affirm every idea.*

Step 2: Clarifying Questions (Five Minutes)

Appendix A (page 221) offers insight into this step.

Step 3: Description—What? (Four to Six Minutes)

Appendix A (page 225) offers insight into this step.

Step 4: Interpretation—So What? (Four to Six Minutes)

Appendix A (page 227) offers insight into this step.

Step 5: Presenter Check-In (Two Minutes)

Appendix A (page 229) offers insight into this step.

Step 6: Evaluation of Next Steps—Now What? (Five to Seven Minutes)

Appendix A (page 230) offers insight into this step.

Step 7: Presenter Reflection (Five Minutes)

Appendix A (page 231) offers insight into this step.

Step 8: Debrief (Five Minutes)

A quick reminder about debriefing. Debriefing is discussing the process of learning for individuals and the groups, not reopening the content that was just discussed. See the introduction (page 1) for more detail and for possible questions to use to frame a debrief.

Language You Can Borrow: *The debrief is a time to converse about the protocol itself and how we did, not about the content anymore. Remember, we gave it back to* [presenter's name]*! So, how did that go for us today?*

Application Example 1

What a great problem to have—involved parents! However, Joshua is at his wits' end when it comes to the president of the band boosters, Karen. She brings support to a whole new level. Every time Joshua turns around, Karen is there *helping*. Sometimes the help actually is helpful; other times, Joshua is hoping for some breathing space.

Joshua has joked with Karen about her continual presence. He collects a bit of data about the frequency of her visits to the band room. He even talks to her about the situation, in terms he thinks are direct. Whenever she is there, Joshua finds himself unable to think straight—in a rehearsal, on the marching band practice field, and even in his office.

He knows Karen's work output is massive and appreciates the volume of what she can accomplish—thus the tension. He wants to figure out how to set an appropriate boundary without pushing her away.

Other fine arts teachers could relate to this dilemma because many of them have a boosters club, too, so he asks Kendra, the department chair, for some time at the next meeting. When he describes to her what he wants, Kendra asks, "It sounds like you want ideas. Are you fine with that—if we just, in essence, Pinterested all over you?" After a good laugh, Joshua is about to say yes, but instead asks, "Can I be honest?" After an affirmative nod from Kendra, Joshua adds, "I don't think it's just about ideas. Yes, I want to leave with a few ideas, but I think I'm stuck because of what I think about her and the situation. I probably need some help figuring out what I *don't* know."

Kendra volunteers to facilitate a Descriptive Consultancy protocol at the next department meeting for Joshua. Kendra explains a bit more during step 4, interpretation, because she is worried the group will immediately jump to idea generating. Her lead-in has an important impact, as one of the most important things Joshua hears is when one of his colleagues points out, "A possible assumption might be we know why she is hanging around so much. In fact, her presence may be less about us than we think."

Overall, the protocol goes very well. Joshua leaves with better thinking *and* a few ideas. During the debrief, Kendra hears the orchestra teacher say on the way out to another colleague, "Now *that's* what our department meetings should be like."

Application Example 2

Corinne craves feedback. She wanted it as a classroom teacher but didn't often receive it. Now that Corinne is an assistant principal, the principal has recognized her need for productive feedback and obliges her—often.

Now Corinne has turned her sights to the seventh-grade teachers. No matter how she frames the classroom observational feedback, it doesn't seem to quite land. She's starting to think the dilemma includes contributing behaviors on her end and associated behaviors on their end.

Corinne thinks long and hard about with whom she might collaborate about this dilemma. After coaching from her principal, she decides to ask the four seventh-grade collaborative team leads. Corinne wants to keep the circle small for this experience, so she starts planning to be the presenter and the facilitator. However, she quickly realizes it will be very difficult to meet the responsibilities for both jobs simultaneously. Pam, the media specialist, completed a facilitation training last summer, so Corinne asks her to serve as facilitator.

As Corinne and Pam preconference, Corinne is quite focused on which discussion protocol will best meet her goal. Corinne had been part of a professional development session where another principal used the Consultancy protocol. Pam has come prepared and focuses the conversation more on the dilemma question (purpose first, then protocol). They draft the question many times, starting with Corinne-first iterations (What might I do to help teachers want feedback?) and resulting in a larger, more culture-focused question (What would have to change for our seventh-grade team to productively give and receive feedback?). Only then do Pam and Corinne delve into choosing a discussion protocol.

Time becomes one of the deciding factors. Pam recommends Descriptive Consultancy, as she thinks it has all the necessary components, some gentle pushing against Corinne's assumptions, a check-in to make sure the teachers are on a productive track, idea generating, and, critical in this situation, a time frame of forty minutes.

The teachers are a bit hesitant in the first part of the protocol—as one of them says in the debrief, "I wasn't sure if this was a trap—just a way for Corinne to get information out of us." The important shift for them is step 4, interpretation. One teacher mentions, "I really felt like we were trying to think this through. It was hard! It wasn't just a brainstorm of a bunch of lofty ideas which wouldn't be implemented anyway." Corinne leaves renewed—her desire for feedback definitely filled.

Issaquah

Educators often ask about the namesake of the Issaquah protocol, thinking there may be some cultural connection to indigenous people. Although the word *Issaquah* does, in fact, have indigenous origins, the naming of the protocol comes from the original developers, Nancy Mohr, Debbie Bambino, and Daniel Baron (n.d.), who were in Issaquah State

Park, Washington, at the time they developed the protocol. The present version is my own adaptation. *Coaching* is the one-word descriptor for Issaquah.

Expanded Supports for Issaquah

Figure 5.5 shows the anchor chart you can post for the Issaquah protocol.

Purpose: To coach a presenter to think deeply	
Sequence:	
1. **Presentation**	Less than seven minutes
2. **Clarifying Questions**	Three to five minutes
3. **Description: What?** *I heard . . .*	Four to six minutes
4. **Interpretation: So What?** *What this might mean . . .* *What might be under this . . .* *A possible assumption . . .* *Something I'm thinking . . .*	Five to seven minutes
5. **Presenter Check-In**	Two minutes
6. **Interpretation: Probing Questions**	Ten minutes
7. **Presenter Check-In**	Two minutes
8. **Evaluation of Next Steps: Now What?** *We could . . .* *What if we . . .*	Ten minutes
9. **Presenter Reflection**	Five minutes
10. **Debrief**	Five minutes

Figure 5.5: Issaquah anchor chart.

Visit go.SolutionTree.com/leadership for a free reproducible version of this figure.

Scaffolded Steps for Facilitators

Like Descriptive Consultancy, Issaquah is built on DIE—just like a coaching conversation. Issaquah is slightly longer, adding two steps. These steps 6 and 7, Probing Questions and the corresponding Check-In, provide a second opportunity within the protocol for participants to engage in interpretation.

Step 1: Presentation (Less Than Seven Minutes)

The Issaquah protocol has ten steps. If a facilitator talks about each step at length as the protocol begins, the group will lose its focus and engagement. For this particular process, I sometimes point toward the chart and offer the group fifteen seconds to read the steps, and then we move on.

Appendix A (page 219) offers additional insight into this step.

Language You Can Borrow: In addition to the possible language choices in appendix A, the following could be helpful choices for a facilitator to use in Issaquah.

In this structure, we will slow down our gut response to offer ideas. We begin with hearing from our presenter, then following up with any clarifying questions we might have. Next comes a what, so what, now what framework. These coaching behaviors first use the exact words from [presenter's name], *then use our own words to offer possible interpretations.*

We will quickly check in with [presenter's name] *to make sure we are on the right track. A step called Probing Questions stretches out the interpretative step. We will use a resource to help us craft the very best questions for* [presenter's name]. [Preferred pronoun] *will listen to our questions and decide which one or two questions really helps* [preferred pronoun] *think the most.*

Finally, we will use that question to guide our now what? or idea-generating step. [Presenter's name] *will gift us this dilemma for a while, then take it back to offer a reflection. As with all protocols, we end with a debrief of the process.*

What questions do you have about these steps before we begin?

Step 2: Clarifying Questions (Three to Five Minutes)

Appendix A (page 221) offers insight into this step.

Step 3: Description—What? (Four to Six Minutes)

Appendix A (page 225) offers insight into this step.

Step 4: Interpretation—So What? (Five to Seven Minutes)

Appendix A (page 227) offers insight into this step.

Step 5: Presenter Check-In (Two Minutes)

Appendix A (page 229) offers insight into this step.

Step 6: Interpretation—Probing Questions (Ten Minutes)

Probing questions are a critical step in using the Issaquah protocol, similar to the Consultancy protocol. Thus, the white space learning for both protocols and most of the Language You Can Borrow have been consolidated into appendix A (page 219).

Language You Can Borrow: In addition to the possible language choices in appendix A, the following could be helpful choices for a facilitator to use in Issaquah.

It's about time to have our gift-giving session with [presenter's name]. *In Issaquah, the asking of the questions, rather than the answers, is the gift. In fact, in this developmental coaching sequence, please ask a question and then pass in your sticky note. We won't note the reaction nor response to each question. Instead, [presenter's name] will collect the questions, then respond in the next step. [Presenter's name], you might find it helpful to start creating some categories of these questions as they are handed to you. The categories might be topical or content related, or you might make groupings of which questions really made you think the most. After we hear the first question, we will proceed to the left, one question at a time. Who will begin?*

[Ten minutes]

Our time for this step has ended, but right now you can still hand in any questions you didn't ask. They are still potential fodder for [presenter's name]'s thinking.

Step 7: Presenter Check-In (Two Minutes)

Issaquah has a second time to check in with the presenter; both check-ins occur after interpretive steps. The originally developed protocol does not have an explicit purpose for this step. The directions read, "Which question was the one that made you think the hardest? Why?" (Mohr et al., n.d.). It could appear almost like a game show for the presenter—which question will they choose?

Instead, the step can be set up for multiple benefits: for the presenter, to engage in some deep thinking about the dilemma and possible blind spots, but also for the participants. When a presenter chooses a probing question, the question can become a platform from which to generate ideas in the next step, Evaluation of Next Steps: Now What? Some ideas a participant may have developed earlier may no longer be as aligned to the presenter's current thinking.

It is fine if presenters need a minute or so to organize their thoughts. They may have fielded a fair number of sticky notes! Then the response should be brief. They have a choice whether or not to actually answer the question; it is enough to just read aloud the most provoking question.

Language You Can Borrow: *So, [presenter's name], we have offered several gifts, and it's time for us to hear a reaction. Rather than talk about each one, which question or category of questions is causing the most thinking?*

Step 8: Evaluation of Next Steps—Now What? (Ten Minutes)

Appendix A (page 230) offers insight into this step.

Step 9: Presenter Reflection (Five Minutes)

Appendix A (page 231) offers insight into this step.

Step 10: Debrief (Five Minutes)

A quick reminder about debriefing. Debriefing is discussing the process of learning for individuals and the groups, not reopening the content that was just discussed. See the introduction (page 1) for more detail as well as possible questions to use to frame a debrief.

Language You Can Borrow: *The debrief is a time to converse about the protocol itself and how we did, not about the content anymore. Remember, we gave it back to [presenter's name]! So, how did that go for us today?*

Application Example 1

Susan is a risk taker. She has plowed a tough row as a female superintendent in the southern United States. Although she is not afraid to make decisions, she also acknowledges when it is important to bring others into the decision-making process.

A potentially important piece of state legislation has been recently passed, and the state department of education is still working on creating the corresponding rules and procedures. On paper, Susan thinks the district could be a good match for the innovation that is now permissible. In preparation for a conversation she needs to have with the school board, she chooses to use a regularly scheduled administrative staff meeting to gather feedback.

Originally, Susan thought a large-group open conversation might be in order, as she wants to make sure no one is feeling pressure to agree with her. The more she thinks about it, the more concerned she grows that she may not hear honest opinions. With that in mind, she chooses Issaquah to structure the conversation.

Susan knows it will not be easy nor wise to be both the presenter and the facilitator. In fact, it may prevent her goal of her staff members from speaking honestly. Trevor, the associate superintendent, volunteers to facilitate. In planning for the Issaquah, he knows strategic grouping will be an important factor. Although he could make specific groups, naming specific leaders in each group, instead, he chooses to explicitly share the rationale with the group. After explaining why he thinks heterogeneous groups will be important, he asks his colleagues to make sure each group of three to four leaders includes three perspectives: (1) building leader, (2) central office instructional leader, and (3) central office operational leader. Satisfied with his explanation, the seven building principals and twelve central office leaders create their groups.

Facilitating for his supervisor is proving trickier than Trevor thought it would. When Susan answers a clarifying question, she often continues talking, adding much more detail than what the asker desired. During step 3, Description: What? Susan wants to immediately redirect any slight misunderstanding of the context.

After using several prompts Trevor thinks are subtle, he notices a slight smirk from a few of his central office colleagues. He begins to worry Susan will start to notice, too, thus negatively affecting the possible impact of the discussion protocol.

After Susan wants to respond to the first probing question, Trevor chooses to make his discomfort public, saying, "This is more difficult than I expected. Sitting in this seat when you [referring to Susan] are sitting in that seat makes it difficult for me to know when to intervene. I want to make sure we are honest; with no appearance I am trying to censor anyone. At the same time, I know these discussion protocols are intentionally designed so that learning is a running dialogue in my head, too. I will do my best, and I welcome your help toward our goal."

The risk pays off with Susan and Trevor's colleagues. The rest of the protocol proceeds smoothly, including raw, honest moments when Susan hears some leaders questioning the district's readiness for such a radical innovation.

At the end of the protocol, Susan genuinely thanks the group, and shares the notes she will bring to the board later that month. Notwithstanding the critical feedback the protocol brings forward, perhaps more important is the debrief. The team members note they were better able to tolerate risk this time. They are creating a culture where they can have difficult and productive conversations.

Application Example 2

James has seen it all, or so he thought. He has said that so many times in his career. When he transitioned from teacher to department chair, he was surprised to find other teachers didn't teach like he does. When he became an assistant principal, he was again surprised other departments didn't run things like he does. The line of incredulity continued as he progressed through other positions, principal, executive director, and assistant superintendent.

Now retired from full-time school leadership, James works for an external agency, providing principal mentoring and support. In this part-time role, James coaches eight current building principals in two different school districts. The job hours are appealing, the commitment level is just right—he generally feels quite successful.

Once each quarter, he and other principal mentors gather. After various business items, the team provides space for one principal mentor to bring forth a puzzling issue or a conundrum. James raises his hand.

Seven of the eight sitting principals on James's caseload respond well to James and his style. They have provided anecdotal feedback to James and the program director about how they don't see James as an extra task or meeting. Alexa is not one of those principals.

Alexa has resisted James's support from the onset of their meeting, and all of James's attempts have been unsuccessful. In fact, several of his attempts didn't get off the ground, as Alexa frequently does not return his phone calls, texts, and emails.

James chooses Issaquah to support his coaching needs. The six other coaches, collectively with just over one hundred years of principal experience, waver in their fidelity to the process, often wanting to jump to offering ideas. Jessica, the program director, holds fast, often joking with them, "We're not at step 8 yet . . ."

Her steadfastness yields productive results. During step 6: Probing Questions, one of James's colleagues asks, "As you and Alexa are different people, what have you assumed is not part of the dilemma, but you may have been too cursory in eliminating that potential factor?" James chooses to reflect that question back to the group in step 7: Presenter Check-In, offering his risky thinking as he says, "I believe race may be a factor in my perceived inability to connect deeply with Alexa."

With this insight, the principal mentors meet the challenge of identifying possible ideas, but only for the few minutes Issaquah offers. During step 9: Presenter Reflection, James profusely thanks the group members for their thinking and ideas, and knows the process, due to the willingness of his colleagues to show fidelity to the steps, will make a significant difference in his approach to working productively with Alexa.

Peeling the Onion: Defining a Dilemma

The Peeling the Onion protocol was developed by Nancy Mohr (McDonald et al., 2013), and I have adapted it to its present form. Peeling the Onion has a unique position in the dilemma family of discussion protocols. It contains some similar steps to the other members of this family, but the purposes of using the protocol are different, which leads to an important optional step near the end. The subtitle of this discussion protocol is quite informative: Defining a Dilemma.

There are two times when Peeling the Onion may be particularly helpful. First, a potential presenter may have difficulty determining a dilemma question. In a preconference, it might sound something like this.

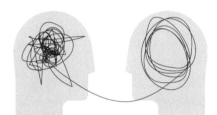

Thomas:	We used the four criteria to identify that you have a dilemma. Now we need to craft a dilemma question—something the group will use to focus its efforts. Do you have one on the tip of your tongue, or might you want to hear what I have as a possible draft?
Emily:	I'd like to hear yours.
Thomas:	Perhaps your dilemma question is something like, How might I develop a shared responsibility among departments regarding the strategic plan?
Emily:	Hmmm. That seems like it's part of it, but not quite right.
Thomas:	Here's another that is bubbling in my mind: What might be at the heart of why the strategic plan doesn't seem to have clear and dedicated ownership?
Emily:	That's good, but . . . I'm not sure that is really it either.
Thomas:	Would you like to hear another, or do you have a suggestion?
Emily:	I honestly don't know—let's hear another.
Thomas:	What conditions exist in our organization around strategic planning?

| Emily: | That's interesting, but—I guess I just don't know. Am I doing this wrong? |
| Thomas: | Not at all! This indicates to me we aren't quite sure how to name the dilemma. Guess what? There's a protocol for that! |

Emily is quite certain she has a dilemma, but even with a preconference, she is unable to sign off on the dilemma question. The fog she is in is palpable—as *fog* is the one-word descriptor for Peeling the Onion.

The second situation where Peeling the Onion may be helpful is if presenters are unsure if they really want better thinking (Consultancy), ideas (Descriptive Consultancy), or coaching to action (Issaquah). The scaffolded steps for Peeling the Onion later in this chapter include an optional step in which the presenter can decide whether to pursue further ideas.

Expanded Supports for Peeling the Onion

Figure 5.6 shows the anchor chart you can post for the Peeling the Onion protocol.

Purpose: To truly understand the complexity of a dilemma before attempting to offer solutions	
Sequence:	
1. **Presentation**	Less than ten minutes
2. **Clarifying Questions**	Five minutes
3. **Discussion Rounds** *I heard . . .* *An assumption I hear . . . or An assumption I hold . . .* *A question this raises for me . . .*	Fifteen minutes
4. **Presenter Check-In**	Five minutes
5. (Optional) **Presenter and Group Discuss Possibilities Together** *We might . . .* *What if we . . .*	Five minutes
6. **Debrief**	Five minutes

Figure 5.6: Peeling the Onion anchor chart.

*Visit **go.SolutionTree.com/leadership** for a free reproducible version of this figure.*

Scaffolded Steps for Facilitators

After the group offers several rounds to assist the presenter in better exploring the dilemma, the facilitator checks in with the presenter. In this check-in, the presenter has a choice to make: ask the group to engage in the next idea-generating step or do not ask. The Peeling the Onion protocol acknowledges that after a presenter gains clarity about a dilemma, it *may* or *may not* be productive to ask the group to generate ideas. I have presented using this protocol and graciously passed on the idea-generating step. After the group helped me better understand the dilemma, I wanted space and time to generate and implement my own ideas. I would have appreciated their ideas; however, it didn't match my needs in that moment.

Step 1: Presentation (Less Than Ten Minutes)

Of all the dilemma-based protocols, Peeling the Onion is the one where presenters may be the most confused—they might say, "Did I already say that?" or "I feel like I'm talking in circles." This protocol is often chosen because presenters aren't quite sure what to name the dilemma—they appear to be in a fog due to the complexity of the situation. They may inadvertently be using the first step to try and name it, rather than allowing the protocol and the group to do some of that heavy thinking for them.

Language You Can Borrow: In addition to the possible language choices in appendix A (page 219), the following could be helpful choices for a facilitator to use in a Peeling the Onion protocol.

- *Peeling the Onion seeks to help our presenter understand the complexity of a dilemma before trying to find next steps. In other words,* [presenter's name] *is in a dilemma, however,* [preferred pronoun] *may not be quite clear what the dilemma completely entails or encompasses.* [Presenter's name] *understands a great deal of the dilemma, but is here to better understand it, not necessarily solve it.*

- *We will peel away the layers (hence the name of this protocol) of this dilemma today.* [Presenter's name] *will be silent, taking notes as these layers are pulled away.*

Step 2: Clarifying Questions (Five Minutes)

Appendix A (page 221) offers insight into this step.

Step 3: Discussion Rounds (Fifteen Minutes)

There are usually four segments in this series of discussion rounds that constitutes step 4. The total step lasts fifteen minutes, so a facilitator might divide them equally—just short of four minutes for each step. Because at this point in the protocol Peeling the Onion is less about solving and more about exploring, I tend to give more credence and time to the second and third discussion stems (assumptions and questions). At times, a group might not get to the final stem of "What if . . ."

Another way of organizing the time is to give more time for the probing questions round, as designing effective probing questions is complex. If you choose to do so, consult appendix A (page 219) regarding how you might facilitate similar steps in a Consultancy protocol. An additional resource is in appendix C: Excerpts From the *Pocket Guide to Probing Questions* (page 240).

Language You Can Borrow: In addition to the possible language choices in appendix A (page 219), the following could be helpful choices for a facilitator to use in a Peeling the Onion protocol.

To begin this step, we will begin by starting with the literal. What did we hear? The anchor chart uses "I heard . . ." as our sentence starter. Starting with the literal helps both [presenter's name] *to ensure what* [preferred pronoun] *thought* [preferred pronoun] *communicated is what we heard, and it also ensures we have collective brainpower to make sure we heard everything we need. We will start this stem in go-rounds, where one person says one thing, then the next person speaks, and so on. This helps us ensure equity as* [presenter's name] *is seeking many perspectives to better explore and manage this dilemma. So, who will begin?*

[Transitioning to next round]

If you still have more literal information to add, that is fine, but as we continue to participate in a predictable order, let's add in the next prompt. It may feel uncomfortable talking about assumptions, yours or those others may have, but it is vital to the success of our work today to do so. It may be helpful to think of assumptions as either being heard *or* held. *Notice the slightly different stem options. Starting this round with someone different from the first round, let's keep going.*

[Transitioning to next round]

In this next round, we will ask questions for [presenter's name]. *They are called probing questions. Asking and answering probing questions is a hallmark of this protocol. When leveraged well, these questions channel insight not just for the group but also for the presenter. In fact,* [presenter's name] *may find more value in this round than anything else we do today.*

Probing questions are crafted to be powerful and open. They resist the tendency to assume there is one right answer. Specifically, they do not *recommend. We are often quite good at using questions to recommend others to do something, such as, "Addison, could you take out the trash? Julie, why is the fridge door open?" These sorts of responses are not helpful at this stage in this process. Instead, we want to craft better, more helpful questions.*

A support document called the Pocket Guide to Probing Questions *will be our guide today as we channel our energies toward* [presenter's name]*'s dilemma. Please find the bulleted list near the beginning. These are characteristics of what constitutes a probing question. Take a few quiet moments and scan those bullets, searching for a descriptor that clearly sets the bar for what we want and need our probing questions to accomplish.*

[Time to read]

As you consider the dilemma posed today and our posted question, use the fantastic set of question stems in the Pocket Guide to Probing Questions *document. These stems are extremely helpful as you seek to bring your potential questions to life.*

Think more about the quality *of your questions, instead of attempting to raise the* quantity. [Presenter's name] *will not respond to our questions;* [preferred pronoun] *just gets to listen and reap their depth.*

Who will begin? After we hear the first question, we will proceed to the left, one question at a time.

[If there is time left in this round, then the last prompt may be considered.]

With the few moments left before we give this dilemma back to [presenter's name], we can think together about potentials and possibilities. This can be a back and forth conversation. Who has something now for this fourth bullet, such as, "What if we . . .?" "We might . . ." "A possibility could be . . . "

Step 4: Presenter Check-In (Five Minutes)

Helpful information about the presenter reflection is found in appendix A (page 231). Additionally, in Peeling the Onion, the end of this presenter reflection also requires the facilitator to ascertain whether or not the presenter wants the group to continue into the optional step. This may organically happen, or the facilitator may need to prompt the question.

Language You Can Borrow: [Presenter's name], *as you turn back to the group, please know we got some stuff wrong! We aren't you. Think of yourself like a duck; some of the feedback rolled right off your back, and some of it may have gotten stuck in your tail feathers. Feel free to hold onto what seems helpful; no need to defend anything to us. This step is called presenter* reflection, *not presenter* defense, *or presenter* response. *You now have a few moments to tell us what resonates with you, what, in other words, got* stuck—*what you are leaving thinking the most about. Since you showed discipline by not interrupting us, we won't interrupt you now.*

[If the presenter doesn't move into directing the group]

So, you now get to decide, are you full and just need us to step away so you can do your own thinking, or do you want us to talk for just a few moments about something you heard? What are your druthers?

Step 5: (Optional) Presenter and Group Discuss Possibilities Together (Five Minutes)

Presenters may be happy the group helped push the fog away in order to make the dilemma clear. At this point, they may or may not need the group to offer some ideas in this step. If a presenter chooses to ask the group for ideas, this step can be tricky to navigate. In most protocols with generative steps, presenters are turned away from the group, so they do not need to respond to each idea. This move also helps the participants be bold in their idea generation.

This step in Peeling the Onion invites the presenter to generate ideas *with* the group. The time frame is limited (five minutes) so that fact can help alleviate potential tension. However, I find it helpful to discuss the trickiness of the step with the group.

Language You Can Borrow: [Presenter's name] *asked us to engage with* [preferred pronoun] *in some idea generating. We have a few minutes for this step, so all of our ideas may not end up being shared. Please keep in mind* [presenter's name] *may not respond to every idea, as* [preferred pronoun] *may be writing down the ideas or just plain thinking. So, what ideas do we now have based on what* [presenter's name] *said during the presenter reflection?*

Step 6: Debrief (Five Minutes)

A quick reminder about debriefing. Debriefing is discussing the process of learning for individuals and the groups, not reopening the content that was just discussed. See the introduction (page 1) for more detail as well as possible questions to use to frame a debrief.

Language You Can Borrow: *The debrief is a time to converse about the protocol itself and how we did, not about the content anymore. Remember, we gave it back to* [presenter's name]*! So, how did that go for us today?*

Application Example 1

Julianne is a bit shell-shocked as she walks out of the assistant principal's office. After a colleague quit midyear, she has been named the case manager for a very tricky case, according to her administrator. Julianne has heard the stories about Alissa, but when she sees her in the hall—a bubbly, blonde, blue-eyed seventh grader—Julianne can't believe all those stories are true.

What also makes this situation tricky are Alissa's parents. They fully advocate for Alissa and her unique needs; unfortunately, these moments of advocacy are often at the expense of staff members. Julianne remembers her former colleague frequently being in tears after meetings. One of those meetings even took multiple days.

One bright spot is Julianne's relationship with her former colleague, Kameron. In hearing the news, Julianne calls Kameron for advice. Kameron is very willing to discuss the situation and will even come back to school to talk if it will help Julianne.

Thankful for her willingness, Julianne decides to call a meeting where Kameron and some of Alissa's teachers can help her prepare for an introductory meeting with Alissa's parents.

As Julianne walks through the halls the next day, multiple teachers raise their eyebrows or touch her arm, and one teacher mouths, "Good luck." Julianne then knows she will need to carefully structure this meeting if she wants something productive to emerge. She chooses a Peeling the Onion protocol.

At first, Julianne thinks she would be the obvious presenter, as the current case manager. However, the more she thinks about the process, the more she feels like she doesn't know enough about this dilemma—but Kameron does.

Julianne calls Kameron and tells her about the protocol she is planning. Before Julianne even asks, Kameron volunteers to be the presenter. In Kameron's words, "I would love to get at the root of Alissa's issues. I'm game."

Peeling the Onion is a great choice for the conversation. The teachers who attend don't have a "lightbulb" strategy for Alissa; instead, they are interested in a conversation with colleagues who are also trying to figure her out.

The goal of this meeting is met: to prepare for the next IEP meeting. Julianne leaves the meeting with a potential root cause that could have a positive impact the next time the parents join.

Application Example 2

Kathy is stuck. As a grant writer in a large school district, she has a history of helping people come together. A strong listener, she hasn't had difficulty in the past building consensus with various departments when vying for a grant. Unfortunately, her streak has been broken, and she is not sure why a particular workgroup is so troubling for her.

Over the years, she has developed a network of colleagues who work at different levels (that is K–12, college, and early childhood). They formed a voluntary learning community several years before and work hard to meet five to six times a year at a local coffee shop. In each gathering, one person brings forward an issue with which he or she needs help. Kathy believes her colleagues are strong thinkers and could help her navigate this situation.

Betty, one of the group's members, volunteers to facilitate a discussion protocol for Kathy. In their preconference phone call, Kathy can't quite put her finger on naming the dilemma. Since that is so tricky, Betty suggests using the Peeling the Onion protocol, so the group can help Kathy name what is going on—then Kathy can develop strategies to address the named dilemma.

Kathy is appreciative about bringing her dilemma to the group, but doesn't find affirmation throughout the whole meeting! Her respected colleagues cause some tension in her as they raise possible assumptions she may be making about the work as well as her colleagues. When Betty asks at step 5 if Kathy wants the group to offer some ideas, Kathy says, "Thanks, but no thanks!" and moves into her reflection of her current thinking. The conversation has given her enough to think about, and she doesn't want to consider any pragmatic ideas until she feels comfortable with the true root cause of the dilemma. It feels freeing to be able to make that choice.

Thoughtful Protocol Selection

The matrix in figure 5.7 was originally provided earlier in the chapter with only the first two columns. Now that you have read more of the protocol-specific steps, this expanded version provides more insight as a facilitator and presenter choose a protocol during a preconference. To illustrate, presenters may decide a protocol with probing questions will be helpful for their thinking. They also sense their groups may be potentially sidetracked because the dilemma is important to several participants. Therefore, having a presenter check-in seems important. In that short step, a facilitator turns to the presenter and asks if anything currently being discussed is far afield or unrelated to the dilemma at hand. Once the protocol is chosen, figure 5.7 can benefit the facilitator in looking for any new skills or steps a group may have never experienced. For example, a group may have never used a dilemma-based protocol with probing questions. A facilitator could choose to prep the group prior to the protocol or stop at that step and engage in some skill building.

	One-Word Why	Concrete, Named Dilemma	Probing Questions Asked	Probing Questions Answered	Presenter Check-In	Optional Step: All Generate
Consultancy	Depth	X	X	X		
Descriptive Consultancy	Ideas	X			X	
Issaquah	Coaching	X	X		X	
Peeling the Onion	Fog		X			X

Figure 5.7: Choosing a dilemma-based protocol—Expanded version.

Explore and Manage Dilemmas in an E⁴ Way

I described dilemmas earlier in this chapter as unworkable puzzles or tangled clumps of yarn. When educators face dilemmas of practice, all four Es suffer: efficient, effective, equitable, and excellent.

Efficiency becomes improbable as the group spends valuable time pondering and re-pondering the dilemma. Instead of focused time, it seems every waking hour circles back to the dilemma. Working effectively is difficult when your mind is dragged in different directions. Ask workers who tried to be productive at home with their families during COVID-19! Issues of equity—equity of support, equity of access, and equity of resources—are often embedded somewhere in dilemmas. Finally, groups often do not feel excellence when discussing dilemmas without a protocol (structured conversation) to guide them. Emotions run high when a presenter or facilitator brings a dilemma forward, and emotions often manifest some of our worst group behaviors.

The four foundational protocols discussed in this chapter create productive spaces to explore and manage dilemmas. Three of the protocols have specific steps to generate ideas only after the group has thoroughly dissected the dilemma. Chapter 6 focuses on the generation of ideas—using the collective wisdom of the group to develop multiple options.

6

Protocols to Generate Ideas

Idea-rich websites like Pinterest (www.pinterest.com) or Teachers Pay Teachers (www .teacherspayteachers.com) have shrunk the world of education. Gone are the days of teachers going into one another's classrooms to look in four-drawer file cabinets for ideas about a topic. Electronic tools can be extremely valuable, especially as educators work outside of school hours: at home, at a son's baseball practice, during a daughter's violin lesson, or even in the line at the grocery store.

Teams of educators spend time engaging in collective idea generation, too. Unfortunately, there are limitations in effectiveness and efficiency in many of those interactions. The generative protocols in this chapter are face-to-face experiences that ameliorate those gaps.

Every discussion protocol in this book might produce ideas. A Tuning protocol (chapter 3, page 95) intentionally creates space for cool feedback so presenters can decide how to plug the holes in their written work. Examining running record scores with an ATLAS: Looking at Data protocol (chapter 4, page 128) should create some ideas. Some dilemma-based protocols (chapter 5, page 147) include actions where participants intentionally offer potential next steps.

The generative family honors the desire of educators to desire and accept ideas but only does so after carefully considering the other protocol family options. It is intentional that this family appears in chapter 6, after we have already examined numerous other discussion protocols. Instead of *defaulting* to an idea-generating protocol, this family requires an explicit choice by the presenter: *I want ideas—and that's all I want.*

This chapter contains two foundational protocols: (1) Wagon Wheels and (2) Charrette. Both include expanded supports for facilitators, many of which are found in appendix A (page

232). Both situations that follow would benefit greatly from a discussion protocol described in this chapter.

SITUATION A

Nick prides himself on reaching the tough-to-teach students. He has been a classroom teacher for multiple grades in K–5 and gifted students in a pull-out setting, and now he is an interventionist, mostly in mathematics.

A voracious researcher, Nick can get lost in hours of internet and resource searching, trying to find a strategy that will unlock a learning gap for his students. People know this about him and use him as a resource for their own students who befuddle them.

Nick loves Vanessa as a student. A high-energy third grader, she loves to learn and really wants to do well. Unfortunately, learning does not come easily for Vanessa, and Nick is determined to make sure Vanessa progresses this year.

As part of his determination, Nick has tried various strategies and pathways with Vanessa, most with very short-term results. He has never seen a gap quite like Vanessa demonstrates.

The elementary interventionists meet monthly at one another's schools to compare progress monitoring data and check in on response to intervention practices. Nick is thinking this might be a good opportunity to hear some ideas about what others may think about Vanessa's gap. What he's most worried about is having a never-ending idea-fest. Since he has tried so many things already, he doesn't want to waste his time nor the time of his colleagues.

SITUATION B

Cindy has been given a significant task to transition teachers at her school to standards-based grading. A district study team has met and revised the grading policy. The new board-approved policy comes with a time line for training she needs to enact. As a high school assistant principal, Cindy is used to directives and deadlines, but this one seems particularly tricky.

Although she knows the end result is not flexible, she believes this is a perfect opportunity to differentiate professional development. Having been the administrator of several content departments, she is not only aware of individual teacher differences on this concept but varying content approaches as well.

Thank goodness it is only February, and the professional development won't begin until the summer! District assistant principals meet monthly, and she thinks they might be a perfect group from which to harvest ideas. Some of them work in buildings where they have been piloting standards-based grading, so she is sure they will have important perspectives to bring. She wants to leave the meeting with a basketful of ideas to consider in creating a menu of teacher learning for the summer.

Nick and Cindy both have clarity about what they need: ideas and only ideas. It is possible that later on in the development of their ideas, they may have a document to tune or a dilemma to work through. However, right now, they just want a discussion protocol that helps them meet their request for ideas.

The Protocols

Educators are at risk. I realize that is a hilarious sentence in and of itself. We talk about students being at risk but rarely think of ourselves in those ways. We are at risk of being idea junkies. It seems almost sacrilege for teachers not to say, "Yes," when someone asks them, "Would you like a few ideas?"

Generative in this context means to create, produce, and design. The generated content totally depends on what the presenter asks the participants to generate. As the situations at the beginning of the chapter depict and the application examples later describe, generative protocols are applicable in wide-reaching and diverse situations.

As the book's introduction (page 1) indicates, preconferencing is essential to matching a discussion protocol to the presenter's purpose. Generative protocols raise the explicit question, It sounds like you want ideas—is that all you want? If this answer is in the affirmative, two foundational options exist in this protocol family.

To help understand the main conceptual difference between the two protocols in this family, let's consider probably the number one website people visit when they need some ideas to spark their excitement: Pinterest. Launched in 2010, Pinterest has been a repository of ideas, faves, and likes ever since. Individuals may use Pinterest in their professional lives to curate resources and references, and in their personal lives to remind themselves of what inspires them or even to create a wish list of potential purchases.

Julie, my wife, was a latecomer to Pinterest, probably not beginning to pin pictures and websites until 2017. Once a user, I quickly sensed her use would adversely affect me. At first, she told me about her escapades into the world of fancy stationery, monogrammed apparel, and teaching ideas. However, it grew troubling when she learned how to share certain pins with me. I should have rejoiced in those simpler days.

It started innocuously, with a variety of pins that showed beautiful master bathrooms. Not being savvy enough to know this was a trap, I showed genuine interest, and, you guessed it, eighteen months later, we had a remodeled master bathroom. Don't overlook that this was a major hit to our bank account. This master bathroom example will serve as the perfect extended metaphor for this chapter, comparing the two foundational protocols in this family, Wagon Wheels and Charrette.

Wagon Wheels

The Wagon Wheels brainstorming protocol (SRI, n.d.k) was designed to capture the collective ingenuity and intelligence of a group. I first used a Wagon Wheels protocol in a professional development institute I was leading. My co-facilitator had engaged in a preconference (see appendix B, page 237) and found the participants only wanted ideas. I wasn't sure what protocol would really work—it turned out that Wagon Wheels worked beautifully! It is built on a simple premise: the room is smarter than any one individual person. To the participants, this process feels like a low-risk idea-fest; to presenters, it feels like a huge weight is lifted off their shoulders as they realize they don't have to come up with every possible idea on their own.

Wagon Wheels can feel like a live version of Pinterest. When Julie first started to explore Pinterest for master bathroom remodel ideas, she broadly cast her net, pinning beautiful tile patterns, vanities that looked more like pieces of furniture, curbless showers, and chrome fixtures. She didn't know exactly what we might need, so all ideas were initially potentials.

In a Wagon Wheels discussion protocol, efficiency stems from the group as it helps the pinning process. The presenter poses the situation, the participants gain clarity, and then they let their idea-generating juices flow—all ideas are possibilities, even the ludicrous. Participants keep a written record of their ideas, stop when they don't have any ideas left, and hand their ideas to the presenter, hoping something may be a golden nugget for their colleague.

Pre-Protocol Preparation

The Wagon Wheels discussion protocol has a few unique preparation decisions, one to be made during the preconference and one just prior to the discussion protocol itself.

During the preconference, it is important to consider how the participants will respond to the request for ideas. Perhaps the topic seems more single-faceted, like some of the following.

- I need some ideas about how to start a STEM Night at my school. What are all the logistics I need to contemplate?

- I have forty-five minutes with a school staff right before the December holiday break. What meaningful work might we accomplish, considering their probable frenetic spirits due to the holidays?

- I want my students to show their learning in our current unit of study in a variety of ways. I need some ideas about broad rubric categories because I don't want to create a unique rubric for each product choice.

In single-faceted, idea-generating Wagon Wheels, no modification of the process is necessary. However, sometimes the generative need may best be described in various dimensions or categories.

- For our parent engagement event, I want to have three specific experiences with parents and need ideas in these three areas: (1) parent education topics they may want, (2) ways to help students with homework, and (3) our technology resources they can access at home.

- We have one opportunity to launch a perception survey with our high school students this year. I am looking for questions in these two categories: (1) student-teacher relationships and (2) student-student relationships.

- In creating an agenda for a leadership team retreat, I am looking for short community builders, longer community builders, and some that are more physical in nature.

In these cases, the facilitator will need to approach one step in the protocol sequence differently. In the expanded supports that follow, the term *multiple buckets* indicates these sorts of generative needs.

Physical setup is the second decision that needs to be made. Most discussion protocols featured in this book do not have specific physical or environmental requirements. Wagon Wheels, however, does require some planning about the seating of participants.

The facilitator can set up the chairs for Wagon Wheels brainstorming in one of two ways. Each person needs a chair (other than the presenter and the facilitator). In more open spaces or for small groups, using a setup that resembles a Wagon Wheel works well, as demonstrated in figure 6.1.

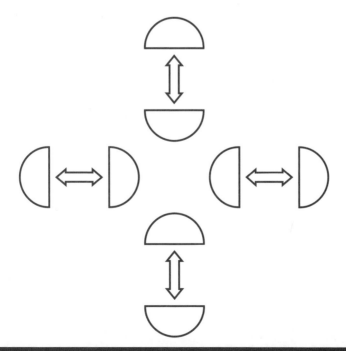

Figure 6.1: Wagon Wheels traditional setup.

The chairs can form multiple wheels, and there is not a particular recommendation for a number for the inside and outside spokes. Place a piece of paper on each chair of the inner spoke of the wheel.

For more narrow spaces or for larger groups, the speed-dating setup, visually represented in figure 6.2, can be more efficient and effective.

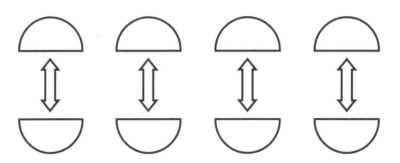

Figure 6.2: Wagon Wheels speed-dating setup.

Choose *one* of the long chair lines and place a piece of paper on each chair.

If an odd number of participants exists, consider creating a conjoined twin pair in two closely grouped chairs. In the situation resembling a wheel, consider having them as an outside spoke as there may be more room on the outside of the wheel. For the speed dating situation, consider having the conjoined twin pair on the chair line that does *not* have paper. In both situations, every time a new brainstorming partner is created, the conjoined twins will move as a unit.

Group size is not an issue for this protocol; it can work with extremely large groups. If it is important to write down all the ideas, large groups might benefit from a technology hack. Consider a one-question Google Form and a QR code that participants can use to document their ideas. Each time a new partnership is formed, a new form is submitted. This way, all the ideas are captured in a Google Sheet and the participants can easily share them, if they desire.

Expanded Supports for Wagon Wheels

The anchor chart for the Wagon Wheels protocol in figure 6.3 could include the following information.

Purpose: To generate more ideas than the presenter could ever need	
Sequence:	
1. **Presentation**	Less than ten minutes
2. **Clarifying Questions**	Five minutes

3. **Generate with a partner**	Two to three minutes
4. **Repeat with a new partner**	Two to three minutes
5. **Assess quantity of ideas left; either repeat step 4 or move to step 6**	Two to three minutes
6. **Hand in ideas**	Thirty seconds
7. **Debrief**	Five minutes

Figure 6.3: Wagon Wheels anchor chart.

Visit **go.SolutionTree.com/leadership** for a free reproducible version of this figure.

Scaffolded Steps for Facilitators

This process can be very engaging and even lighthearted for participants. However, the protocol can also be useful for very serious, urgent issues. Facilitators can model the spirit and intent of the content. For instance, I might not use the speed-dating reference in the protocol setup if the situation was a leadership team generating ideas about how to memorialize a long-standing staff member who has passed. Conversely, I might use that analogy if a department is listing ideas about how to spend time at its annual August retreat.

Step 1: Presentation (Less Than Ten Minutes)

Appendix A (page 232) offers insight into this step.

Language You Can Borrow: In addition to the possible language choices in appendix A, the following could be helpful choices for a facilitator to use in a Wagon Wheel.

[Presenter's name] *needs our help in generating as many ideas as possible about a specific topic. In fact,* [preferred pronoun] *wants more ideas than* [preferred pronoun] *could possibly use. We will use the Wagon Wheels brainstorming protocol to accomplish this outcome. As you come to this area of the room, please bring something to write on and write with. Then select a chair. If you particularly enjoy writing and speaking at the same time, please choose a chair with paper on the seat.*

[After everyone is seated]

Everyone has a job in this protocol. That is, generate ideas. If you sat at a chair with a piece of paper, you have the additional responsibility of taking notes as ideas are exchanged. So, everyone is a generator, and one person is also a writer.

The steps of this protocol, this structured conversation, go like this: first we will hear from [presenter's name] *about* [preferred pronoun] *generative need. Then, because we heard something from* [preferred pronoun]*, we will have a chance to ask a few clarifying questions— questions of fact that are usually simply asked and simply answered. The third step involves us generating ideas with a partner—the person you are currently sitting across from. We will deepen our pool from which to generate ideas by occasionally changing partners. When we have exhausted our ideas, we will be finished. At that point, we will ceremonially pass in our ideas to* [presenter's name]*, and then debrief the process.*

Time for us to hear from [presenter's name]. *You now have up to ten minutes to talk to us about the context and the charge you have for us today. Our responsibility is to take notes if that helps us better understand the context and what we need to do.*

Step 2: Clarifying Questions (Five Minutes)

Appendix A (page 234) offers insight into this step.

Step 3: Generate With a Partner (Two to Three Minutes)

This step seems simple enough, brainstorm some ideas. However, this myopic view doesn't take into account many educators' contexts when they are asked to develop ideas; they then need to implement those very ideas. Rarely would a team of third-grade teachers create a list of ideas without envisioning themselves enacting those ideas. This step asks educators to simply generate the ideas, not judge the veracity of others' ideas nor poke holes in possible implementation. I have found that explicitly raising this difference is a vital step toward ensuring a more fulfilling result for the presenter.

This step also requires the facilitator to remember the preconference decision, single bucket or multiple buckets. If the topic has multiple dimensions or facets, it is important for the participants to be clear on their job for this step.

The original version of this discussion protocol (SRI, n.d.k) articulates five minutes to be spent with each partner, generating and recording ideas. I find that time to be too long; participants tend to either delve too deeply into one idea (not the purpose of Wagon Wheels), or they may veer off course. Five minutes is a long time for two adults to stay focused.

This protocol can feel odd for presenters at times because they may want to walk around and listen in as participants generate ideas. Encourage the presenter to stay away from the group with you at one end of the lines or away from the wheel or wheels. If presenters circulate, the groups tend to want to engage with them to validate their ideas. What results is fewer ideas, which is antithetical to the purpose.

Keep your eyes and ears out for confusion in the first round. This confusion could be as overt as participants raising their hands and wanting to talk to the presenter or as subtle as a set of partners not talking nor writing anything down. It may be helpful to insert a short step of clarifying questions before switching partners.

Finally, in many discussion protocols where a presenter is asking for feedback, I recommend facilitators invite presenters to relinquish their work or dilemma to their colleagues and turn ninety degrees. This move can help the presenter feel less prone to interrupt and redirect the group and can help the participants show more ownership of the borrowed work. In a Wagon Wheel, the ninety-degree rotation isn't necessary, as the presenter is not seated as part of the group. However, I still find it helpful for the group members to assume a point of view where they see themselves as owners of the work, more as *we*, *me*, and *I*, and less *they*, *he*, *her*, or *them*. Language support for this move can be found in appendix A, Discuss and Evaluate Next Steps: A Facilitator Ownership Decision (page 230).

Language You Can Borrow: *It is now time for us to do some generating together.* [Presenter's name], *is it all right for us to borrow this topic from you for a while?* [If yes] *As we now have our charge, a point-of-view shift occurs: we will use different pronouns as we talk—less of the* *following:* they, them, her, she, him, *and* he, *and more of these:* we, our, me, my, *and* I. *This collective ownership not only helps* [presenter's name] *as* [preferred pronoun] *steps out of the conversation, it aids in placing ourselves in* [preferred pronoun] *position, increasing the potential for really thoughtful and helpful feedback.*

We will put some of our ideas on paper. It is important for us to remember the purpose of Wagon Wheels, which is to generate more ideas than [presenter's name] *could ever need. Thus, it is our job to write as many ideas down as we can. What we* aren't *going to do is assess each idea, try to problem solve each idea, or come up with the* best *idea. That is for* [presenter's name] *to do later.*

> ## JUST FOR MULTIPLE BUCKET SITUATIONS:
>
> *Since there are multiple categories for us to generate about, this round will just focus on the first category or dimension, which is _____.*

Writers, please use the piece of paper provided and write your name and your partner's name on the top. Partners, please look at each other, say "Hello!," and begin your first round of generating ideas.

Step 4: Repeat With New Partner (Two to Three Minutes)

Since educators are idea-holics, it also would seem to be bad form for a teacher to say, "I'm out of ideas." Thus, it is important to grant that permission in a Wagon Wheels protocol. What this license offers is not only for educators to admit this outcome but also to not feel obligated to continue regurgitating an idea they have already shared to another partner.

I choose to label this round the *90 percent new round.* It may be impossible for two partners to talk about 100 percent new ideas because they weren't both privy to the previous round, but if they spend a majority of their time generating new ideas, then it serves the presenter's goal.

One method the following Language You Can Borrow offers is asking the writer to render a quick synopsis of previous ideas. That, combined with the non-writer's memory of the previous round, gets this round directed toward new ideas rather quickly.

Language You Can Borrow: *Writers, take a quick moment to dot any Is or cross any Ts.* [A few seconds] *Everyone, please thank your partners with their name.*

[If seating arrangement is shaped like a wagon wheel] *Inside spoke writers, please stay put. Outside generators, please stand and move one spoke to your right.*

[If seating arrangement is shaped like two long lines] *Those of you who were writers can stay put. Now, gently push your chair back slightly so extra space appears between you and your former partner. Those of you who did not write, please now stand and move one person to your right. The person on the end without a partner gets to sashay down the middle to find a new partner.*

As you sit down and greet your new partner, writers, please draw a line across your paper to separate the ideas, then write your name and your new partner's name. [Time] You now have a new partner. If this were a speed dating environment, you might have a tendency to say the same thing over and over again until you have chemistry with someone! Instead, here we have a different goal: let's call this the 90 percent new round. If you already shared an idea and it was recorded, have faith it will be considered. You do not need to resurrect it over and over again with each new partner. We can resist the one-hit wonder tendency.

To help with this goal, when we begin, we will ask the writers to offer a very brief rundown of the ideas already recorded. Look at your partner and say, "Well, hello there!"

Step 5: Assess Quantity of Ideas Left (Two to Three Minutes)

Without a clear reminder of why a presenter wants Wagon Wheels, a well-meaning facilitator may make a classic mistake and have participants keep meeting new partners until they have talked to every other participant. That makes sense, right? We must be out of ideas by then! Having used this protocol once with over 125 teachers in a cafeteria, I saw the fear in their eyes the second time I asked them to move to a new partner. I soon learned it was important to clearly indicate to the group when a Wagon Wheel will be finished.

The Language You Can Borrow at step 1 indicates this ending with *When we have exhausted all of our ideas, we will be finished.* However, at that juncture, the participants may not have been concerned about the end of the protocol because it had yet to begin. At this point, participants start to care—about the efficiency and their own effectiveness.

Since a Wagon Wheels protocol ends when the participants are out of ideas, it makes sense to check on their progress toward that end. A facilitator could do that in a variety of ways—one visual method from the Language You Can Borrow may be helpful for this step.

Once those data are collected, a facilitator needs to choose whether to continue with another round or stop. Having facilitated upwards of one hundred Wagon Wheels, I can safely say educators underestimate their idea-generating powers. Early in my facilitation experience, I would ask the group members if they had any ideas left, and if they said they didn't, we stopped. I made a change in a Wagon Wheel when a presenter was particularly concerned she wouldn't get one workable idea from the group. When participants said they didn't have any ideas left, I said, "Excellent. Let's find one last partner—just half the time." A collective groan ensued, participants moved, and we started the timer again. During the debrief of that protocol, it didn't take long for someone to say, "I hate to say it, but I'm surprised. I was not thrilled we were going for an extra round at the end because I was out of ideas . . . turned out, I wasn't." Her sentiment is common, and for that reason, I now employ the one-last-half-round decision quite often. Additionally, this decision matches the purpose of Wagon Wheels, which is to generate more ideas than the presenter could ever need.

It is hard to know how many times a group may need a formative check-in. It could be the group is empty at the first juncture, leading the facilitator to engage one last round. A facilitator also may gauge other factors.

- Excitement

- Flourish of pens or clicking of keys as ideas are generated

- Volume of talk all the way through the two to three minutes

Based on indicators like these, the facilitator may choose to *not* check in until a later round.

Language You Can Borrow: *Writers, take a quick moment to dot any Is or cross any Ts.* [A few seconds] *Everyone, please thank your partners with their name.*

Before we proceed, let's check on our progress. Imagine you had a glass full of ideas, and you can use your thumb and forefinger to show how full your glass was when this protocol began. [Show with your hands as in figure 6.4.] *Please, everyone now show your glass—how full is it now? Our goal is to evaporate every idea out of our glasses because that is our charge from* [presenter's name].

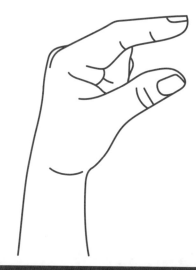

Figure 6.4: How full are you?

[If seating arrangement is shaped like a wagon wheel] *Inside spoke writers, please stay put. Outside generators, please stand and move one spoke to your right.*

[If seating arrangement is shaped like two long lines] *Those of you who were writers can stay put. Now, gently push your chair back slightly so extra space appears between you and your former partner. Those of you who did not write, please now stand and move one person to your right. The person on the end without a partner gets to boogie down the middle to find a new partner.*

As you sit down and greet your new partner, writers, please draw a line across your paper to separate the ideas, then write your name and your new partner's name. [Time] *Writers, please start by offering a very brief rundown of the ideas already recorded. First, look at your partner and say, "You come here often?"*

Step 6: Hand in Ideas (Thirty Seconds)

Wagon Wheels is one of the few discussion protocols in chapters 3–6 where a presenter doesn't speak at the end. There is no step called presenter reflection because the presenter doesn't yet know what he or she thinks about the collected ideas. However, this doesn't mean the participants don't want it to happen.

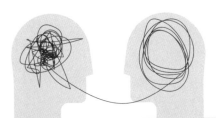

Presenter:	(having just been handed the ideas) *Thank you so much for these! I'm excited.*
Participant:	Well? Tell us what you think? We're dying to know!
Presenter:	Um . . .

Unfortunately, this scenario depicts me early in my facilitation career. Since I did not deeply understand the nuances and potential pitfalls of Wagon Wheels, I was unprepared. I would love to say I rescued this presenter out of this uncomfortable situation, but that isn't true. I was unprepared for this possibility, so after several moments of quiet from the presenter, I simply invited everyone to bring their chairs back to the tables so we could debrief. It was super clunky. The words in the subsequent Language You Can Borrow section offer an explicit way to waylay this prospect.

Language You Can Borrow: *Writers, take a quick moment to dot any Is or cross any Ts.* [A few seconds] *We now get to pass our ideas to* [presenter's name]. *Although* [preferred pronoun] *is very excited to absorb all of these ideas,* [preferred pronoun] *won't—at least not now. Instead, the purpose of Wagon Wheels is to generate more ideas than could ever be used, then leave and ponder. So, please thank your partners with* [preferred pronoun] *name, and let's talk about how this went.*

Step 7: Debrief (Five Minutes)

A quick reminder about debriefing. Debriefing is discussing the process of learning for individuals and the groups, not reopening the content that was just discussed. See the introduction for more detail as well as possible questions to use to frame a debrief.

Language You Can Borrow: *The debrief is a time to converse about the protocol itself and how we did, not about the content anymore. Remember, we gave it back to* [presenter's name]! *So, how did that go for us today?*

Application Example 1

Alejandro is in a rut. He knows it; his students know it. Every time a summative assessment rolls around, he always does the same thing he did the time before. He has told himself the students find comfort in routine, but now he's not so sure the story he is telling himself is actually true.

During the next in-service day without students, groups of teachers are getting together and using discussion protocols to have cross-department improvement sessions. Alejandro signs up to bring an issue or concern to the group. Test reviews are going to be his topic.

Claudia is his assigned facilitator, and they agree to talk during lunch the day before to make sure they have a meaningful plan for their group. As Claudia hears Alejandro's goal for the session, she thinks a generative protocol might serve him (and the group) well.

As part of this protocol preconference, Claudia uses the Preconference Key Words and Actions planner (appendix B, page 237). She asks, "Are you satisfied with ideas—nothing else?" and Alejandro agrees.

In deciding how many ideas might be his goal (*a few* or *a bunch*), Alejandro isn't sure. "I could go with either. Whatever you think is best," he says.

Just like in a coaching conversation, the best advice is usually no advice at all, so Claudia follows up with, "Would you immediately know the idea you want to implement if you heard it?"

"Probably not," Alejandro says after a moment of thought. Wagon Wheels it is, thinks Claudia.

Fast forward. Not only did the Wagon Wheels protocol produce several viable options for Alejandro in his Spanish classes, three group members email him later to ask for copies of the generated ideas, as they are planning for their own content.

Application Example 2

Brenda is a planner. She loves to plan to plan—is even known to write *make a plan* as an item on a checklist about the plan. Thus, she is dumbstruck when Yvette, her assistant principal, reminds her about Family Math Night. It had been completely off her radar, even though she was part of the school improvement team that wrote it into its yearly plan.

The date had been secured at the beginning of the school year, but now there are only four weeks until it takes place—too late to get a committee or workgroup together. Yvette does say Brenda can have a piece of the upcoming faculty meeting to try and elicit some volunteers.

Resisting her normal urge to just plan everything herself, Brenda knows it would be better to avail herself of all the experience in the room. Having been at her school for only one year, her potential planning may be beautifully aligned—just for her previous school. She decides a Wagon Wheel brainstorming protocol would serve three purposes: (1) build ownership from many of the staff members who probably are required to attend the night anyway, (2) get direction toward certain activities and away from others, and (3) create some goodwill with some staff members who tend to find her style too directive.

Yvette is a logical facilitator choice, but instead, Brenda decides to ask Addison, a new grade-level chair who really loved the fourth-grade meeting when Brenda brought Wagon Wheels to their collaborative team. Addison agrees.

Initially, Brenda only thinks she will need help with the kinds of mathematics activities the family members and their students might do during the evening, but during the preconference, as Addison asks simple questions about logistics and communication, Brenda realizes Wagon Wheels could help her on many fronts. They decide to use the multiple buckets approach and ask staff to generate ideas for the following three areas.

1. Big picture agenda (What might be the "big rocks" of the evening?)

2. Specific content for specific grade levels (How and who will decide what content each grade level might feature?)

3. Communication (What are the best ways in our school context to get the word out?)

For the actual protocol, some setup is required. Addison and Brenda have asked Yvette if they could be first on the agenda so the chair setup can take place in advance. Creating wheels of six (three inside and three outside) will work well in the media center. Addison has even asked Yvette to be logistical help, to add or delete chairs to wheels as needed and be a fill-in—joining any Wagon Wheel that has an odd number of people to prevent the conjoined twin situation if at all possible.

Brenda pulls up the meeting slide deck and projects the first slide where she has created a greeting that says, "Please find a chair and mix up our circles so grade levels aren't sitting together. Thanks!" While Brenda is handling their minimal technology needs, Addison places three different colored pieces of paper under the inside circles of each Wagon Wheel. Confused, Brenda asks Addison why she isn't putting the same color with each wheel, to which Addison replies, "I thought we could use a different color for each prompt, making it easier for you to sort the ideas later. Is that OK?"

The Wagon Wheel lasts longer than they anticipated because when Addison checks in two different times during the first prompt, her colleagues still have more ideas to share! It doesn't appear anyone seems to mind as Yvette whispers to Addison and Brenda, "I can't remember the last time I have seen each staff member so engaged. This is good."

Charrette

The Charrette protocol was developed by Kathy Juarez (National Turning Points Center, 2001) of Piner High School in Santa Rosa, California. The most recent revision, by Kim Feicke (2007), is the base I used in my adaptation. *Charrette* is a French word meaning *small cart*. The charrette has two back wheels and two long poles in the front (a quick online image search can be helpful to picture it if necessary). The poles might be tethered to a donkey or a horse, or the poles could be held by a human.

Knowing the etymology of the word *charrette* is extremely helpful for both the facilitator and participants. Since many teacher teams are dominated by talk where the purpose is unclear, without a firm grasp of this backstory, a Charrette can simply turn into generalized brainstorming.

When introducing Charrette to a group for the first time, an extended metaphor is often helpful. Let's imagine Tyese. As her facilitator, I might prepare the group in this way.

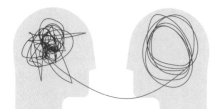

Presenter:

Some of you may not know Tyese is French. Did you know that? She actually is a French peasant woman, living near the Rhine River Valley. She has had a rough go of it, now widowed, living on her farm by herself. All she has to support herself is her farmland.

So, she harvests her fields of cabbages, radishes, and carrots, and loads them in her cart, called a charrette. On Market Day in the local village, she walks the charrette to town, as she is too poor to own a donkey or a horse.

Once in town, she sets her charrette down, and people begin to walk by. What does that look like when people buy produce? What exactly might we see?

Participants:

[Typical responses: examining, holding, shaking, thumping, tasting (a grape!)]

Presenter:

Let's take a momentary break from Tyese's story. My wife grew up on a farm, and she informed me watermelons are ready for eating if you scratch them and just a bit of the rind comes off in your fingernail. Every person decides to interact with fruits and vegetables in different ways.

Now back to Tyese's story. On Market Day, we might see all of those kinds of actions occurring with her fruits and vegetables, and Tyese is OK with this because that's what she expects.

However, there is something unique to the vendors on Market Day in that village. They probably didn't sign a contract to be there or leave at certain times. When Tyese is done with the villagers examining her fruits and vegetables, she will simply leave, take her charrette, and go home. That's what happens in this discussion protocol called Charrette.

This metaphor of Tyese as a French peasant farmer works beautifully when imagining Tyese as an elementary school principal, too. She will bring her current thinking, her work, in a metaphorical charrette and place the charrette in front of the group. The group will take her current thinking, examine it, thump it, scratch it . . . As Tyese steps back from her charrette and her colleagues step closer, she eventually will gain the clarity she needs. At that point, she will thank the group and let them know what she has decided.

If you have read this chapter from the beginning, you might remember the Wagon Wheels protocol ends when the *participants* are out of ideas because that matches the presenter's goal. In a Charrette, the protocol ends when *presenters* say they know what they are going to do next.

Architects use charrettes in their work, bringing three-dimensional models to each other or groups of constituents, asking for help in a particular area. For instance, an architect might be trying to provide solar power to one area of the house and is stuck on how to do so. A few moments in a Charrette around a conference table in the office might provide the architect just what's necessary to move forward.

Expanded Supports for Charrette

The anchor chart for the Charrette protocol in figure 6.5 could include the following information.

Purpose: To identify and commit to a few next steps	
Sequence:	
1. **Presentation**	Less than ten minutes
2. **Clarifying Questions**	Five minutes
3. **Generate**	About five to twenty minutes
4. **Presenter Next Steps**	Five minutes
5. **Debrief**	Five minutes

Figure 6.5: Charrette anchor chart.

*Visit **go.SolutionTree.com/leadership** for a free reproducible version of this figure.*

Scaffolded Steps for Facilitators

The Charrette is a deceivingly tricky protocol to facilitate. I often experience educators who *love* Charrette when we use it together. They often characterize it as *easy* or *relaxed*. What they don't know in that moment is that I am recovering from the Charrette facilitation! These explanations help facilitators take their job seriously.

Step 1: Presentation (Less Than Ten Minutes)

Appendix A (page 232) offers insight into this step.

Perhaps the most important move a facilitator must make is to ensure the group is clear about what the presenter wants the group to generate. If at the end of the Presentation step, presenters have not explicitly named what they are looking for from the group, ask them.

Language You Can Borrow: *Charrette is a protocol that will help* [presenter's name] *gain the idea or ideas* [preferred pronoun] *needs to move forward on a project. A charrette is a French word for a wheelbarrow or cart. Today* [presenter's name] *is putting some of* [preferred pronoun] *work in* [preferred pronoun] *Charrette and allowing us to work with it for a while. When* [preferred pronoun] *doesn't want us doing that anymore,* [preferred pronoun] *will simply take the Charrette and go home.*

So, here's how this protocol might go. First, we will hear from [presenter's name]. [Preferred pronoun] *will tell us as much as* [preferred pronoun] *can about this situation or idea. After a few minutes of that, we will move to asking a few questions about the project or lesson. At that point,* [presenter's name] *will step out from the conversation and give it over to us to design for a while. When* [preferred pronoun] *gets what* [preferred pronoun] *needs, we will stop and hear* [preferred pronoun] *next steps. What questions do you have that you need to resolve before we begin?*

Please tell us about the lesson or project you wish for us to consider. While [presenter's name] *is talking, we will take detailed notes.*

Step 2: Clarifying Questions (Five Minutes)

In addition to the text in appendix A, the end of the clarifying questions in a Charrette asks the facilitator to ensure the group is clear on what exactly the participants are generating in the Charrette.

In the Clarifying Questions step, the facilitator needs to meet one of the many responsibilities in a Charrette: ensure someone takes a second set of notes in step 2. As participants generate ideas, the facilitator may choose to document the ideas or a participant might volunteer to fulfill the responsibility. Often this can occur with a large piece of sticky paper on a wall or a projected word processor document. At this point in the protocol, the group needs this document to be titled. For instance, see the following examples.

- Shawnda wants some ideas on how to redesign her website so parents have fewer clicks to find the most important information (which she has identified). The title of the poster is *Navigation Ideas for Efficiency*.

- Toby needs a decision on how to organize the administrators' learning team next year. As the executive director of schools, he wants ideas from the current school administrators from around the district about how they might spend their learning time. The title of the poster is *Next Year's Learning Designs for Leaders*.

- Becky has always given a traditional test at the end of her unit on East Asia. She wants something more technology infused. The title of the poster is *Techy Assessments to Be Used Summatively*.

Usually, presenter and facilitator discuss the title during the preconference. However, during the Presentation step, a presenter may end up confounding the goal, perhaps adding irrelevant details or complicated layers. It may take thirty to sixty seconds of dialogue between the facilitator and presenter to ensure the title is what they want *at this point in time.*

Language You Can Borrow: *Before we move to the next step, we want to make sure the group is clear on the focus for this Charrette.* [To presenter] *What exactly do you want us to generate ideas about today?*

Create a title on whatever document will be used to record the ideas in the next step.

Additional language is offered in appendix A (page 232).

Step 3: Generate (About Five to Twenty Minutes)

As the preconference discussion in the introduction (page 1) mentions, and as the "Preconference Key Words and Actions" document (appendix B, page 237) indicates, generative protocols are used when the presenter wants ideas—and that's all they want. The Wagon Wheels protocol certainly meets that criteria with the volume of ideas it produces. Charrette also meets the goal, though with fewer ideas; by the end of the Charrette the presenter is committed to act on specific ideas.

The Charrette protocol is quite unique due to the interplay among the three jobs in this step. Because the goal is to find actionable ideas that prompt the presenter to commit, the presenter is not removed from the conversation for long periods of time, as in protocols in other families (for example, Consultancy, Tuning, or ATLAS). Instead, the facilitator needs to be quite skillful in this protocol, particularly in checking in with the presenter.

The goal of this protocol is to provide ideas, and there are not multiple steps for the participants to arrive at this place. In protocols to seek perspective, the descriptive and interpretive steps provide a foundation for the evaluative step. In protocols to explore and manage dilemmas, participants think in similar ways, sometimes using probing questions. In Charrette, participants immediately jump in with their idea-generating selves.

It is important for a facilitator to provide space for the group to redirect or even reset if the ideas they are constructing are not aligned with the presenter's intended goal. Similarly, a check-in can create more confidence in participants to ensure the presenter is receiving their thoughts productively.

I find the current version of the Charrette protocol (Feicke, 2007) to be unclear about what a check-in looks like or sounds like. If educators hastily read the Charrette protocol, they may even miss this necessity. Offering a presenter three choices during a check-in provides a structure for effectiveness and efficiency.

1. **More of the same:** Most of the ideas are proving helpful for the presenter, and no redirect is necessary. The presenter wishes the group to keep on keeping on.

2. **A refocus:** A presenter might choose to refocus the group if a pivot is necessary—perhaps the group became excited over a few ideas that might not work for sundry reasons, and it is unproductive to talk about them anymore. Or a presenter may have heard a specific idea that he or she would now like the group to operationalize and explore further. A refocus is not a rebuke—instead, it increases efficiency for all group members.

3. **Celebrate and cease:** It is a job hazard for educators to develop many ideas, often more than what is needed. In a Charrette, presenters can call it quits when they have identified actions to which they commit. I surmise many readers right now can identify times when well-intentioned colleagues kept *idea-ing* all over us even though we had given many nonverbal cues (such as looking at phones or stopping writing) and verbal cues (such as saying, "Thanks!" or "That could work" or "I really appreciate those ideas"). We must keep in mind the question, Why continue to offer ideas when the presenter already knows what he or she is going to do?

Check-ins can occur approximately every five minutes. This is not a hard and fast rule: a lull may take place three minutes into the generative step, which could be a ripe opportunity to check in. Or perhaps the facilitator sees the presenter stop writing ideas: those are actionable, observational data that could warrant a check-in! Perhaps the group is becoming dangerously focused on one idea or one vein of ideas. A check-in can prove helpful then, too. I think of five minutes as the maximum amount of time before a check-in.

The protocol poster includes some wiggle room for this step, about five minutes to twenty minutes. Imagine the following.

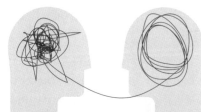

(Five minutes of generating ideas)	
Facilitator:	Kirsten, we would love to check in and see what you need. Here are the three options: . . .
Kirsten:	This is great! I'd love some more.
Facilitator:	All right! Let's keep going!
(Five more minutes of generating ideas)	
Facilitator:	Kirsten, we would love to check in and see what you need. Here are the three options: . . .
Kirsten:	This is great! I'd love some more.
Facilitator:	Glad these are helping. Who's next with another idea?
(Five more minutes of generating ideas)	

continued →

Facilitator:	Kirsten, we would love to check in and see what you need. Here are the three options: . . .
Kirsten:	This is great! I'd love some more.
Facilitator:	Uh . . .

This Charrette can occur, but it is a rarity. Since you would have explained ≥20 earlier in the protocol, the group might generate one last time, letting the presenter know this will be our last hurrah.

Many participants in professional development have described Charrette as *loose*, *conversational*, and *less protocol-y*. Remember our definition of a discussion protocol. It is a structured conversation. Charrette *has* inherent structures—what's different in this discussion protocol is that the facilitator holds most of the responsibility. For instance, in a Tuning protocol, feedback is divided between warm and cool feedback. There's even a step for participants to plan out their varied responses. In an Issaquah protocol, there are several steps, each asking the participants to do a different kind of thinking and responding. Even the Charrette protocol poster looks simple—there are only five steps and none of them have particular sentence stems included. However, Charrette can be deceptively complex to facilitate well. The proficiency lies in the responsibilities.

Embedded in several paragraphs of the original version of Charrette is one critically important sentence: "It is the facilitator's job to help the group stay focused on the requesting team's/individual's questions or issues, observe the Charrette, record information that is being created, ask questions along the way, and occasionally summarize the discussion" (National Turning Points Center, 2001).

You may notice checking in is not even included in this list! I contend the check-in is the most important element that differentiates Charrette from a brainstorming session. The other tasks in the quoted list all help the participants meet the presenter's needs. I accept many of these facilitative actions would help almost any group (using a protocol or not), but these actions are critically important in a Charrette.

The word *job* appears in the quotation, but I believe *responsibility* is more apropos. Facilitators must ensure these actions take place, but it doesn't mean *they* need to personally do the work. For each of the actions listed next, consider whether or not you might give away this responsibility when you facilitate Charrette.

- **Stay focused on the question or issue:** In the Clarifying Questions step, the facilitator is prompted to title the page. Just like in other protocols, the presenter identifies his or her focus (for example, goals in a Tuning or a dilemma question in a Consultancy) and the facilitator makes this focus public by writing out on a whiteboard, posterboard, or projected screen. Charrette is no different. Just saying, "Go—generate some ideas!" will not yield efficiency and effectiveness.

- **Observe the Charrette:** Voice equity is not built into a Charrette. The openness participants feel can also be detrimental to groups that have been relying on a protocol to make sure certain voices don't dominate and others find space to speak. I sometimes draw the group (the table and each person's name in sequential order around the table) in a notebook, and while participants generate ideas, I might place small tally marks next to names to show the quantity of their contributions. If a troublesome pattern emerges, I might use a check-in to make a participation change by saying, for instance, "Now that we've just checked in with Sarah, we have a new focus. Let's use a go-round now, starting with Kendra. We can take twenty to thirty seconds now for each of us to plan what we might say."

- **Record information that is being created:** Although the presenter is taking notes of the ideas participants are generating, it's helpful to have a second set of notes. Sometimes when presenters hear an idea that really has potential, their eyes look up to the right, or they pensively purse their lips—they are starting to operationalize that particular idea, and . . . they are no longer writing anything down. At the end of the protocol, whoever is taking the second set of notes might take a picture of a poster, fold up the document, or email the projected list of ideas to the presenter.

- **Ask questions along the way:** Charrette facilitators are not engaged in group coaching. These questions are not meant to be deep reflective questions that prompt slow responses. Instead, a facilitator might ask factual, implementation-type questions such as, "When might that happen? Who could be involved? Which might make more sense to come first?"

- **Summarize the discussion:** I suspect many of you have been part of a brainstorming session when you or someone else felt overwhelmed. A presenter is not immune from this emotion, and in some ways the presenter may be even more susceptible. Summaries can help presenters, giving them a moment to think. I find a quick summary before checking in can be an opportune time. However, the summaries are not just for the presenter; they can help the participants, too! I sometimes use summaries to help a group hear its patterns. Consider saying something like, "Sorry to interrupt this excitement! Let's take a quick moment to look at our list. It appears we were quite excited about two particular ideas, offering [presenter's name] a few logistical details about those two ideas. Let's check in with [preferred pronoun] now . . ." The check-in here gives the presenter a chance to affirm the group's excitement or redirect its enthusiasm in another direction.

I often feel a bit spent after I facilitate a productive Charrette. As you decide which of these responsibilities you will shoulder, remember the key action of checking in with a presenter. I remember one Charrette experience when I was the presenter and I didn't know my facilitator very well. Thus, I was afraid to advocate for myself. She became invested in the generating of ideas and forgot her important task of checking in. In fact, the first check-in happened after eighteen minutes. By this point, I had settled on an idea, then lost that one and decided on another, went back to the first one, then finally gave up, just writing down everything I heard instead. When she paused the group and asked me, "So, Thomas, now you have three options: more of the same, refocus the group, or have us stop. Which do you need?" All I could muster was, "I have no idea."

I could have stepped in, gently interrupted the group, and asked for a check-in, but I didn't, and I learned a valuable lesson. As a facilitator, I now use a stopwatch and look for five-minute intervals. As mentioned previously, this time is not firm, but it is an acceptable guide. It may be helpful for facilitators to ask for help with timing these intervals in order for them to focus their energy on the other facilitative responsibilities.

Without a clear understanding of a Charrette, some may equate it to brainstorming. These three crucial differences will help facilitators realize how their actions make a Charrette far better than brainstorming.

1. The cardinal rule of many brainstorming sessions is this: *every idea is a good idea.* In a Charrette, that is just not true. The presenter will interject occasionally in a Charrette to help the participants know which ideas are helping the presenter get closer to committed actions.

2. In many brainstorming sessions, everyone in the room is welcome to generate ideas. In a Charrette, group members abide by the distinct jobs, facilitator, presenter, and participants, in a mode of operation reminiscent of many discussion protocols. Presenters, possibly the people most connected and passionate about the topic, step out of the generating step, relying on the group to provide the clarity they have not been able to find on their own.

3. Brainstorming sessions often have unpredictable, much less graceful, methods of ending. In a Charrette, the facilitator and presenter partner together to ensure the group stops when the partner has identified committed actions.

Language You Can Borrow: *We now have a chance to generate ideas on* [presenter's name]*'s behalf.* [Presenter's name]*, if you would be willing to scoot away from the group and turn ninety degrees, that will help us better own the* [lesson or project] *as our own and for you to simply listen to the ideas without feeling like you need to judge each one in the moment. While you are listening, please be sure you have a place to write notes on the promising ideas we offer. Don't fear, we will also document a second set of notes for you.*

Every so often, the group will pause, and we will check in with you to see what you need.

At a check-in, consider saying the following.

This seems like a ripe time to check in with [presenter's name]. *So, you have three options: (1) this is working for you and you would like more of the same, (2) you would like to refocus the group and hear something more specific in a particular area, or (3) you would, frankly, like us to stop talking! You know what you're going to do, and you're ready to tell us about it. What's your choice?*

Step 4: Presenter Next Steps (Five Minutes)

Many discussion protocols in which a presenter is asking for feedback on a personal data set, dilemma, or document include a step where the presenter speaks at the end. The language is specific for that step, the presenter reflection. I mentioned in various places that the word *reflection* is not synonymous with *response* or *defense*.

Notice the language for this reflection step in a Charrette is different. Here it is called Presenter Next Steps. The phrase reminds us a Charrette protocol isn't finished until the presenter has made a commitment to action. The Language You Can Borrow for this step makes sure presenters realize if they choose option 3 during a check-in, that means they are ready to commit.

Since a Charrette feels loose to many participants, it can be tempting for participants to still want to help presenters once they turn back to the group. A reminder about expectations at this point is often helpful.

Even with a gentle (or not so gentle) poke, sometimes well-intentioned educators continue with their brainstorming selves. One strategy I might consider in those moments is implementing a delay tactic. You might say, "It appears there is still excitement and enthusiasm about this topic! Let's debrief the protocol first, then we can decide what to do next."

Language You Can Borrow: *So,* [presenter's name]*, since you chose the third option to stop our generating, what do you commit to do? Since you showed discipline by not interrupting us as we generated, we won't interrupt you now.*

Step 5: Debrief (Five Minutes)

A quick reminder about debriefing. Debriefing is discussing the process of learning for individuals and the groups, not reopening the content that everyone just discussed. See the introduction for more detail as well as possible questions to use to frame a debrief.

Language You Can Borrow: *The debrief is a time to converse about the protocol itself and how we did, not about the content anymore. Remember, we gave it back to* [presenter's name]*! So, how did that go for us today?*

Application Example 1

Veronica is in a quandary. As the district foreign language specialist, she knows she doesn't have enough time with the high school foreign language department chairs, but she also can't find any way to cut any items from her agenda. It is so rare they meet, she wants to make sure this time is valuable to them, and that it helps her meet the expectations the curriculum director has placed in front of her.

She is quite confident she is not unique in this struggle, so she decides to bring her agenda to the weekly meeting of curriculum coordinators. Leila, her partner and friend who manages English to speakers of other languages, first recommends Tuning as a protocol to use, but at the end of their preconference, Veronica knows she is willing to scrap all the draft processes she had for the topics. None of the topics can be deleted, but she is willing to change how she approaches them. Since significant segments of the agenda may be blown up by the time this protocol is finished, Charrette seems to be a better choice.

As she is presenting, she realizes how much time and thought she has already invested in this half-day agenda. Although she knows her fellow coordinators will have some sage ideas, it does worry her they might just tell her to cut items she knows she can't cut. Good thing Leila has spent so much time with Veronica—Leila senses the concern and reiterates prior to the generative step that the team should not touch the content of the agenda—the *what*, as she coins it. Instead, the coordinators will focus more on the *how*—the processes and methods Veronica might use to promote engagement and work efficiently.

The topic is certainly relevant to the coordinators, for they each work with department chairs in the various contexts. Thus, it is tough for Leila to carve out a break in the conversation to perform a check-in with Veronica. Leila is thankful she had delegated several responsibilities in this Charrette, including taking notes, timing, and making sure everyone has a chance to speak. This helps her focus on summarizing prior to the first check-in.

At the first check-in, Veronica chooses option 2: refocus the group. She is elated one of the ideas will help with several agenda items, where the department chairs need to offer feedback but also realize they are not the decision makers. She tells the group she is going to place posters around the room with the different topics and offer two different times for department chairs to record their feedback with markers. This time-saving strategy will allow her to dedicate more time to the more complex topics.

Those two topics drive the redirection Veronica requested, taking form in these questions: How might I structure the conversation I need around those two topics? What protocols or strategies should I consider?

The group does not disappoint, and approximately three minutes in, Veronica stops typing. Leila notices the slight change and makes eye contact with Veronica, who smiles. "This might be a great spot to circle back to Veronica," Leila chimes in. This time, Veronica chooses the third option and proceeds to relay her draft agenda to the group.

The debrief is joyous, partially due to the camaraderie the group shares, feeding from Veronica's infectious smile. Also, several members of the group relay their own takeaways, indicating specific changes they are going to make to upcoming agendas.

Application Example 2

As Misty, a principal, sits down in her car after exiting the central office, she exhales deeply. She has just learned about two new district initiatives that could jeopardize the positive movement her campus has been experiencing. The time line is urgent, as the district is going to start its own communication plan soon, and Misty wants to ensure the staff hear about the new work from her.

She calls Amy, a fellow principal, on the way back to her campus. She knows they will devolve into complaining if she doesn't immediately state her hope for this conversation. She does so, saying, "Amy, I need a protocol match. Will you please help me?"

As Misty discusses the situation from her perspective, Amy initially thinks this might be a dilemma—how to communicate these changes to the staff without squelching positivity. However, as Amy starts to apply the four dilemma criteria, she realizes the last criterion is not true. "Misty," she asks, "have you tried anything about how to communicate these changes yet?" Not shockingly, Misty hasn't—they both had *just* heard the news.

Misty instantly knows a Charrette would provide a better match. Thanking Amy as she pulls into her campus driveway, Misty parks her car and then texts her three assistant principals, asking if they could meet after dismissal.

Not having time to preconference ahead of time, she asks the first to arrive, Matt, if he will serve as the facilitator. Although this sort of "combat facilitation" is not ideal, Misty does not want to wait any longer. Her only advice to Matt is the following: "Y'all will want to talk about what I'm going to tell you. You will probably have some opinions about what we will now be required to do. Instead of going down that trail, please keep everyone focused on the communication—how and when we can talk to the staff, so this doesn't become a distraction."

Matt knows his two fellow assistant principals well and is able to meet Misty's expectations. More than once, he points back to the poster where he has been collecting ideas, rereading the title: *How and when to communicate to the staff.*

Matt chooses to wait an extra minute until the first check-in, due to his multiple redirections. The tenacity pays off—Misty calls the Charrette a success at the first check-in. The group has found a connection to an existing campus initiative that Misty had not deeply considered. Hearing the group members talk, she finds an opening.

The debrief is short, as they now need to prepare for this communication, but Misty insists they still debrief. She admits to her administrative team how important Charrette was to her today, saying, "I am quite confident if I had been talking *with* you, instead of listening, I probably would have steered you away from where we ended up. Such a great reminder how protocols can really help us make better decisions!"

Generate Ideas in an E⁴ Way

I bet many readers who are educators have been thinking about meetings where generating ideas was unproductive—perhaps unfocused, untimed, inequitable, or even all three. Strategically choosing a generative eprotocol like Charrette or Wagon Wheels can make a palpable difference. These choices aren't trying to handcuff educators (who often are natural idea generators)—rather the protocols harness their power and create more E⁴ experiences.

It could be tempting to stop reading now. After all, introductions and afterwords are just filler, right? In this text, they absolutely are *not*. In facilitator terms, the introduction represents the setup of the protocol—absolutely essential for a protocol to do its job well. The next pages represent the debriefing of a protocol, which includes processing the *how* of an experience, as well as the *next steps* for participants. Keep reading.

Afterword

Debriefing

A protocol is not an event.

When a protocol becomes the focus, the real meaning and learning have been obscured. The protocol may have been performed flawlessly based on an observer's judgment; the problem is the protocol was *done*, not *used*.

As chapter 1 contends, using protocols presupposes a meaningful and purposeful agenda. Protocols become the method, the avenue toward learning, rather than the actual learning itself. Using protocols rather than simply doing them shows the transformation discussion protocols can produce in educators (Kersey, 2014).

As the introduction was named "Grounding," it shouldn't surprise you the afterword is named "Debriefing." The essential question the facilitator asks of many groups, "How did this go for us?" is now germane to ask yourselves as you close this book—albeit temporarily, I hope. Let's think about how to organize implementation of protocols, and then take a final look at how to apply E^4 to this journey.

An Implementation Organizer

When I first learned about protocols in 2001, I was immediately hooked. I started using them in multiple spheres of my life, and without a framework, my implementation seemed to appear haphazard. I also realized my expectations of others when I used discussion protocols were different than their expectations of both the protocol and me. I chose to strategically organize my use of the tools around three outcomes.

1. To accomplish a task with a single-time group
2. To improve work in existing groups
3. To engage in a voluntary learning community

It would be adult learning malpractice to offer you learning without opportunities to plan your own implementation. The rest of the afterword gives you a lens into my implementation and use, as well as a few methods to consider in planning your own.

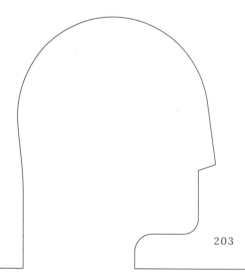

To Accomplish a Task With a Single-Time Group

I have no doubt you will find a protocol in this book to use with a group that meets once (or quite infrequently) for a specific purpose. A parent education event will benefit from a text-based protocol (chapter 2, page 37). A group of parents called together to give feedback on the Title I plan will be thrilled to use a Tuning (chapter 3, page 95) rather than just have an unstructured conversation for an hour. Teachers who volunteer to come to the district office and brainstorm with the human resources director about how to effectively recruit high-quality teachers will love a Wagon Wheels brainstorming (chapter 6, page 180).

In these situations, I usually do not take time to develop norms with the group. The individuals who are there are ready for the content of the meeting. Instead, I might pose a few draft norms for their consideration, quickly check in (possibly with a Fist to Five strategy—see appendix E, page 247), and move on.

In these groups, I generally don't even use the term *protocol*. I might use *experiences* or *processes*. As mentioned in the introduction, many educators have now been protocoled, and using a high-stress word when it might not be necessary seems foolhardy.

To Improve Work in Existing Groups

I am quite confident you will use protocols in this book (and others from the SRI website at www.schoolreforminitiative.org) with existing groups. A leadership team will need to use a dilemma-based protocol (chapter 5, page 147) in its work. Entire school faculties will explore cultural competence with protocols that explore equity (chapter 2, page 58). Collaborative teacher teams have data to examine with ATLAS: Looking at Data (chapter 4, page 128).

These groups usually have mandatory membership, and as I often remind teams in schools, "Here's the good news—you are paid to collaborate with your colleagues! Let's go earn it." These teams stay together throughout the course of weeks and months, so it is important to develop norms that are meaningful and useful to the team. Compass Points (page 69) and Group Juggle (page 74) both appear in chapter 2 as protocols to assist in creating group norms.

I would use the term *protocols* in these groups, as the frequency of meeting gives the group opportunities to use the debrief steps at the end of each experience. During that time, group members can discuss the constraints of discussion protocols. Those process conversations can help groups improve their work in subsequent sessions. Doing one protocol with a group of educators would certainly feel like a performance or a novelty; using protocols over the longevity of a group shows their usefulness toward specific purposes and goals.

Application examples abound throughout this book in order to give you a plethora of potential implementation ideas. These situations are singly offered, none within the sequence of learning or producing work in a group. It seems important to show you a longer agenda, annotated with the facilitator's thinking of why certain protocols were used and why other spaces in an agenda didn't use a protocol at all.

An In-Depth Agenda Example

An expanded version of this section and the next, Agenda Excerpts, appears as a three-part series on the Solution Tree blog. Visit www.SolutionTree.com/blog/MeetingGoals for a deeper look at agenda planning.

As the Baby Boomer principal population began retiring, this district saw the need for a structured program of principal support. In this first year of the program, newly hired principals received coaching support as well as engaged in intentional learning quarterly with one another. Several retired district principals were asked by the superintendent to mentor the newly hired principals by visiting the campus and providing on-the-ground coaching as well as phone support. The agendas presented in this section represent the required quarterly meetings with other newly hired principals. Dr. Shawna Miller, chief executive director of Organizational Learning (and a former district principal), and I served as the facilitators for this group. In the annotations that follow, the word *we* refers to our thinking as we constructed agendas.

Principals completed the following prior to coming together.

- Designed their one hundred–day entry plan with principal supervisors
- Read chapters 1–4 of *The Principal 50* (Kafele, 2015)
- Met together during the summer leadership conference

The agenda shows how protocols are *used* for a purpose, not simply *done*. In fact, over 90 percent of the fifteen principals in this cohort had previously completed three days of professional development about how to use protocols as effective leaders. Thus, the intent of these sessions was not to teach protocols, rather, it was to use protocols for the work they needed to accomplish as school leaders.

As you examined prior agendas in this book (chapter 1, page 21), you saw the term *connective tissue*, which is a method of sequencing an agenda to ensure tighter purpose, rather than sets of activities. To help the reader better understand the decisions that informed each agenda item, these important notions have been removed from the planning template itself and placed just prior to each agenda item.

The terms *tight* and *loose* show up again here. In the introduction, these words are descriptors to categorize a protocol in the amount and types of constraints it asks of participants. When designing agendas, it is healthy to hold tight and loose as a tension. As the introduction mentions, perpetual users of protocols need to know their own tendencies and habits in designing agendas. We tend to design agendas with experiences *we* would enjoy and find meaningful, thus already creating a biased agenda as a first draft.

Agenda Excerpts

One guiding principle in our planning was to ensure the agendas are responsive to principal needs for two reasons: (1) this was the first year of this support iteration, and (2) responsive agenda setting is a best practice for adult learning, and we wanted to help these leaders see this support mechanism as a microcosm of the adult learning they could design for their own school staffs.

We knew effective learning communities include rituals and procedures. How to begin our day-long experiences together would be important, as seen in figure A.1. We knew of a specific protocol we planned to use on the second day we were together but did not want to introduce that experience too early. We decided to help ground these principals with a process that was not unique to their context: they could lift the experience and use it in a variety of settings with a variety of groups if they wished. Using a variety of items (for example, stress balls or fidget toys) at each table, the first round of Synectics (see appendix E, page 250) created a personal connection. The second round met our real goal of using a grounding experience to advance our day's agenda, which included campus improvement planning and change management.

Why	When	What and How	What Happened
To ground	8:30 a.m.	Synectics Make a connection with one of the items on the table. Partner talk Round 1: Open connection Round 2: Connection to something you're trying to change on your campus	Participants enjoyed the items, made meaningful connections, and articulated several possible applications for the experience.

Figure A.1: September 20 agenda excerpt 1.

As new principals continue to find their sea legs, prioritizing demands to focus on instruction is a challenge and stopping to assess seems to be a luxury. Days are filled with dousing operational fires, and many new principals are quite adept at that work, which can lead them to a false sense of accomplishment. We knew an important function of this learning community was to personally and collectively assess our instructional leadership.

The specific items listed in figure A.2 were chosen as they fit into the district vision of campus needs assessments. In order to set a vision for the campus, examining stakeholder relationships and needs was critical.

Finally, we made an intentional choice regarding the process of this experience: rank ordering. Assessing in schools often involves sorting into categories that have positive and negative connotations, such as effective or not effective and glow or grow. It could also involve using a rubric with multiple levels. Asking learners to rank order a list does not assume deficit (or success) on any specific item; rather, it asks them to assess each item in light of each other item. This kind of higher-order thinking was helpful for these principals for this immediate content, and it also provided a clear model of creating thinking environments for teachers in their buildings.

Why	When	What and How	What Happened
To assess	8:45 a.m.	Have the following ten items on strips of paper and ask participants to rank order how well you are engaging in the following leadership behaviors. 1. Determining which staff have the most influence in the building 2. Looking for and celebrating small wins 3. Taking specific steps to build trust with parents 4. Taking specific steps to build trust with other administrators (assistant principals and so on) 5. Taking specific steps to build trust with teachers 6. Taking specific steps to build trust with support staff 7. Consistently starting with the why 8. Verifying your assumptions about which staff may be on board with your vision 9. Clearly modeling the behaviors you seek in staff 10. Determining more root causes, rather than treating symptoms Show your list to a partner and discuss the question, What are the factors that led you to order this way (for example, time, energy, or contextual complexity)?	In written reflections at the end of the day, these few minutes had been poignant for a few principals. One mentioned she knew she had been spending extra time on a specific behavior, but it hadn't occurred to her what was *not* happening as often as a result.

Figure A.2: September 20 agenda excerpt 2.

While confronting current reality, it is also important not to lose sight of successes along the way. Many newly hired principals are in fix-it mode, so their minds move from one problem to the next. It's easy to be overwhelmed by what needs to happen, and in turn overlook or miss the positive steps and small wins. We wanted to ensure protected time away from their campuses when they could process a success with others, as seen in figure A.3 (page 208). The Success Analysis protocol (chapter 2, page 56) was a perfect fit for our hope. We availed ourselves of the last step in the protocol when groups looked for commonalities across their successes to develop a set of success criteria. We intended for these criteria to be a longstanding artifact as the principals met over the course of the next several months.

Why	When	What and How	What Happened
To build shared success criteria as new principals	9:00– 10:15 a.m.	Success Analysis (for mentor follow-up) Connection to Conscious Competence (Mind Tools, n.d.; Van Soelen, 2016)	As expected! No modifications needed to be made—thank goodness we had a number of principals divisible by three! During the debrief, a principal mentioned how this protocol would be a perfect fit for her campus. She has been asking teachers how their student achievement data improved so much last year, but no one seems to have a clear answer.
	10:15– 10:30 a.m.	Break	

Figure A.3: September 20 agenda excerpt 3.

Each of the principals had a one hundred–day entry plan that included a campus needs assessment. Although it would have been tempting to always provide new learning and new tasks each time these principals convened, we wanted them to see the value of these sessions in helping them work on their current work, possibly in more effective and efficient ways.

The rest of the day, as well as the next three gatherings with this group (in November, January, and March) continued with a similar trajectory. Some structured protocols from this book were included in future agendas (from chapter 2: Chalk Talk [page 47], Microlabs [page 52], and The Text Rendering Experience [page 41]; from chapter 3: Gap Analysis [page 89]; and from **go.SolutionTree.com/leadership**, Connections, Defy Gravity, and Planting the Seed). At their request, we spent each afternoon in small groups, examining dilemmas they were experiencing at their campus (from chapter 5: Consultancy [page 153], Descriptive Consultancy [page 159], Issaquah [page 162], and Peeling the Onion [page 168]).

However, we did not spend every moment using a discussion protocol. For instance, some direct instruction occurred. In the second meeting, we showed participants how to create sociograms of their faculty members. A *sociogram* is a visual representation of the interactions between members of a group. They then set one-day, one-week, and one-month plans of how to use the graphic toward leveraging relationships with staff in their campus improvement plan efforts.

Well-intentioned educators can sometimes go overboard once they learn about the power of discussion protocols. Simply *doing* protocol after protocol in a meeting does not create effective adult learning. In fact, a deluge of protocol after protocol can overwhelm participants. Instead, when used judiciously and with clear purpose, the habits and dispositions participants demonstrate in discussion protocols simply become the way a group works. Sometimes the group demonstrates these habits within the constraints of a particular protocol; other times participants demonstrate these behaviors in a general conversation or an informal collaboration. In these moments, protocols can be transformative (Kersey, 2014).

To Engage in a Voluntary Learning Community

Finally, you may choose to find others who wish to use discussion protocols in a voluntary learning community. Sometimes called a *reflective learning community*, an *intentional learning community*, or *being in a critical friendship*, a *voluntary learning community* is a place where educators work together to develop their reflective and collaborative skills. These groups require the highest level of trust and risk among members. Some of the experiences and protocols may look similar to other groups (reading professional texts, giving and receiving feedback, looking at examples of adult-generated and student-generated work), but the variable of voluntary membership makes a difference. When participants *choose* to spend their time engaged in these learning experiences, their level of investment is higher and thus, they may be more prone to render tough-to-say feedback or offer unpopular but important-to-consider perspectives. I have seen school leaders in groups like this try out an idea they have yet to bring forth in their own school. I watched teachers admit their inability to voice their disapproval regarding inequitable structures and practices. I myself, in my own district, have brought forth issues that confounded me, and in voicing them, made me feel vulnerable.

Some principals in Gwinnett County, Georgia, chose to practice critical friendship with one another. The National Association of Elementary School Principals published a two-part blog post about their experiences in this voluntary collaboration (Van Soelen, 2019a, 2019b). Among the themes in their written reflection are the following.

- Tight on time
- Facilitator of adult learning
- Relevance
- Ownership
- Risk taking

These principals *chose* to be together. The word *voluntary* is a critical characteristic of this level of discussion protocol use. When individuals choose to add a meeting to an already tight calendar, the return on the investment better be there! As one of these principals wrote, "It is always the right call to make time for this meeting" (Van Soelen, 2019a).

Meaningful norms are an essential part of the success of groups such as these. These agreements were tested as courageous educators brought the hardest and most complex issues to the table. Figure A.4 (page 210) represents the norms the way they read after the group had been together for six years.

Group Norms

"We prioritize our learning, risking and challenging ourselves as we do the following:

present *(bring work that matters to us);*

facilitate *(hone our skills); and*

participate *(listen deeply and openly and give and receive purposeful and constructive feedback),*

all the while, being trustworthy with what we discuss as we grow as leaders."

Source: Van Soelen, 2019b.

Figure A.4: Group norms.

I was the convener of this group, not the facilitator for each discussion protocol. We rotated responsibilities so each of us would be able to benefit from the purposeful and constructive feedback our norms required of us. Each of us served as chief adult developers (Fahey et al., 2019), so we wanted double learning in these sessions, including the learning about content (for example, a dilemma about scheduling, an artifact about how to write effective observational feedback, or a blog post about leading second-order change) and the learning about how to effectively lead processes. We were in a critical friendship together, so we used the term *critical friendship protocols.* The term *critical friendship* was not used lightly—these principals would not refer to the grade-level teams or collaborative groups at their schools as being critical friends because those groups lacked the important feature of voluntary membership. Our group was special, important, and different. And all it took to start was an email, a location, and a few doughnuts for a 7:30 a.m. start time.

Our agenda each month was intentionally repetitive. We started with Connections (**go .SolutionTree.com/leadership**) as a way to ground our frenetic minds. A second opening experience is called "It mattered we met . . ." In these three to four minutes, individuals who were at the last gathering (usually at least 85 percent of our members had regular attendance) might choose to speak, using that specific prompt. A few sample responses to that prompt might sound like the following.

- "It mattered we met because Tonya's dilemma helped me work out something at my own school."

- "It mattered we met because the article Bo chose was just what I needed. I ended up using it with my leadership team—thanks, Bo!"

- "It mattered we met because I needed a breath—just some time for myself."

- "It mattered we met because we laughed together!"

The third agenda item included a time to use a text-based protocol (chapter 2, page 37) to read a text. The responsibility to choose a text rotated each month. People who chose the text might choose to facilitate, they might ask a colleague to help choose a protocol and facilitate, or they might call me ("phone a friend") to help decide on a protocol that I would then facilitate.

The final item was the longest part of the meeting: using a process from chapters 4–6 to look at a piece of student or adult work in order to give and receive feedback. In the first year of this team, we tried to work, meeting to meeting, over email. We soon abandoned this method as it proved frustrating for many. From that point onward, at the beginning of the school year, we would collaboratively set our dates and decide on presenters and facilitators. If members had something urgent on which they wanted feedback, they could call the presenter scheduled and ask for a switch.

These four items took just under two hours, and as the principals reflected (Van Soelen, 2019a, 2019b), this time was necessary and well spent.

Your First Step Toward E^4

Where and how will you take the next step? Perhaps choosing one of the following three outcomes could be a helpful method to ensure this book doesn't become just another literary conquest on your packed bookshelf.

If discussion protocols are new in your context, you might use them to accomplish certain tasks. Chapter 2 (page 35) offers many application examples to which you could relate.

Perhaps an existing group may be your Petri dish—a place to try out some of the processes that intrigue you? An administrative team, a leadership team, or a school-improvement committee might all be logical next steps. You may also think about some of these practices and protocols as interventions for groups. There may be a particular teacher collaborative team that is in need of effectiveness and efficiency. You might assume primary facilitation for this team for a period of time and use many discussion protocols in this book to create a positive trajectory.

Finally, you might choose to jump in with both feet—finding some other courageous educators who are seeking a community where they can take risks. Although no one seems to have time for another meeting, to repeat what a principal in the aforementioned group wrote, "It is always the right call to make time for this meeting" (Van Soelen, 2019a).

Whatever way you start, that is the key—starting. Rather than setting the book on the corner of your desk and looking for the right opening, open up your calendar, look at collaborative gatherings coming up in the next few weeks, create a purpose-driven agenda (chapter 1, page 21), and go for it. E^4 is worth it!

Appendices

Appendix A

Consistent Approaches to Common Steps in Protocols

Just like learners write in the white spaces of a handout as they experience insights, this appendix offers my white space learning from almost twenty years of facilitating the foundational protocols from chapters 4–6.

Consistent Approaches to Common Steps in Protocols to Seek Perspective

Chapter 4, "Protocols to Seek Perspective" (page 111), discusses four foundational protocols, each focused on a different work product: ATLAS, ATLAS: Looking at Data, Examining Assessments, and Making Meaning. Each of the following headings addresses one or more of them. In addition, a facilitator may choose to study the Language You Can Borrow when preparing to facilitate one of these protocols.

Look

This section includes approaches to the ATLAS, ATLAS: Looking at Data, Examining Assessments, and Making Meaning protocols. Using discussion protocols frequently can help educators become more comfortable with productive silence. A tendency exists among those of us who are educators to fill space with words in order to convince ourselves and others that the collaboration is meaningful and effective. Additionally, ambitious leaders who facilitate meetings tend to skip or reduce the time taken for protocol steps that ask for silence. I've heard the following reasons from these leaders for why they might choose to skip this part of a protocol.

- "It is so awkward to have quiet. People get nervous and fidgety."
- "Our group is high functioning, so we don't need this step."
- "It seems like such a waste of time—just get to it."

I counter these responses with the following.

- "Giving each educator space to examine the work creates a more equitable space later for each person to participate."
- "It seems paradoxical, but taking the private thinking time up front will actually be more efficient. In their estimate, it will take longer for educators to find their opinions and find their points. In my experience, however, when we take time up front to clarify our personal thinking, this creates time for efficient collaborative thinking."

The nature of the work sample informs what participants do during this step. For instance, if the presenter brings multiple copies of a single piece of student work for an ATLAS protocol, participants might write their observations directly on the work sample. If the data for an ATLAS: Looking at Data protocol are digitally presented, participants might take notes on a separate piece of paper or on sticky notes. Similarly, educators would also take their own notes if the sample is visual (2-D or 3-D) or auditory (sound file, video file).

Language You Can Borrow: There are three options, depending on the nature of the work.

1. If the work has been copied for each person, consider saying, *You have a copy of the work in front of you. We are borrowing it temporarily, then will return these copies to* [presenter's name]. *We will have four to eight quiet minutes to examine this piece of student work.*

2. If the work was not able to be copied (for example, electronic document, 2-D product, or 3-D model), then consider saying, *As you examine this work, please be diligent in taking notes, getting ready for our first step of description. We will have four to eight quiet minutes.*

3. If the work was not able to be copied (for example, a video or audio performance), then consider saying, *As we* [listen to or watch] *this product, please be diligent in taking notes, getting ready for our first step of description.* [When finished] *Now we will take two to three minutes to gather our thoughts before moving on to the description step.*

Description

This section includes approaches to the ATLAS, ATLAS: Looking at Data, Examining Assessments, and Making Meaning protocols. Any learning around the acronym DIE is particularly helpful as this step begins. If a group knows DIE, a thirty-second practice to refresh descriptive skills is helpful. Perhaps point at something on the wall or reach into a student's desk and pull out something—even ask someone to fish something out of a purse or school bag—all you need is an object. Many times, there is someone in the group whose brain will move to interpretation, and asking the question from the DIE minilesson, "And what do you *see* that makes you *think* that?" brings everyone back to the point of description—literal, concrete observations without interpretation or evaluation.

Resist shortchanging this step. It is typical in a teacher team to go around the group one time, in the name of equity, with each person having a chance to speak. In this process, the point of extensive description is more than equity—description helps presenting teachers note what they see in the student work and what they have missed. The description becomes non-evaluative feedback for their colleagues.

As a facilitator, it can be tricky to know how to respond when participants venture beyond description during this round. Notice how the Language You Can Borrow for this step approaches this potential complexity.

Deciding whether to use a go-round or popcorn style is important for the facilitator to consider. For the description step, I recommend initially starting with a go-round. This move provides efficiency at a step that doesn't require heavy lifting from the group and may mitigate gaps in experience.

Language You Can Borrow: *Time to start the first round—description. Just like we practiced, we will begin each statement with "I see" or "I notice." These statements are short and to the point. To assist us all in finding what you are describing, you may wish to offer some directional words, like, "I see on the bottom of page 1 . . . or at timestamp 2:35."*

We will go around the group several times, and the rule of no-repeats applies. Once we have seen it, we have seen it! The goal is to see things no one else has seen so [presenter's name] can really find a fresh perspective.

Our brains all move quickly at times, so one or more of us may venture beyond description. Any one of us can bring the group back to description with these lines: "What is your evidence?" or "What did you see to make you think that?"

So, to begin our rounds of description, who will begin?

Evaluate Our Learning

This section includes approaches to the ATLAS and Making Meaning protocols. Several facilitators I know make a particular move in several protocols that includes a presenter. It occurs at different junctures in each one, but it represents the same notion. That is, asking the presenter if it would be permissible for the group to take on their work. This respectful question asks the participants to borrow, to hold someone else's dilemma and care for it as if it were their own. At this point, presenters might turn their chair ninety degrees, now facing the facilitator, so their ear is to the group. This physical shift has two big benefits.

- Presenters can focus on listening and note taking, as their ear is now directed to the group. They do not need to spend cognitive energy thinking about their nonverbal reactions (for example, furrowed or raised eyebrows—basically anything with eyebrows). Presenters report the positive experience of having some space (intellectual and physical) between themselves and the work. It is relieving to give the work away even for a few minutes.

- The group can better own the work instead of looking to the presenter for nonverbal feedback as it offers each piece of feedback. Participants report having more courage to offer tough-to-hear feedback when the presenter is slightly turned.

If a facilitator chooses this method, a pronoun shift occurs with the group. The sentence stems on the anchor chart indicate the change: more *we* and *I*, rather than *she*, *they*, or the name of the presenter. This collective language helps the presenter be in a productively risky space because the group isn't just giving advice with fingers pointed. It also helps the group really ponder its feedback.

With this method, at the end of the feedback step, the facilitator would invite the presenter back into the group, and the point of view switches—the group gives the work back to the presenter, and feedback has a clear stopping point.

Language You Can Borrow: [Presenter's name], *you have described and interpreted with us, but in this step, I think it would be more helpful if we took on this student as if* [preferred pronoun] *were one of ours. Would it be OK for us to now lift this student from your shoulders for a while?* [If yes] *It will be helpful for you and us if you would be willing to turn ninety degrees, so your ear is to the group. You can focus on listening and the group can focus on owning your work rather than talking at you, as you will not be verbally participating for a while.*

As we now have been charged with this student work, a point of view shift occurs. We will use different pronouns as we talk—less of they, them, her, she, him, he *and more of* we, our, me, my, I. *This collective ownership not only helps* [presenter's name] *as* [preferred pronoun] *steps out of the conversation, it helps us place ourselves in* [preferred pronoun] *position, increasing the potential for really thoughtful and helpful feedback.*

Presenter Reflection

This section includes approaches to the ATLAS, Examining Assessments, and Making Meaning protocols; it is optional for ATLAS: Looking at Data. Notice the name of this step: it is presenter *reflection*, not presenter *response*, nor presenter *defense*. If the protocol itself and the people within the structure all did their jobs artfully and skillfully, this step most likely shouldn't be problematic. However, our work as educators is personal. Thoughtfully leading into this step is important. An "OK! That was hard! Joseph, turn on back, what are you thinking about all of our helpful feedback?" doesn't set up Joseph as a presenter very well.

Over the years, participants have shared that my metaphors have been helpful. They allow individuals to hold onto the intent of a step or a concept. At this step, the duck analogy is what I choose to use. Sometimes, presenters feel like a duck during the discussion step. They hear a piece of feedback, and write it down, but in the moment, it is sliding right off their backs. Other notions they heard were also intriguing, memorable, or even obvious—these pieces of feedback catch in their tail feathers.

This analogy helps presenters realize participants do not expect, nor does the protocol have time for, a play-by-play rundown of everything said prior. Another means of helping presenters be ready to reflect to the group is encouraging their focus on their note-taking during the feedback step. Presenters may have starred a few items, underlined something, perhaps their pen hovered a moment as they wrote something down—those could be the items they choose to share during the next step.

Even with a facilitator's beautifully worded entrance, sometimes a presenter ends up offering a lengthy commentary on everyone's feedback. One facilitator move might be to acknowledge what the presenter has said by saying something like, "You heard a lot in this experience!" And use a quantifiable limit, saying, "Perhaps one more thing . . ." to help find an endpoint.

Finally, if the group borrowed the work, don't forget to give it back! The work is physically collected as the presenters turn ninety degrees back to the group in order to share their thinking.

Language You Can Borrow: [Presenter's name], *as you turn back to the group, please know we got some stuff wrong! We aren't you. Think of yourself as a duck: some of the feedback rolled right off your back and some of it may have gotten stuck in your tail feathers. Feel free to hold onto what seems helpful; there's no need to defend anything to us. This step is called presenter* reflection, *not presenter* defense, *or presenter* response. *You now have a few moments to tell us what got stuck—what you are leaving thinking most about. Since you showed discipline by not interrupting us, we won't interrupt you now.*

Consistent Approaches to Common Steps in Protocols to Explore and Manage Dilemmas

Chapter 5, "Protocols to Explore and Manage Dilemmas" (page 147), discusses four foundational protocols that are like biological cousins: Consultancy, Descriptive Consultancy, Issaquah, and Peeling the Onion. Several aspects of their anatomy and mannerisms are similar. Each of the following headings addresses one or more of them. In addition, a facilitator may choose to study the Language You Can Borrow as he or she prepares to facilitate one of these dilemma-based protocols.

Presentation

This section includes approaches to the Consultancy, Descriptive Consultancy, Issaquah, and Peeling the Onion protocols. It is helpful for participants if the facilitator gives a brief rundown of the steps before the presenter starts the protocol. Simply reading a printed anchor chart is not enough or valuable enough to spend time doing. Make sure what you do say prior to handing it over to the presenter is a value add to the process. Additionally, your words are not designed to foreshadow or replace what the presenter is about to say. The group doesn't yet need to know the content of the document or the dilemma question.

A tangible task would be to time yourself rehearsing this opening. It shouldn't take longer than sixty seconds to give a preview of the steps.

Then comes step 1: Presentation, which is included in each of the four foundational dilemma-based protocols. Sometimes presenters feel like they should limit their presentation to a *brief* summary of the dilemma, even though the group would benefit more from a detailed account. If the presenter stops talking (and usually looks at you!), you may wish to employ a few different strategies.

- Offer fifteen to twenty seconds of quiet for presenters to work through a mental checklist, making sure they communicated everything they wanted. When I create this space for the presenter, 95 percent or more of the time, they end up saying more.

- You may know something about the work due to a previous conversation you had with the presenter. It may be helpful to prompt presenters to speak about one or more of those insights or facets if they wish.

Even with some of these strategies, the presentation may end up being shorter than anticipated. Some discussion protocols ask the participants to have the discipline to hold tight to the time frame, even sitting in silence if needed. That is not the case for dilemma-based protocols. If a presentation only takes five minutes, that is fine—just be ready for the next step (Clarifying Questions) to perhaps extend past five minutes. The net result of the time spent for both steps combined will not extend beyond the protocol's time frame.

Perhaps the most important move a facilitator must make is to ensure the group is clear about the dilemma question the presenter is choosing. If, at the end of the Presentation step, presenters have not explicitly named the dilemma question, ask them. If they need assistance, you might reference the preconference and name the draft dilemma question, asking if that still gets at the heart of the dilemma.

A small but meaningful shift for some facilitators is to *not* overprepare posters for these sessions. For instance, some of my colleagues love having a poster ready with the dilemma question already scribed. This facilitative move is designed to produce efficiency, but it can inadvertently limit the presenter. I have seen presenters change their questions at the end of their presentation because they gained clarity as they were talking, uninterrupted, during the first step. If we have the poster pre-prepared, presenters may not feel they have the liberty to alter the question. *Note*: For the Peeling the Onion protocol, a dilemma question may not be present because the intent of that protocol is to help the presenter *define* the dilemma.

Language You Can Borrow: As you are thinking about how to frame your first sixty seconds of introducing the steps, here are some phrases and sentences that may be appropriate for your specific dilemma-based protocol.

- *If what we talk about today was a problem, a solution would exist and probably would already be implemented! Instead, we will treat this as a dilemma, a thorny, complicated issue that takes our best thinking to move forward.*

- *In this structure, we will slow down our gut response to offer ideas. We begin with hearing from our presenter, then follow up with any clarifying questions we might have.*

- *When we get to the Probing Questions step, I will help us create really helpful probing questions.*

- *After the presenter answers some of our probing questions, we will ask if we can borrow the dilemma as if it is our own. Then,* [preferred pronoun] *can turn to the side so* [preferred pronoun] *ear is to the group, listening but not feeling like* [preferred pronoun] *needs to affirm everything we say.*

- *Finally, our presenter will turn back, let us know* [preferred pronoun] *current thinking, then we will end with a debrief about the process. What questions do you have about these steps before we begin?*

- [Presenter's name], *thank you for bringing such a meaningful issue to us today. In this first step, several minutes have been carved out for you to tell the context of your dilemma. Participants will work hard, taking notes, as we will be hearing much detail about your thinking.* [Presenter's name], *please give us all the background you can possibly think of regarding your dilemma.*

Clarifying Questions

This section includes approaches to the Consultancy, Descriptive Consultancy, Issaquah, and Peeling the Onion protocols. Unfortunately, educators frequently use questions as a method of recommending. A colleague might ask, "Did you use the district item bank for the assessment?" which (whether or not it was intended) may sound like a recommendation or even an accusation. A broader question, such as, "What resources did you use to create the assessment questions?" feels less prescriptive.

Clarifying questions are designed for the asker to receive information. *Quickly asked, quickly answered* is a familiar mantra I use. It is not the goal here for the presenter to think. If a question inadvertently causes the presenter to furrow the brows, lift the chin, or look up to the right . . . some facilitators may choose to intercept the question and judge it to be out of alignment with the intent of the step. Although the facilitator may be correct in this judgment, the consequence of correcting a participant is risky—it could cause a decrease in participation from not only that participant but others as well.

Watching presenters is another way to manage a question that, in your opinion, is not clarifying. If they choose to start answering it (within a few seconds), then it may have been clarifying *to them*. Remember, the goal of the facilitator is to make *facile* (make easy) the process for each person involved. It is far simpler to let the presenter be the arbiter of which questions feel clarifying or not.

Utilizing a go-round is a popular way to ensure voice equity. Start with one person, then after that person's participation, proceed to the left or right, going all the way around. Many discussion protocols use this method. Consider the risk when soliciting clarifying questions: it may inadvertently pressure participants to come up with a clarifying question when they really don't have one. Simply opening this up to the group popcorn style may be more aligned to the step's intent. It also shows the group you want to be as authentic as possible—not forcing anyone to make up anything.

Language You Can Borrow: *Now, we each have a chance to ask any clarifying questions, so we more completely understand the context of this work. These sorts of questions are simple questions of fact. They might start with* who, what, how many, where, *or* when. *We will resist asking a question that is a disguised recommendation, such as "Did you ever think about using . . . ?" Some may think a question with a* yes *or* no *answer is automatically clarifying. Instead, think about your intent. A good rule of thumb for clarifying questions is that these questions are for you to understand the situation, not for the presenter to think deeply. That will happen later.*

What clarifying questions does the group have?

Probing Questions

This section includes approaches to the Consultancy, Issaquah, and Peeling the Onion protocols. Designing effective probing questions is complex. It seems educators have a default mechanism to give ideas. Considering this along with many educators' penchant for accomplishing tasks, it's no surprise that they are often found outside of school working as designers and implementers of work (for example, Cub Scout leader, sports team snack organizer, or treasurer of a booster club).

These habits *are* helpful in identifying and solving problems; however, those behaviors work against them in dilemma-based protocols. Even when the name of this step seems clear (Probing Questions), the interpretation of that step is where the complexity lies.

This family of protocols is the only one that explicitly uses probing questions. The nature of a dilemma (determined as such through the four-step criteria) makes it appropriate and welcome for the group to ask probing questions of the presenter. Therefore, it is critical participants have a clear understanding about the intent and design of an effective probing question.

The intent of a *clarifying* question is for a participant to acquire missing information while a *probing* question serves as a platform for pondering. Table A.1 shows the two ways these types of questions differ.

Table A.1: Differences Between Clarifying and Probing Questions

	Purpose	Main Beneficiary
Clarifying Question	To fill in details	Participant
Probing Question	To inspire thinking	Presenter

As a facilitator, you may have already informed or reminded the group participants about how, if they're not careful, clarifying questions could be suggestive. The same result can inadvertently occur with probing questions. If a participant is asking a probing question and has a desire for what the answer *should* be, the question probably isn't authentically probing. It may be a disguised recommendation (and maybe not disguised that well).

It is still often troublesome to work against the tendency for educators to offer ideas. Even with the purpose *to inspire thinking* an educator might say, "Sure, my question had an idea embedded in it, but then the presenter can think about whether or not that is a good idea." Further criteria may help explicate the characteristics of a probing question (Thompson-Grove & Frazer, n.d.).

- Allows for multiple responses

- Encourages perspective taking

- Challenges assumptions

- Creates a paradigm shift

- Promises insight

Many facilitators find it helpful to pause at the probing question step, offering resources to assist the participants. Time may be the first gift. In these dilemma-based protocols, the Probing Questions step is one of the longest—that signifies importance. Rather than immediately asking questions as soon as the Probing Questions step begins, segmenting that time may be beneficial. Offering two to four minutes for participants to silently write probing questions is an effective facilitator move.

The second resource that can counteract participants' propensity to ask ineffective questions is the *Pocket Guide to Probing Questions* (appendix C, page 240). Originally developed by Gene Thompson-Grove and Edorah Frazer (n.d.) exactly for this purpose, it can serve as an invaluable support to increase the number of probing questions that feel genuinely probing to the presenter. I find this resource so beneficial in a discussion protocol that I had the sentence stems for probing questions laminated on the corner of my desk as a central office leader. I used them during impromptu or planned coaching conversations, as well as a method to self-coach and make better decisions.

In the learning trajectory of a group over time, a facilitator may find the Probing Questions step is consistently problematic. Some of these actions may prove helpful.

- Use the Pocket Guide in the protocol itself, asking participants to create at least one of their probing questions with the sentence stems.

- Keep a written record and analyze either after the discussion protocol or during another gathering.

- Keep a written record and ask the presenter to place some of them on a continuum from least probing to most probing.

Because I'm never sure if the written questions may be helpful to the group's development, I consistently ask groups to write their probing questions on sticky notes—even if the discussion protocol doesn't require it or if the presenter answers the questions. Additionally, the probing questions allow the presenter to listen to the question, not worry about writing it down.

Making connections to content is a skill many high-quality teachers do naturally— they are unconsciously competent. For instance, a teacher may use hand motions to teach the various ways tectonic plates interact with each other. That same kind of attention to learning is often needed in a discussion protocol. I'm not lobbying for hand motions! However, the use of figurative language can inspire group members to truly understand the intent of a particular step. For instance, the following Language You Can Borrow uses the metaphor of a gift.

Language You Can Borrow: The Consultancy and Issaquah protocols each have a step for the participants to ask probing questions of the presenter. Peeling the Onion has a specific round dedicated to these kinds of questions. The construction of probing questions is similar in all three protocols—I highly recommend copying or projecting the *Pocket Guide to Probing Questions* from appendix C (page 240) for participants.

We asked clarifying questions that were for us. *We needed clarity, so we asked. Now, we will ask questions for* [presenter's name]. *They are called probing questions. Asking and answering probing questions is a hallmark of this protocol. When leveraged well, these questions channel insight not just for the group but also for the presenter. In fact,* [presenter's name] *may find more value in this step than in anything else we do today.*

Probing questions are crafted to be powerful and open. They resist the tendency to assume there is one, or a right, answer. Specifically, they do not recommend. *We are often quite good at using questions to recommend others to do something such as when we say, "Addison, could you take out the trash?" or "Julie, why is the fridge door open?" These sorts of responses are not helpful at this stage. Instead, we want to craft better, more helpful questions.*

A support document called the Pocket Guide to Probing Questions *will be our guide today as we channel our energies toward* [presenter's name]*'s dilemma. As you examine the first section, please look toward the set of bullets that describe the characteristics of probing questions. Take a few quiet moments and scan those bullets, searching for a descriptor that clearly sets the bar for what we want and need our probing questions to accomplish.*

[Thirty seconds]

These are not the run-of-the-mill questions we ask each other every day! Instead, these are well-crafted, highly intentional gifts for [presenter's name]. *Thinking of them as gifts helps me. I usually plan the giving of a gift, and thoughtfully consider what I will buy, how I will wrap it, and the possible reactions. We will now use that metaphor of gift giving as we create probing questions for* [presenter's name].

Please have a few sticky notes near you for the first part of this step. As you consider the dilemma posed today and our posted question, use the fantastic set of question stems toward the end of the Pocket Guide to Probing Questions *document. These stems are extremely helpful as you seek to bring your potential question to life. I think of these stems as wrapping paper samples. We must ask, "How will I wrap up my present (my idea) for* [presenter's name]*?"*

As you write, the first draft may not be awesome—in fact, it usually isn't. Feel free to crumple it up and draft again. That sound isn't interruptive to us, for it is the sound of revision. *You may have wrapped a present before and then noted evidence of where you could have done better—so you undid the wrapping and tried again.*

We will take the next three to five minutes to quietly prepare and write our probing questions.

Description: What?

Description is an explicit step in the Descriptive Consultancy and Issaquah protocols. The concept of description is a prompt within the discussion step in the Consultancy protocol. Some of the ideas listed in this section may also help a facilitator in a Consultancy.

A dilemma is like being in a personal tornado. The noise is so significant that presenters might not really know what they said. The first prompt: "What did you hear?" ensures the presenter has a very literal hearing of the dilemma. Secondly, dilemmas often raise emotions, as the content is generally tricky (by definition, it is a dilemma) or complex. When those emotions surface, listening often suffers. In Descriptive Consultancy and Issaquah, the unvarnished and unexaggerated replaying of the dilemma is critical to ensure each member of the group truly understands the dilemma. The rest of these protocols hold these understandings as a foundational step.

For groups who have used discussion protocols presented in chapter 4, "Protocols to Seek Perspective" (page 111), the Description step is an application of a learned and practiced skill. Although that sounds simple, participants with this past experience may still struggle. Description seems to be easier for educators when a document (for example, an assessment, student work, an article, or adult-generated work) is used. When participants are asked to describe what they heard in a dilemma, it is easy to accelerate to subsequent steps (Interpretation and Evaluating Next Steps). Consider this example; this group is using Descriptive Consultancy, but this phenomenon can happen in all four of the dilemma-based protocols.

> Luis has just told a group about a thorny situation he has with a particular team at school. As the assistant principal, he feels like he should be able to sometimes leverage his positional authority, and other times, not have to use it, relying on relational capital. After some minutes of clarifying questions, the facilitator moves into the Description step without any instructive lead-in or commentary, saying, "OK, thanks, everyone. Let's move into the Description step. What did we hear Luis say? Who will begin?"
>
> Although his colleague group of assistant principals from other schools has extensively used the ATLAS: Looking at Data discussion protocol and even facilitated teacher groups using the same process, the first response in the Description step sounded like this.
>
> Participant 1: "I heard Luis has a dilemma we all experience, too!"

continued →

Although "I heard . . ." was the chosen prompt by participant 1, the words are not descriptive. A better response would have been more literal, such as "I heard Luis say he is sometimes stuck knowing when to use his position." Since Luis said those exact words, "when to use my position," the response fits the expectation of this step.

Just as I recommend in chapter 4 (page 111), an instructive moment (short or long) will position the group to better show fidelity to the intent of this step. Longer instruction could include a minilesson on the DIE acronym; something shorter could involve literally describing an object in the room.

If you use this step well, it can go rather quickly, as participants are reading directly from their notes, rather than extemporaneously speaking. It is helpful to prompt the presenter to a potential expectation or action during this step. If the step's function is for the presenter to hear how well the dilemma was communicated, then it may not be necessary or helpful to write everything down. Additionally, it may be important to assure the group and the presenter there is not a need to wait for confirmation after each participant offers a descriptive statement. The check-in step creates space for the presenter to clarify, if needed.

Some facilitators choose to scribe everything group members say at various steps in numerous protocols. This action seems to come from a well-intentioned place—often to honor each person's contribution. However, a consequence is a considerable slowing down of the process and the more troublesome outcome of a growing suspicion that the facilitator might not know the intent of each step.

Deciding whether to use a go-round or popcorn style is important for the facilitator to consider. For the description step, I recommend initially starting with a go-round. This move provides efficiency at a step that doesn't require heavy lifting from the group and may mitigate experience gaps.

Educators generally choose to collaborate with homogeneous groups when asked. For instance, a science teacher often likes to talk to other science teachers. Even more specifically, assistant principals at the middle school level would often select a group with other middle school assistant principals. Even one more sorting could happen, where an elementary principal in a school with a high English learner population would choose to talk with principals who serve similar populations. These behaviors are based on a common assumption that homogeneous groups are more helpful.

Due to this assumption, when educators are placed in heterogeneous groups, and they feel like they cannot relate to the topic and content, engagement suffers. The description step prevents this by asking all participants to set aside their possible backgrounds with the topic and *just describe what they hear*. This is just like a job posting that clarifies that no previous experience is required. That perspective also fuels the next interpretive step, which may be the most important step of the entire protocol.

Language You Can Borrow: *Time to start the first round—description. We will begin each statement with, "I heard" or "I noticed." These statements are short and to the point. This does not ask for reading between the lines; instead it is simply reading the lines! Look at your notes and say something you wrote down. During this step, our presenter will simply listen in. You* [to the presenter] *might find it helpful to write down anything that* doesn't jibe *with your memory. The rest of us won't talk at* [presenter's name] *because* [preferred pronoun] *won't be able to respond . . . at least, at this step in the process. So, for this round, who will begin?*

Interpretation: So What?

This section includes approaches to the Descriptive Consultancy and Issaquah protocols. Although presenters may choose a Descriptive Consultancy or Issaquah because they want to leave with a few ideas regarding their dilemma, this process is not in the generative family of discussion protocols (chapter 6, page 177). Instead of being all about the ideas, these coaching protocols ensure a robust understanding of the dilemma before offering any ideas. Jumping too quickly to ideas happens in other settings, too. For example, consider a teacher team meeting in which members open a data portal to discuss the most recent United States history assessment scores and someone begins with, "We really need to go back and reteach the Reconstruction period." The next ten minutes are spent brainstorming different reteaching methods to do so. This team hasn't engaged in any root cause analysis (interpretation) of data, so the ideas the members are generating aren't grounded in anything. The ideas may or may not be worthy of implementing, but they don't have a focused lens through which to view them.

In a network of schools called Uncommon Schools, headed by Paul Bambrick-Santoyo (2019), teacher teams examine student work and identify a gap; they attempt to *stamp* the understanding the students are missing. Many teams initially struggle with this process, identifying an entire standard as the gap. Saying, for instance, "We need to reteach ELAGSE6L2 again." A standard isn't a gap—it is a chasm far too wide through which to be productive. Peeling away layers to identify a small, teachable gap is critical.

In this process that Uncommon Schools uses, the teacher team works to build consensus on the gap. Although that is not the goal in a Descriptive Consultancy, the Interpretation step can help presenters focus on what is underneath the dilemma that may be getting in the way of them better managing it.

It might be easy to assume the goal of the deep understanding is only for the participants— almost like it's a gatekeeper that won't accept ideas until they *really* understand this situation. Although there certainly is some merit in the notion, the Interpretation step creates great value for the *presenter*, too. In fact, as a presenter in many coaching protocols, I often find more value in this step than the idea generation coming up two steps from now. Hearing different perspectives on the *why* of the dilemma helps me hear ideas in more prescriptive ways—just like the history teacher team focused on a teachable gap in learning.

Whereas the Description step gave the presenter a literal hearing of their contributions, the Interpretation step seeks to use the *participants'* words. Some educators who have experienced professional development around instructional coaching may equate this step to paraphrasing. Some characteristics of paraphrasing that are helpful for this step include the following.

- Capture the essence of the message (Costa & Garmston, 2010).

- Use more of your words rather than the words of the presenter.

- Speak using tentative language (for example, *possible*, *perhaps*, and *could*).

If facilitators choose to use paraphrasing as a mental hook for participants in this step, they may wish to parallel description or interpretation with parrot-phrasing or paraphrasing (Garmston & Wellman, 2013). My wife might call me and say, "Please pick up some chicken breasts for dinner." My parrot-phrase uses her words: "We need chicken breasts from the grocery store." There is no interpretation there! Although parrot-phrasing is generally considered a strategy to avoid, the Description step is designed to sound just like a repetitive parrot, only able to say what has been heard.

Versions of Descriptive Consultancy (Parrish & Taylor, 2013) and Issaquah (Mohr et al., n.d.) offer the one-sentence starter, "What this means to me . . ." A possible limitation of this prompt in this context is it can lead to premature idea generation. For example, someone might say, "What this means to me is we need to bring all the students together in third period in order to . . ." The prompt isn't at fault because it could also produce some deep thinking by the presenter, such as, "What this means to me is we have a gap between our understanding of the literacy expectations document and what the seventh-grade team is thinking."

If the true intent of this step is to create space for the group to consider alternative views of the dilemma (remember the protocol family name, *Exploring* and Managing Dilemmas), then having multiple prompts can further that goal. The anchor charts provided in chapter 5 (page 147) for these protocols specifically include a prompt about assumptions, as the articulation of assumptions in the original Consultancy protocol is a key benchmark.

Groups who are novices at this protocol may be hesitant to be courageous in their identification of possible root causes, worried they need immediate feedback from the presenter if they are on the right track. Just like in the description step, waiting for affirmation from the presenter after each person speaks can cause significant fatigue to the group and impede the process. Instead, it is important for the group to know a check-in occurs immediately after interpretation—a space for the presenter to identify any key understandings and rein in the group from venturing down rabbit holes.

Language You Can Borrow: *Time to start the second round—interpretation. This is arguably the most important step in helping our presenter think about the dilemma. We wish to massage this dilemma—push it around a bit. We are not trying to push around* [presenter's name], *just the dilemma.*

This is where we read in between the lines. High risk, high reward is the motto for this step. If participants do not work hard enough in this step, then their ideas will suffer later in the protocol. Please be bold and think of all the possibilities and interpretations of this particular dilemma. If we interpret too far, the worst thing that could happen is [presenter's name] *will rein us back during the next step.*

We have a few choices of how we might each participate, displayed on the anchor chart. Please consider starting with one of these sentence stems. [To the presenter] *Please take notes during this step. All right, who will begin?*

Presenter Check-In

This section includes approaches to the Descriptive Consultancy and Issaquah protocols. Since Descriptive Consultancy and Issaquah include a step in which the team offers ideas to better manage the dilemma, it is critical to have a clear understanding prior. The check-in creates a small space for the presenter to jump back in with two very clear jobs. The first of these is to identify any areas that were inaccurate or unessential to the dilemma. This may include things the facilitator heard during either the description or interpretation steps. The second is to identify any important a-ha moments or insights that could help focus the idea generation about to happen.

The timing of this step matters. If a presenter uses the next ten minutes to offer a line-by-line, play-by-play analysis of the last two steps, the group loses its momentum and energy. Instead, this should be similar to checking the oil by lifting the dipstick and noting the level.

A possible outcome of a presenter check-in is a change in the dilemma question. The root cause and interpretive discussion by the group may have helped the presenter narrow and focus the scope of the dilemma. If so, a revision of the question will only help the group do the same in the next step, narrow and focus its ideas to help manage the dilemma.

Language You Can Borrow: *So, it is time to check in with* [presenter's name].

[To the presenter] *This is designed to be quick. Two jobs here: one, anything that, in your opinion is far off and isn't helpful for us to consider moving forward? and two, any really important insights you have already had?*

Evaluate Next Steps: Now What?

This section includes approaches to the Descriptive Consultancy and Issaquah protocols. It is a misunderstanding to think of this step as an unabashed idea-fest. The spirit of this step differs from generative protocols (chapter 6, page 177) in that the ideas now generated stem from the deep analysis that just occurred. Ideas in dilemma-based protocols are more about possible next steps. For instance, in a generative protocol, ideas might be quite action oriented (for example, call this person, or make this product). In a dilemma-based protocol, ideas could be reflective (for example, think about the impact of X, or consider how to alleviate the tension regarding Y), but still actionable.

Language You Can Borrow: Consider the Facilitator Ownership Decision in the next section. Some of the language in that section may be helpful here.

We have come to the idea step, evaluating next possible actions. As we now have been charged with this dilemma, a point of view shift occurs. We will use different pronouns as we talk—less of they, them, her, she, him, *and* he *and more of* we, our, me, my, *and* I. *This collective ownership not only helps* [presenter's name] *as* [preferred pronoun] *steps out of the conversation, it aids us in placing ourselves in* [preferred pronoun] *position, increasing the potential for really thoughtful and helpful feedback.*

Let's start with everyone offering one idea, then we talk without going around the circle. You might build on what someone else says or raise something new. Just keep in mind the norms that we have set in place.

Discuss and Evaluate Next Steps: A Facilitator Ownership Decision

This section includes approaches to the Consultancy, Descriptive Consultancy, and Issaquah protocols. Several facilitators I know make a particular move in each of the four foundational protocols. It occurs at different junctures in each one, but it represents the same notion of asking presenters if it would be permissible for the group to take on their work. This respectful question asks the participants to borrow, to hold someone else's dilemma and care for it as if it were their own. At this point, presenters might turn their chair ninety degrees, now facing the facilitator, so their ear is to the group. This physical shift has several benefits.

- Presenters can focus on listening and note-taking, as their ear is now directed to the group. They do not need to spend cognitive energy thinking about their nonverbal reactions (for example, furrowed or raised eyebrows—basically anything with eyebrows). Presenters report the positive experience of having some space (intellectual and physical) between themselves and the work. It is relieving to give the work away even for a few minutes.

- The group can better own the work, instead of looking to the presenter for nonverbal feedback as members offer each piece of feedback. Participants report having more courage to offer tough-to-hear feedback when the presenter is slightly turned.

If a facilitator chooses this method, a pronoun shift occurs with the group. The sentence stems on the anchor chart indicate the change: more *we* and *I*, rather than *she, they,* or the name of the presenter. This collective language can have a broad impact. It helps the presenter be in a productively risky space because the group isn't just giving advice with fingers pointed. It also helps the group members really ponder their feedback.

With this method, at the end of the feedback step, the facilitator would invite the presenter back into the group, and the point of view switches—the group gives the work back to the presenter, and feedback has a clear stopping point.

Language You Can Borrow: [Presenter's name], *thank you for doing some of your thinking about this dilemma out loud. Would it be OK for us to now lift this heavy dilemma from your shoulders?* [If yes] *It will be helpful for you and us if you would be willing to turn ninety degrees, so your ear is to the group. You can focus on listening, and the group can focus on owning your work rather than talking at you, as you will not be verbally participating for a while.*

As we now have been charged with this dilemma, a point of view shift occurs. We will use different pronouns as we talk—less of they, them, her, she, him, *and* he *and more of* we, our, me, my, *and* I. *This collective ownership not only helps* [presenter's name] *as* [preferred pronoun] *steps out of the conversation, it aids in placing ourselves in* [preferred pronoun] *position, increasing the potential for really thoughtful and helpful feedback.*

Presenter Reflection

This section includes approaches to the Consultancy, Descriptive Consultancy, Issaquah, and Peeling the Onion protocols. Notice the name of this step: presenter *reflection*, not presenter *response*, nor presenter *defense*. If the protocol itself and the people within the structure all did their jobs artfully and skillfully, this step most likely shouldn't be problematic. However, our work as educators is personal. Thoughtfully leading into this step is important. An "OK! That was hard! Joseph, turn on back, what are you thinking about all of our helpful feedback?" doesn't set up Joseph as a presenter very well.

Over the years, participants have shared that my metaphors have been helpful. They allow individuals to hold onto the intent of a step or a concept. At this step, the duck analogy is what I choose to use. Sometimes, presenters feel like a duck during the discussion step. They hear a piece of feedback, and write it down, but in the moment, it is sliding right off their backs. Other notions they heard were also intriguing, memorable, or even obvious—these pieces of feedback catch in their tail feathers.

This idea helps the presenter realize we do not expect, nor does the protocol have time for, a play-by-play rundown of everything said prior. A more concrete way to help presenters be ready to reflect to the group is focusing on their note-taking during the feedback step. Presenters may have starred a few items, underlined something, perhaps their pen hovered a moment as they wrote something down—those could be the items they choose to share during the next step. That specific idea can help a presenter who seems to not know how to start verbally reflecting to the group.

Even with a beautifully worded entrance by the facilitator, sometimes a presenter ends up offering a lengthy commentary of everyone's feedback. One facilitator move might be to acknowledge what participants are saying with, "You heard a lot in this experience!" and use a quantifiable limit, saying, "Perhaps one more thing" to help find an endpoint.

Finally, if the group borrowed the work, don't forget to give it back! If there is any physical work that was examined as part of the protocol, the artifacts are now collected as presenters turn ninety degrees back to the group in order to share their thinking.

Language You Can Borrow: [Presenter's name]*, as you turn back to the group, please know we got some stuff wrong! We aren't you. Think of yourself like a duck: some of the feedback rolled right off your back and some of it may have gotten stuck in your tail feathers. Feel free to hold onto what seems helpful; no need to defend anything to us. This step is called presenter* reflection*, not presenter* defense, *or presenter* response. *You now have a few moments to tell us what got stuck—what you will leave thinking most about. Since you showed discipline by not interrupting us, we won't interrupt you now.*

Consistent Approaches to Common Steps in Protocols to Generate Ideas

Chapter 6, "Protocols to Generate Ideas" (page 177), discusses two foundational protocols, each focused on a different quantity of ideas: Charrette and Wagon Wheels. Each of the following headings addresses one or more of them. In addition, a facilitator may choose to study the sections called Language You Can Borrow as they prepare to facilitate one of these protocols.

Presentation

This section includes approaches to the Charrette and Wagon Wheels protocols. It is helpful for participants if the facilitator gives a brief rundown of the steps before the presenter starts the protocol. Simply reading a printed anchor chart is not valuable enough to spend time doing. Make sure what you do say prior to handing it over to the presenter is a value add to the process. Additionally, your words are not designed to foreshadow or replace what the presenter is about to say. The group doesn't yet need to know the content of the document or the dilemma question. A tangible task would be to time yourself rehearsing this opening. It shouldn't take longer than sixty seconds to give a preview of the steps.

Presentation is included in each of the four foundational dilemma-based protocols. Sometimes presenters feel like they should limit their presentation to a *brief* summary of the dilemma, even though the group would benefit more from a detailed account. If the presenter stops talking (and usually looks at you!), you may wish to employ a few different strategies.

- Offer fifteen to twenty seconds of quiet for presenters to work through a mental checklist, making sure they communicated everything they wanted. When I create this space for the presenter, 95 percent or more of the time, they end up saying more.

- You may know something about the work due to a previous conversation you had with the presenter. It may be helpful to prompt presenters to speak about one or more of those insights or facets if they wish.

Even with some of these strategies, the presentation may end up being shorter than anticipated. Some discussion protocols ask the participants to have the discipline to hold tight to the time frame, even sitting in silence if needed. That is not the case for generative protocols. If a presentation only takes five minutes, that is fine—just be ready for the next step (Clarifying Questions) to perhaps extend past five minutes. The net result of the time spent for both steps combined will not extend the protocol.

Perhaps the most important move a facilitator must make is to ensure the group is clear about what it needs to be generating ideas about. If at the end of the Presentation step, presenters have not explicitly named what they want ideas for, ask them. If they need assistance, you might reference the preconference and name the specific gap they identified.

Language You Can Borrow: As you think about how to frame your first sixty seconds of introducing the steps, here are some phrases and sentences that may be appropriate for your specific dilemma-based protocol.

- *If what we talk about today was a problem, a solution would exist and probably would already be implemented! Instead, we will treat this as a dilemma: a thorny, complicated issue that takes our best thinking in order to move forward.*

- *In this structure, we will slow down our gut response to offer ideas. We begin with hearing from our presenter, then follow up with any clarifying questions we might have.*

- *When we get to the Probing Questions step, I will help us create really helpful probing questions.*

- *After the presenter answers some of our probing questions, we will ask if we can borrow the dilemma as if it is our own. Then, [preferred pronoun] can turn to the side so [preferred pronoun] ear is to the group, listening but not feeling like [preferred pronoun] needs to affirm everything we say.*

- *Finally, our presenter will turn back, let us know [preferred pronoun] current thinking, then we will end with a debrief about the process. What questions do you have about these steps before we begin?*

- *[Presenter's name], thank you for bringing such a meaningful issue to us today. In this first step, several minutes have been carved out for you to tell the context of your dilemma. Participants will work hard taking notes, as we will be hearing much detail about your thinking. [Presenter's name], please give us all the background you can possibly think of regarding your dilemma.*

Clarifying Questions

This section includes approaches to the Charrette and Wagon Wheels protocols. Unfortunately, educators frequently use questions as a method of recommending. A colleague might ask, "Did you use the district item bank for the assessment?" which (whether or not it was intended) may sound like a recommendation or even an accusation. A broader question, such as, "What resources did you use to create the assessment questions?" feels less prescriptive.

Clarifying questions are designed for the asker to receive information. *Quickly asked, quickly answered* is a familiar mantra I use. It is not the goal here for the presenter to think. If a question inadvertently causes presenters to furrow their brow, lift their chin, or look up to the right . . . some facilitators may choose to intercept the question, and judge it to be out of alignment with the intent of the step. Although facilitators may be correct in their judgment, the consequence of correcting a participant is risky—it could cause a decrease in participation from not only that participant but others as well.

Another way to manage a question, which in your opinion is not clarifying, is to watch presenters. If they choose to start answering it (within a few seconds), then it may have been clarifying *to them*. Remember, the goal of the facilitator is to make *facile*, make easy, the process for each person involved. It is far simpler to let the presenter be the arbiter of which questions feel clarifying or not.

Utilizing a go-round is a popular way to ensure voice equity. Start with one person, then after that person's participation, proceed to the left or right, going all the way around. Many discussion protocols use this method. Consider the risk of this method for clarifying questions. It may inadvertently pressure participants to come up with a clarifying question when they really don't have one. Simply opening this up to the group popcorn style may be more aligned to the step's intent. It also shows the group you want to be as authentic as possible—not forcing anyone to make up anything.

Language You Can Borrow: *Now we each have a chance to ask any clarifying questions, so we more completely understand the context of this work. These sorts of questions are simple questions of fact. They might start with* who, what, how many, where, *or* when. *We will resist asking a question that is a disguised recommendation, such as "Did you ever think about using . . . ?" Some may think a question with a* yes *or* no *answer is automatically clarifying. Instead, think about your intent. A good rule of thumb for clarifying questions is that these questions are for you to understand the situation, not for the presenter to think deeply. That will happen later.*

What clarifying questions does the group have?

Generate

This section includes approaches to the Charrette and Wagon Wheels protocols. Several facilitators I know make a particular move in several protocols that includes a presenter. It occurs at different junctures in each one, but it represents the same notion, asking presenters if it would be permissible for the group to take on their work. This respectful question asks the participants to borrow, to hold someone else's dilemma and care for it as if it were their own. At this point, presenters might turn their chair ninety degrees, now facing the facilitator, so their ear is to the group. This physical shift has several benefits.

- Presenters can focus on listening and note-taking, as their ear is now directed to the group. They do not need to spend cognitive energy thinking about their nonverbal reactions (for example, furrowed or raised eyebrows—basically anything with eyebrows). Presenters report the positive experience of having some space (intellectual and physical) between themselves and the work. It is relieving to give the work away even for a few minutes.

- The group can better own the work, instead of looking to the presenter for nonverbal feedback as members offer each piece of feedback. Participants report having more courage to offer tough-to-hear feedback when the presenter is slightly turned.

If a facilitator chooses this method, a pronoun shift occurs with the group. The sentence stems on the anchor chart indicate the change: more *we* and *I*, rather than *she, they,* or the name of the presenter. This collective language can have a broad impact. It helps the presenter be in a productively risky space because the group isn't just giving advice with fingers pointed. It also helps the group members really ponder their feedback.

With this method, at the end of the feedback step, the facilitator would invite the presenter back into the group, and the point of view switches—the group gives the work back to the presenter, and feedback has a clear stopping point.

Language You Can Borrow: [Presenter's name], *you have described and interpreted with us, but in this step, I think it would be more helpful if we took on this student as if they were one of ours. Would it be OK for us to now lift this student from your shoulders for a while?* [If yes] *It will be helpful for you and us if you would be willing to turn ninety degrees, so your ear is to the group. You can focus on listening and the group can focus on owning your work rather than talking at you, as you will not be verbally participating for a while.*

As we now have been charged with this student work, a point of view shift occurs: we will use different pronouns as we talk—less of the following: they, them, her, she, him, *and* he *and more of these:* we, our, me, my, *and* I. *This collective ownership not only helps* [presenter's name] *as* [preferred pronoun] *steps out of the conversation, it aids in placing ourselves in* [preferred pronoun] *position, increasing the potential for really thoughtful and helpful feedback.*

Preconference Key Words and Actions

J ust using a protocol doesn't necessarily equate to helpful feedback. Matching *protocol* to *purpose* is key for a successful experience. This tool (page 238) can increase the probability that presenters will receive the feedback they seek. Start in the middle by deciding on a protocol family, then move outward, following the arrows.

Matching Protocol to Purpose (P²): Preconference Key Words and Actions

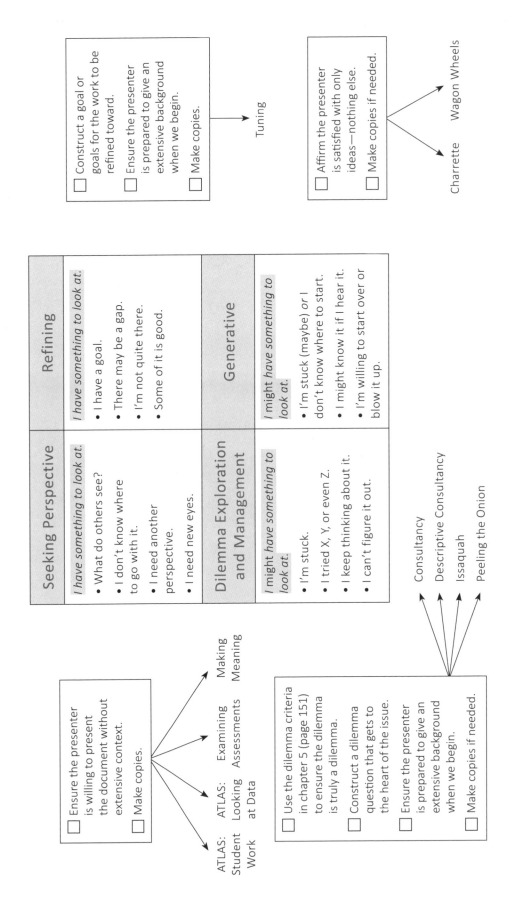

Seeking Perspective

I have something to look at.
- What do others see?
- I don't know where to go with it.
- I need another perspective.
- I need new eyes.

Refining

I have something to look at.
- I have a goal.
- There may be a gap.
- I'm not quite there.
- Some of it is good.

Dilemma Exploration and Management

I might have something to look at.
- I'm stuck.
- I tried X, Y, or even Z.
- I keep thinking about it.
- I can't figure it out.

Generative

I might have something to look at.
- I'm stuck (maybe) or I don't know where to start.
- I might know it if I hear it.
- I'm willing to start over or blow it up.

□ Construct a goal or goals for the work to be refined toward.

□ Ensure the presenter is prepared to give an extensive background when we begin.

□ Make copies.

→ Tuning

□ Affirm the presenter is satisfied with only ideas—nothing else.

□ Make copies if needed.

Charrette   Wagon Wheels

□ Ensure the presenter is willing to present the document without extensive context.

□ Make copies.

Making Meaning
ATLAS: Examining Assessments
ATLAS: Looking at Data
ATLAS: Student Work

□ Use the dilemma criteria in chapter 5 (page 151) to ensure the dilemma is truly a dilemma.

□ Construct a dilemma question that gets to the heart of the issue.

□ Ensure the presenter is prepared to give an extensive background when we begin.

□ Make copies if needed.

Consultancy
Descriptive Consultancy
Issaquah
Peeling the Onion

Appendix C

Facilitation Tools

These tools are here to aid you when facilitating protocols. The first offers some notes and discussion about modifying protocols to use with larger groups. The second draws from a resource by Thompson-Grove and Frazer (n.d.) to provide some guidance on conceiving probing questions.

Using Protocols With Large Groups

Many of the protocols to build shared understanding (chapter 2, page 35) can be modified to use with large groups with little to no substantive changes. For instance, Microlabs can be effective for any size group that can be divided by three or four—no modification required. Chalk Talk, on the other hand, could benefit with a slight revision with groups over fifteen: multiple pieces of paper.

Most of the protocols in chapters 3–6 are designed to be used in smaller groups (usually less than fifteen people). First we'll consider an overarching principle to consider when facilitators believe they have a strong protocol match to be implemented in a large group. That is, purpose. Then we'll address some misconceptions of using protocols with large groups.

Overarching Principle: Consider the Step's Purpose

For each step for which you are considering a modification, articulate the purpose. For instance, the Clarifying Questions step in most protocols is for individuals to fill a basic informational gap in their thinking. If you are considering doubling the amount of time for clarifying questions due to the size of the group, another option (which wouldn't adversely affect engagement) would involve small groups asking their clarifying questions of one another. Then the only questions that would be raised in the large group are those the group could not answer. In extremely large groups, I have used a backchannel website (for example, Mentimeter [www.mentimeter.com] or Backchannel Chat [www.backchannelchat .com]) to raise clarifying questions, as another educator sorts through the channel, grouping questions in efficient ways.

Misconceptions

There are two common misconceptions facilitators should ponder when choosing to use a discussion protocol with a large group: (1) more is better and (2) all steps are for everyone.

More Is Better

The temptation in a large group is to assume more of any step is a value add. In a Tuning protocol (chapter 3, page 95), more warm and cool feedback is better; in an Issaquah protocol (chapter 5, page 162), more probing questions are a boon—right? I would argue, not necessarily. In a Tuning with twenty educators, I might create groups of four to five at the warm and cool feedback step and ask them to engage in go-rounds that last three to four minutes (just enough for everyone to speak once). Then gathering their attention, I may give them thirty seconds to pick two. They quickly decide on two notions that will be raised in the large group. After the presenter hears the notions, the groups reconvene either with a new focus (perhaps now cool feedback) or more time for warm feedback. A similar notion could happen in most protocols in chapters 3–6. Of particular urgency in considering modifications is Charrette (chapter 6, page 190). If the ideas become voluminous, the Charrette will no longer meet its purpose (to identify and commit to a few next steps)—it is inadvertently turning into a Wagon Wheel (page 180; to generate more ideas than the presenter could ever need).

All Steps Are for Everyone

There are times when a portion of a discussion protocol could benefit from a large group presence but not necessarily the entire process. In an Issaquah (chapter 5, page 162), a presenter may want to hear from an entire staff through Probing Questions, then call an end to the required part of the meeting. After some educators choose to exit, those who stay participate in the remaining idea generation step.

Excerpts From the Pocket Guide to Probing Questions

This guide was developed by Gene Thompson-Grove and Edorah Frazer (n.d.). It can be used with protocols to explore and manage dilemmas (chapter 5, page 147). See table C.1.

Table C.1: Differences Between Clarifying and Probing Questions

Clarifying Questions	Probing Questions
• Asked for *participants* to fill a gap in their contextual understanding • Factual in nature • Presenters generally shouldn't have to think; they generally respond quickly after the question is asked	• Asked for the *presenter* to think • Participants do not have an answer they *hope* the presenter gives—truly inquiry in nature • Not a disguised recommendation

Probing questions may meet one or more of the following criteria.

- Allows for multiple responses
- Avoids yes-or-no responses
- Empowers the person being asked the question to solve the problem or manage the dilemma (rather than deferring to someone with greater or different expertise)
- Stimulates reflective thinking by moving thinking from reaction to reflection
- Encourages perspective taking
- Challenges assumptions
- Channels inquiry
- Promises insight
- Touches a deeper meaning
- Creates a paradigm shift
- Evokes more questions
- Is concise
- Prompts slow response

Possible probing question stems include the following.

- Why do you think this is the case?
- What would have to change in order for . . . ?
- What do you feel is right?
- What's another way you might . . . ?
- How is . . . different from . . . ?
- What sort of an impact do you think . . . ?
- When have you done or experienced something like this before? What does this remind you of?

- How did you decide, determine, or conclude . . . ?
- What is your hunch about . . . ?
- What was your intention when . . . ?
- What do you assume to be true about . . . ?
- What is the connection between . . . and . . . ?
- What if the opposite were true? Then what?
- How might your assumptions about . . . have influenced how you are thinking about . . . ?
- What surprises you about . . . ? Why are you surprised?
- What is the best thing that could happen?
- What are you most afraid will happen?
- What do you need to ask to better understand?
- How do you feel when . . . ? What might this tell you about . . . ?
- What is the one thing you won't compromise?
- What criteria do you use . . . ?
- Do you think the problem is X, Y, or something else?
- What evidence exists . . . ?
- If you were X, how would you see this situation?
- If time or money were not an issue . . . ?

Matrix for Building Shared Understanding: When to Use

Due to the sheer quantity of protocols in this family, I created this table (page 244) to help you choose the best protocol for your given situation. Once you have determined the challenge you wish to address, look for something similar in the first column, then note the relevant protocol. Since there are so many protocols in this family, the associated category is also included as a way for you to ensure you have made a solid protocol choice.

When to Use Protocols to Build Shared Understanding

Challenges	Protocol Match	Building Shared Understanding Category
Team having difficulty making a decision with many variables	Affinity Mapping (page 46)	Reflection
Want broad-based feedback but not multiple pages of survey responses	Affinity Mapping (page 46)	Reflection
Team members need to listen to each other more.	Chalk Talk (page 47)	Reflection
Synthesizing learning	Chalk Talk (page 47) Creating Metaphors (**go.SolutionTree.com/leadership**)	Reflection
Teachers having trouble being honest with each other	Continuum Dialogue (page 50)	Reflection
Team needs to assess and talk together (not just take a survey)	Continuum Dialogue (page 50)	Reflection
Not owning new strategies and work	Creating Metaphors (**go.SolutionTree.com/leadership**)	Reflection
Starting to think about a new topic or practice	Microlabs (page 52)	Reflection
Need to check in on an initiative or practice	Microlabs (page 52)	Reflection
Wrap up current strategy or inquiry	Microlabs (page 52)	Reflection
Listening	Microlabs (page 52) Connections (**go.SolutionTree.com/leadership**) Verbal Legos (page 79)	Reflection Community Building Community Building
Group not feeling effective at anything right now	Success Analysis (page 56)	Reflection
Starting something new after a very successful implementation	Success Analysis (page 56)	Reflection
Only using one way to describe self or others (for example, "I am a third-grade teacher," "He is Hispanic," or "She is poor")	Diversity Rounds (page 59)	Equity and Diversity
Lack of acknowledgement or sensitivity to other cultures and races	History of Your Hair (page 61)	Equity and Diversity
Educators needing multiple ways to talk about identity (for example, race, gender, or culture)	Paseo (page 63)	Equity and Diversity

Meeting Goals © 2021 Solution Tree Press • SolutionTree.com
Visit **go.SolutionTree.com/leadership** to download this free reproducible.

Group members unable to understand each other's perspective	Paseo (page 63)	Equity and Diversity
Group members unable to understand one another's *why* or perspective	Passion Profiles (**go.SolutionTree.com /leadership**)	Equity and Diversity
Campus needing ideas on how to connect with students or each other	Student Profiles (page 65)	Equity and Diversity
Group not learning from its previous processes and work	Balloon Bounce (**go.SolutionTree.com /leadership**)	Community Building
Campus has many changes happening and needs clarity about which changes to focus on.	The Change Activity (**go.SolutionTree .com/leadership**)	Community Building
Not having group norms	Compass Points (page 69)	Community Building
Labelling each other's work style and pigeonholing others into specific work (for example, "You keep all the notes in our meetings because you love details")	Compass Points (page 69)	Community Building
Groups are unable to move from big ideas to details or vice versa.	Compass Points (page 69)	Community Building
Humanizing each other	Connections (**go.SolutionTree.com /leadership**)	Community Building
Group members respond to each other even when not desired.	Connections (**go.SolutionTree.com /leadership**)	Community Building
Group working individually instead of collectively during stress	Defy Gravity (**go.SolutionTree.com /leadership**)	Community Building
Group seeing each other in one-dimensional ways	Football Spoons (**go.SolutionTree.com /leadership**)	Community Building
Not having group norms	Group Juggle (page 74)	Community Building
Unarticulated, implicit expectations with each other	Group Juggle (page 74)	Community Building
Managing the chaos of projects or tasks (primary tasks, curve balls, distractions, and daily responsibilities)	Group Juggle (page 74)	Community Building
Lack of trust	Hog Call (**go.SolutionTree.com /leadership**)	Community Building
Not working collaboratively with each other; afraid to make mistakes	Say, Say, Do (page 78) or Say, Say, Do: Leadership Version (**go .SolutionTree.com/leadership**)	Community Building
Not using each other as resources	Say, Say, Do (page 78)	Community Building

Meeting Goals © 2021 Solution Tree Press • SolutionTree.com
Visit **go.SolutionTree.com/leadership** to download this free reproducible.

Introduce the concept of conscious competence.	Say, Say, Do: Leadership Version (**go .SolutionTree.com/leadership**)	Community Building
Not giving respectful, actionable feedback to each other	Verbal Legos (page 79)	Community Building
Not enough collegiality in a group	What's in Common? (**go.SolutionTree .com/leadership**)	Community Building
Pressure on a team to be friends and socialize together outside of work	What's in Common? (**go.SolutionTree .com/leadership**)	Community Building
Team members have very different ways of taking risks.	Zones of Comfort, Risk, and Danger (page 81)	Community Building
A team is risk-adverse.	Zones of Comfort, Risk, and Danger (page 81)	Community Building
Team facilitators are not sure how to help others take risks.	Zones of Comfort, Risk, and Danger (page 81)	Community Building

Source: © 2020 Thomas M. Van Soelen, Jana Claxton, & Kerise Ridinger. Adapted with permission.

Appendix E

Supplemental Strategies

Discussion protocols are structured conversations. The following strategies are slightly different. First, Fist to Five is a facilitation method participants can use to gain consensus—sometimes without much conversation at all. Second, Synectics is an instructional strategy adapted from use with students.

Fist to Five

Richard DuFour, Rebecca DuFour, Robert Eaker, Thomas W. Many, and Mike Mattos (2016), among many others, have done important work on developing and using the Fist to Five strategy; here I offer my own insights. Rather than offering this in sequential form, the following scenario shows the usefulness (and misconceptions) in this powerful strategy.

On a summer day, I offer to buy lunch for a group of teachers if they will work on pacing charts through the midday hours. I have a gift card to a restaurant just down the road. I ask, "Do you agree to a working lunch?" Fifteen minutes later, after extensive discussion from only some of the teachers about the type of food and looking up health ratings for the restaurant, we still haven't ordered food.

Rewind. This time I explicitly decide to ask for consensus instead: "I will buy lunch if you will stay and work on your pacing chart the next few hours. Can you live with this decision? Please offer fist to five."

Fist to Five is a popular strategy to use for consensus building. Either the facilitator or a member of the group mentions a possible solution, then each member puts up a hand to represent his or her level of consensus.

- Five fingers mean, "I like this a lot; I think it's the best possible decision."
- Four fingers mean, "This is fine."
- Three fingers mean, "I'm in the middle somewhere—like some of it, but not all."
- Two fingers mean, "I don't much like it, but I'll go along."
- One finger means, "I don't like this, but I could be swayed."
- A fist means, "I definitely disagree—NO."

I have found an extensive discussion of how this strategy works is often not necessary. Using the anchor chart shown in figure E.1 is usually my chosen method in those moments. Notice the case of the letters and the differences in punctuation. I have a picture of it labeled as a favorite on my phone so I can easily find it.

5	I'M IN!
4	I'M IN.
3	I'm in.
2	I'm in . . .
1	I'm out . . .
Fist	I'm OUT!

Figure E.1: Anchor chart for Fist to Five strategy.

The use of the Fist to Five strategy is not magical. It does not automatically work just because it exists. Stipulated differently, putting up hands is only the data collection; the key to the success of this process is what the facilitator does with the displayed data.

Back to the offer to purchase lunch: the group of ten teachers puts up their hands, and this is the result (figure E.2).

Hand	Number of Teachers
5	2
4	2
3	2
2	3
1	
Fist	1

Figure E.2: Fist to Five result.

Inexperienced facilitators (seen frequently in teacher leaders) see the fists and grow fearful. They may take these data as a repudiation of their leadership. Often their next move is where the process is misunderstood. A fist is not simply indicating being out, it shows a significant distance away from the proposal. Well-intentioned teacher leaders may now ask the colleague directly, "No lunch with us today? Why not? Any way you might change your mind?"

Recently I asked a group what might happen next, and an instructional coach stood up, held her fist out, looked me square in the eye, and raised the other fist! After the group laughed, she explained, "You just asked me my opinion on an issue without any expectation of saying why, and now you are calling me out in the group. I may not have physically raised both my fists in a grade-level meeting, but in my mind, another barrier just went up."

A more data-informed move would be to simply pause or table the subject, saying "OK—so that won't work out, but that is fine. We will stick with our original plan. Thanks." The choice of the fist, rather than holding up one finger, should inform the facilitator to make a different decision.

So, let's change the data collection. Rewind. What if the fist actually put up a 1 instead (figure E.3)?

Hand	Number of Teachers
5	2
4	2
3	2
2	3
1	1
Fist	0

Figure E.3: Hypothetical result 1.

Now, directly asking someone about their data seems like a calculated risk. After all, the teacher who put up a 1 could have put up a fist but chose not to. To me, the ellipsis after "I'm out" represents hope.

Finally, let's try one last rewind. This time the person who put up a 1 put up a 2 (figure E.4).

Hand	Number of Teachers
5	2
4	2

continued →

3	2
2	4
1	0
Fist	0

Figure E.4: Hypothetical result 2.

Now what? Someone who understands the consensus tool deeply will internally (and perhaps externally) celebrate because we have a decision—food will be ordered. However, what I tend to see in groups where this tool has been introduced, but not clearly understood, is the following comment. "Wonderful! No fists or 1s, so others, what would it take to move you up?"

The misunderstanding is clear: the facilitator believes the goal is for everyone to reach a five. The deeper problem is the lack of understanding about consensus versus agreement. If the goal is five, then we are no longer working in consensus; we took a tool designed for consensus and forced it into agreement.

Synectics

Synectics acknowledges that long-term memory is often hooked to images and personal connections. You may have learned a list of conjunctions with a particular rap, or the difference between simile and metaphor due to an image a teacher used. What makes Synectics different is the use of choice. My version of Synectics derives from the methodology invented by George M. Prince and William J. J. Gordon (Synecticsworld, 2012).

Purpose

Participants aim to make a cognitive link from a concept to an image.

Group Size

Any size group is ideal for this strategy.

Pre-Strategy Preparation

Create an array of images that everyone can see. This might be a presentation slide or an electronic link to a poster or a document with six to eight pictures. The images may be illustrations, but photographs are recommended. As you create the options, resist the urge to strategically choose. Instead, look for random images (perhaps on Google Images) rather than trying to connect the image to the concept you have in mind.

Sequence

1. Display the image and ask participants to silently make a connection between a particular concept and an image. Using a sentence stem is often helpful: "[Concept] is like [particular image] because . . ." (One to two minutes)

2. The facilitator decides whether participants use turn and talk, large group share, electronic survey submission and time for participants to see each other's responses, or a chat box in a videoconference meeting. (Less than five minutes)

Once facilitators have created a Synectics visual, they can use and reuse it for various concepts with various groups. This will help them resist stacking the deck, specifically choosing images they wish participants to use. A sample presentation slide with a Synectics visual is available at http://bit.ly/2YQizLO for your use and consideration.

References
and Resources

Adichie, C. N. (2009, July). *The danger of a single story* [Video file]. Accessed at www.ted.com/talks /chimamanda_ngozi_adichie_the_danger_of_a_single_story?language=en on August 21, 2020.

Allen, D. (1998). The tuning protocol: Opening up reflection. In D. Allen (Ed.), *Assessing student learning: From grading to understanding* (pp. 87–104). New York: Teachers College Press.

Allen, D., & Blythe, T. (2004). *The facilitator's book of questions: Tools for looking together at student and teacher work* (2nd ed.). New York: Teachers College Press.

Allen, D., & Blythe, T. (2015). *Facilitating for learning: Tools for teacher groups of all kinds.* New York: Teachers College Press.

Bambino, D. (n.d.a). *Block party.* Accessed at www.schoolreforminitiative.org/download/block-party / on February 4, 2021.

Bambino, D. (n.d.b). *Collaborative ghost walk.* Accessed at www.schoolreforminitiative.org/download /collaborative-ghost-walk/ on August 20, 2020.

Bambrick-Santoyo, P. (2019). *Driven by data 2.0: A practical guide to improve instruction* (2nd ed.). San Francisco: Jossey-Bass.

Baron, D. (n.d.a). *Gap analysis protocol.* Accessed at www.schoolreforminitiative.org/download/gap -analysis-protocol/ on August 20, 2020.

Baron, D. (n.d.b). *Making meaning protocol.* Accessed at www.schoolreforminitiative.org/download /the-making-meaning-protocol/ on August 20, 2020.

Beers, K. (2002). *When kids can't read: What teachers can do.* Portsmouth, NH: Heinemann.

Bermudez, P., Cabrera, B., & Emm, L. (n.d.). *Passion profiles activity.* Accessed at www.schoolreforminitiative.org/download/passion -profiles-activity/ on August 20, 2020.

Bloom, B. S. (Ed.). (1956). *Taxonomy of educational objectives, handbook I: The cognitive domain.* New York: McKay.

Blythe, T., Allen, D., & Powell, B. S. (2008). *Looking at student work* (2nd ed.). New York: Teachers College Press.

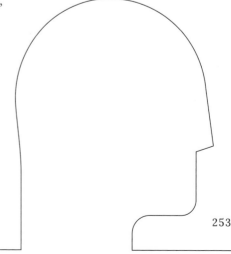

Boogren, T. H. (2018). *Take time for you: Self-care action plans for educators*. Bloomington, IN: Solution Tree Press.

Breidenstein, A., Fahey, K., Glickman, C., & Hensley, F. (2012). *Leading for powerful learning: A guide for instructional leaders*. New York: Teachers College Press.

Bryk, A. S. (2010). Organizing schools for improvement. *Phi Delta Kappan, 91*(7), 23–30.

Bryk, A. S., Sebring, P. B., Allensworth, E., Luppescu, S., & Easton, J. Q. (2010). *Organizing schools for improvement: Lessons from Chicago*. Chicago: University of Chicago Press.

Buchovecky, E. (1996). *Learning from student work*. Newton, MA: ATLAS Communities, Educational Development Center.

City, E. A., Elmore, R. F., Fiarman, S. E., & Teitel, L. (2009). *Instructional rounds in education: A network approach to improved teaching and learning* (6th ed.). Cambridge, MA: Harvard Education Press.

Cochran-Smith, M. (1991). Learning to teach against the grain. *Harvard Educational Review, 61*(3), 279–309.

Costa, A. L., & Garmston, R. J. (2010). *Cognitive coaching foundation seminar: Learning guide* (8th ed.). Highlands Ranch, CO: Center for Cognitive Coaching.

Donohoo, J. (2017). *Collective efficacy: How educators' beliefs impact student learning*. Thousand Oaks, CA: Corwin Press.

DuFour, R., DuFour, R., Eaker, R., Many, T. W., & Mattos, M. (2016). *Learning by doing: A handbook for professional learning communities at work* (3rd ed.). Bloomington, IN: Solution Tree Press.

Dunne, F., Evans, P., & Thompson-Grove, G. (n.d.). *Consultancy protocol: Framing consultancy dilemmas*. Accessed at www.schoolreforminitiative.org/download/consultancy on August 20, 2020.

Dweck, C. S. (2016). *Mindset: The new psychology of success* (Updated ed.). New York: Ballantine Books.

Fahey, K., Breidenstein, A., Ippolito, J., & Hensley, F. (2019). *An uncommon theory of school change: Leadership for reinventing schools*. New York: Teachers College Press.

Feicke, K. (2007). *Charrette protocol*. Accessed at www.schoolreforminitiative.org/download/charrette -protocol/ on August 20, 2020.

Feldman, E. B. (1987). *Varieties of visual experience* (3rd ed.). New York: Abrams.

Fischer-Mueller, J., & Thompson-Grove, G. (n.d.). *Final word*. Accessed at www.schoolreforminitiative .org/download/the-final-word/ on August 20, 2020.

Fullan, M., & Quinn, J. (2016). *Coherence: The right drivers in action for schools, districts, and systems*. Thousand Oaks, CA: Corwin Press.

Garmston, R. J., & von Frank, V. (2012). *Unlocking group potential to improve schools*. Thousand Oaks, CA: Corwin Press.

Garmston, R. J., & Wellman, B. M. (2013). *The adaptive school: A sourcebook for developing collaborative groups* (2nd ed.). Lanham, MD: Rowman & Littlefield.

Gorski, P. (2017). *Reaching and teaching students in poverty: Strategies for erasing the opportunity gap.* New York: Teachers College Press.

Gorski, P., & Pothini, S. G. (2018). *Case studies on diversity and social justice education.* New York: Routledge.

Gray, J. (n.d.). *4 A's text protocol.* Accessed at www.schoolreforminitiative.org/download/four-as-text-protocol/ on August 20, 2020.

Grosvenor, C. (2018, April 9). *"Minute to win it" balloon games: Defying gravity.* Accessed at www.liveabout.com/minute-to-win-it-defying-gravity-1396711 on December 28, 2020.

Heifetz, R., Grashow, A., & Linsky, M. (2009). *The practice of adaptive leadership: Tools and tactics for changing your organization and the world.* Boston: Harvard Business Press.

Hensley, F., Taylor, S. W., & Parrish, C. Z. (n.d.). *Coffee talk (equity focus) protocol.* Accessed at www.schoolreforminitiative.org/download/coffee-talk-equity-focus-protocol/ on August 20, 2020.

Hughes, L. (1968). *The best of Simple.* New York: Hill and Wang.

Johnson, V. (n.d.). *The success analysis protocol with reflective questions.* Accessed at www.schoolreforminitiative.org/download/success-analysis-protocolwith-reflective-questions/ on August 20, 2020.

Kafele, B. K. (2015). *The principal 50: Critical leadership questions for inspiring schoolwide excellence.* Alexandria, VA: Association for Supervision and Curriculum Development.

Kegan, R. (1998). *In over our heads: The mental demands of modern life.* Cambridge, MA: Harvard University Press.

Kegan, R., & Lahey, L. L. (2002). *How the way we talk can change the way we work: Seven languages for transformation.* San Francisco: Jossey-Bass.

Kerr, P. (1983, November 29). NBC comedy "Cheers" turns into a success. *The New York Times.* Accessed at www.nytimes.com/1983/11/29/arts/nbc-comedy-cheers-turns-into-a-success.html on December 20, 2020.

Kersey, S. N. (2014). *Building community in schools: Narratives of possibilities and limitations in critical friends groups.* Unpublished doctoral dissertation, Georgia State University, Atlanta.

Knoster, T., Villa, R., & Thousand, J. (2000). A framework for thinking about systems change. In R. Villa & J. Thousand (Eds.), *Restructuring for caring and effective education: Piecing the puzzle together* (2nd ed.; pp. 93–128). Baltimore: Brookes.

Krownapple, J. (2017). *Guiding teams to excellence with equity: Culturally proficient facilitation.* Thousand Oaks, CA: Corwin Press.

Kruse, S., Louis, K. S., & Bryk, A. S. (1994). Building professional community in schools. *Issues in Restructuring Schools, 6,* 3–6.

Laidley, D., Bambino, D., McIntyre, D., Quate, S., & Quinn, J. (2001). *The paseo or circles of identity.* Accessed at www.schoolreforminitiative.org/download/the-paseo-or-circles-of-identity on August 20, 2020.

Leahy, D. (2004). *ATLAS: Looking at data.* Accessed at www.schoolreforminitiative.org/download/atlas-looking-at-data/ on August 20, 2020.

Liaw, M. L. (2017). Reading strategy awareness training to empower online reading. *English Teacher*, *38*, 133–150.

McDonald, J. P., Mohr, N., Dichter, A., & McDonald, E. C. (2013). *The power of protocols: An educator's guide to better practice* (3rd ed.). New York: Teachers College Press.

Mind Tools. (n.d.). *The conscious competence ladder: Developing awareness of your skill levels.* Accessed at www.mindtools.com/pages/article/newISS_96.htm on February 2, 2019.

Momentous Institute. (2015, June 29). *Blind Lego.* Accessed at https://momentousinstitute.org/blog/blind-lego on August 20, 2020.

Mohr, N., Bambino, D., & Baron, D. (n.d.). *The Issaquah protocol.* Accessed at www.schoolreforminitiative.org/download/the-issaquah-protocol/ on August 20, 2020.

Moss, C. M., & Brookhart, S. M. (2019). *Advancing formative assessment in every classroom: A guide for instructional leaders* (2nd ed.). Alexandria, VA: Association for Supervision and Curriculum Development.

Murphy, S. (2016, September 18). *Grounding: Moving people into space.* Accessed at www.linkedin.com/pulse/grounding-moving-people-space-scott-murphy/?trk=mp-reader-card on July 23, 2019.

National Turning Points Center. (2001). *Transforming middle schools: Looking collaboratively at student and teacher work.* Accessed at www.cce.org/uploads/files/Looking-at-Student-and-Teacher-Work.pdf on December 30, 2020.

Newmann, F. M., & Wehlage, G. G. (1995). *Successful school restructuring: A report to the public and educators by the Center on Organization and Restructuring of Schools.* Madison, WI: Center on Organization and Restructuring of Schools, Wisconsin Center for Education Research.

Oluo, I. (2019). *So you want to talk about race.* Seattle, WA: Seal Press.

Oluo, I. (2020). *Mediocre: The dangerous legacy of white male America.* Seattle, WA: Seal Press.

Palmer, P. J. (1997). *The courage to teach: Exploring the inner landscape of a teacher's life.* San Francisco: Jossey-Bass.

Palmer, P. J. (2009). *A hidden wholeness: The journey toward an undivided life.* San Francisco: Jossey-Bass.

Parrish, C. Z., & Taylor, S. W. (n.d.). *Student profiles.* Accessed at www.schoolreforminitiative.org/download/student-profiles-activity/ on August 20, 2020.

Parrish, C. Z., & Taylor, S. W. (2013). *Descriptive consultancy.* Accessed at www.schoolreforminitiative.org/download/descriptive-consultancy/ on August 20, 2020.

Payne, R. (2005). *A framework for understanding poverty.* Baytown, TX: aha! Process.

Peterson-Veatch, R. (2006). *Affinity mapping.* Accessed at www.schoolreforminitiative.org/download/affinity-mapping/ on August 20, 2020.

Preschool Situational Self-Regulation Toolkit. (n.d.). *Balloon bounce.* Accessed at www.prsist.com.au/balloonbounce.php on December 26, 2020.

Robinson, L., Smith, M., Segal, J., & Shubin, J. (2020, October). *The benefits of play for adults.* Accessed at www.helpguide.org/articles/mental-health/benefits-of-play-for-adults.htm on December 28, 2020.

Routman, R. (2000). *Conversations: Strategies for teaching, learning, and evaluating.* Portsmouth, NH: Heinemann.

School Reform Initiative. (n.d.a). *Change activity.* Accessed at www.schoolreforminitiative.org /download/change-activity/ on August 20, 2020.

School Reform Initiative. (n.d.b). *Compass points: North, south, east, and west—An exercise in understanding preferences in group work.* Accessed at www.schoolreforminitiative.org/download /compass-points-north-south-east-and-west-an-exercise-in-understanding-preferences-in-group -work/ on August 20, 2020.

School Reform Initiative. (n.d.c). *Group juggle.* Accessed at www.schoolreforminitiative.org/download /group-juggle/ on August 20, 2020.

School Reform Initiative. (n.d.d). *Hog call.* Accessed at www.schoolreforminitiative.org/download /hog-call/ on August 20, 2020.

School Reform Initiative. (n.d.e). *Microlabs.* Accessed at www.schoolreforminitiative.org/download /microlabs/ on August 20, 2020.

School Reform Initiative. (n.d.f). *Planting the seed: A text protocol.* Accessed at www.schoolreforminitiative .org/download/planting-the-seed-a-text-protocol/ on August 20, 2020.

School Reform Initiative. (n.d.g). *Questions and assumptions: Adapted for text.* Accessed at www .schoolreforminitiative.org/download/questions-and-assumptions-adapted-for-text/ on August 20, 2020.

School Reform Initiative. (n.d.h). *Say, say, do.* Accessed at www.schoolreforminitiative.org/download /say-say-do/ on February 4, 2021.

School Reform Initiative. (n.d.i). *Slice.* Accessed at www.schoolreforminitiative.org/download/the -slice/ on August 20, 2020.

School Reform Initiative. (n.d.j). *Text rendering experience.* Accessed at www.schoolreforminitiative .org/download/the-text-rendering-experience/ on August 20, 2020.

School Reform Initiative. (n.d.k). *Wagon wheels brainstorm.* Accessed at www.schoolreforminitiative .org/download/wagon-wheels-brainstorm/ on August 20, 2020.

School Reform Initiative. (n.d.l). *Zones of comfort, risk and danger: Constructing your zone map.* Accessed at www.schoolreforminitiative.org/download/zones-of-comfort-risk-and-danger -constructing-your-zone-map/ on August 20, 2020.

Schooling, P., Toth, M., & Marzano, R. J. (2013). *The critical importance of a common language/model of instruction.* Blairsville, PA: Learning Sciences International. Accessed at https://education-store .learningsciences.com/wp/wp-content/uploads/2017/06/Common-Language-of-Instruction-2013.pdf on November 3, 2020.

Southern Maine Partnership. (2003). *Three levels of text protocol.* Accessed at www.schoolreforminitiative .org/download/three-levels-of-text-protocol/ on August 20, 2020.

Synecticsworld. (n.d.). *Founders.* Accessed at https://synecticsworld.com/founders/ on February 5, 2021.

Thompson-Grove, G. (n.d.a). *Connections.* Accessed at www.schoolreforminitiative.org/download /connections/ on August 20, 2020.

Thompson-Grove, G. (n.d.b). *Creating metaphors.* Accessed at www.schoolreforminitiative.org /download/creating-metaphors/ on August 20, 2020.

Thompson-Grove, G. (n.d.c). *Examining assessments.* Accessed at www.schoolreforminitiative.org /download/examining-assessments/ on August 20, 2020.

Thompson-Grove, G. (2000). *ATLAS: Learning from student work.* Accessed at www.schoolreforminitiative .org/download/atlas-learning-from-student-work-protocol/ on August 20, 2020.

Thompson-Grove, G., & Frazer, E. (n.d.). *Pocket guide to probing questions.* Accessed at https:// schoolreforminitiative.org/download/pocket-guide-to-probing-questions on August 20, 2020.

Thompson-Grove, G., Hensley, F., & Van Soelen, T. (n.d.). *Protocol families.* Accessed at www .schoolreforminitiative.org/download/protocol-families/ on August 20, 2020.

Van Soelen, T. M. (2003). *If Polly had been there: An uncommon journey toward teacher induction and development.* Unpublished doctoral dissertation, University of Georgia, Athens.

Van Soelen, T. M. (2013). Building a sustainable culture of feedback. *Performance Improvement Journal, 52*(4), 22–29.

Van Soelen, T. M. (2014, July 24). Livening up the blasé work of mission and vision revision: Part one. *AASA Executive Briefing.* Accessed at http://exclusive.multibriefs.com/content/livening-up-the -blase-work-of-mission-and-vision-revision/education on August 20, 2020.

Van Soelen, T. M. (2016). *Crafting the feedback teachers need and deserve: A guide for leaders.* New York: Routledge.

Van Soelen, T. M. (2019a, May). Talking the talk: Part 2. *Communicator, 42*(9). Accessed at www .naesp.org/communicator-may-2019/talking-talk-part-2-0 on August 20, 2020.

Van Soelen, T. M. (2019b, April). Part 1: Walking the walk. *Communicator, 42*(8). Accessed at www .naesp.org/communicator-april-2019/part-1-walking-walk on August 20, 2020.

Venables, D. R. (2011). *The practice of authentic PLCs: A guide to effective teacher teams.* Thousand Oaks, CA: Corwin Press.

Visual Paradigm. (n.d.). *Cause and effect analysis: Using fishbone diagram and 5 whys.* Accessed at www.visual-paradigm.com/project-management/fishbone-diagram-and-5-whys/ on August 20, 2020.

Weissglass, J. (n.d.). *Microlabs.* Accessed at www.schoolreforminitiative.org/download/microlabs on January 28, 2021.

Wentworth, M. (n.d.a). *Chalk talk.* Accessed at www.schoolreforminitiative.org/download/chalk-talk/ on August 20, 2020.

Wentworth, M. (n.d.b). *Continuum dialogue.* Accessed at www.schoolreforminitiative.org/download /continuum-dialogue/ on August 20, 2020.

Wheatley, M. J. (2002). *Turning to one another: Simple conversations to restore hope to the future.* San Francisco: Berrett-Koehler.

Wiggins, G. (2012). Seven keys to effective feedback. *Educational Leadership, 70*(1), 10–16.

Wiliam, D. (2011). *Embedded formative assessment.* Bloomington, IN: Solution Tree Press.

Wiliam, D. (2018). *Embedded formative assessment* (2nd ed.). Bloomington, IN: Solution Tree Press.

Index

T

Crafting Your Message
Tammy Heflebower with Jan K. Hoegh

Become a confident, dynamic presenter with the guidance of _Crafting Your Message_. Written by expert presenter Tammy Heflebower, this book outlines a clear process for planning and delivering highly effective presentations. More than 100 ideas and strategies help you augment your message.

BKF931

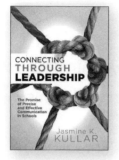

Connecting Through Leadership
Jasmine K. Kullar

The success of a school greatly depends on the ability of its leaders to communicate effectively. Rely on _Connecting Through Leadership_ to help you strengthen your communication skills to inspire, motivate, and connect with every member of your school community.

BKF927

Responding to Resistance
William A. Sommers

Educational leadership is never conflict free. In _Responding to Resistance_, author William A. Sommers acknowledges this reality and presents school leaders with wide-ranging strategies to decisively address conflict involving staff, students, parents, and other key stakeholders.

BKF955

Messaging Matters
William D. Parker

Harness the power of messaging to create a culture of acknowledgment, respect, and celebration. Written specially for leaders, this title is divided into three parts, helping readers maximize their role as chief communicators with students, teachers, and parents and community.

BKF785

Stronger Together
Terri L. Martin and Cameron L. Rains

How do I build collaborative teams that support a common vision? How do I tap into others' skills? New and veteran leaders ask themselves these questions. _Stronger Together_ will help you face your current reality and determine steps for improvement.

BKF792

Solution Tree | Press   _a division of_
Solution Tree

Visit SolutionTree.com or call 800.733.6786 to order.

Wait! **Your professional development journey doesn't have to end with the last pages of this book.**

We realize improving student learning doesn't happen overnight. And your school or district shouldn't be left to puzzle out all the details of this process alone.

No matter where you are on the journey, we're committed to helping you get to the next stage.

Take advantage of everything from **custom workshops** to **keynote presentations** and **interactive web and video conferencing**. We can even help you develop an action plan tailored to fit your specific needs.

Let's get the conversation started.

Call 888.763.9045 today.

 solution-tree.com

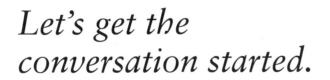